80 Years, A Tribute to the PBY

CATALINA

Z-CAT

80 Years, A Tribute to the PBY

CATALINA

The ultimate color photo album of the best flying boat ever made

HANS WIESMAN

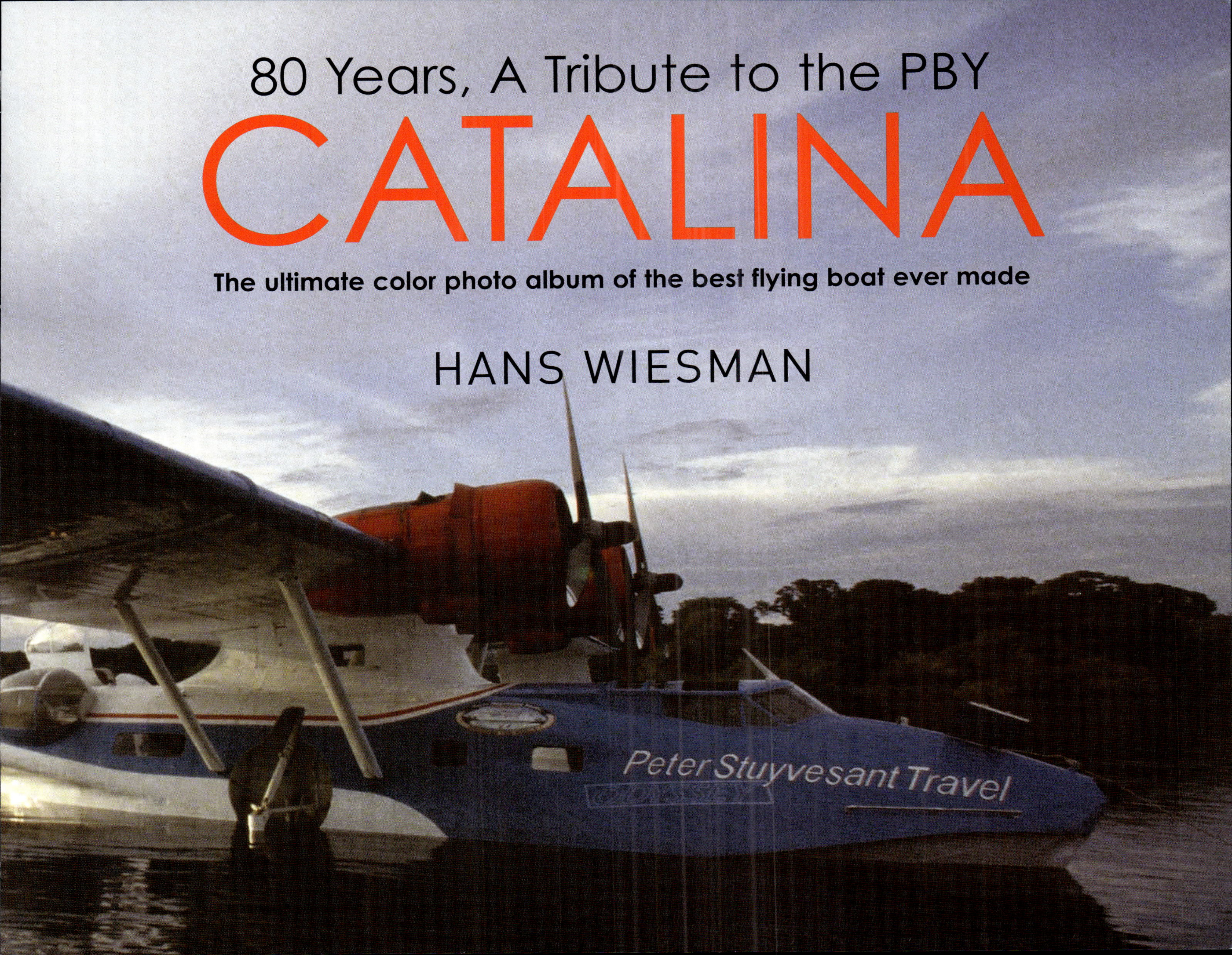

Contents

First published in 2018

Design and typesetting Ian Hughes, www.mousematdesign.com
Historical sourcing and proofreading David Legg, www.catalina.org.uk
Photo upgrading and enhancement Peter Schutte, www.peterschuttebeeldbewerking.nl

ISBN: 978-9-08281-000-4

Printed and bound in the USA

Romancing the Catalina

In a rush, I ran to the river – I could hear the sound of the engines coming closer. It was just at the end of the road, only three minutes walk from our house. I had barely arrived at the muddy bank when there she came, majestically making a low fly-pass over the water of the Mahakam River. In awe, I stood there nailed to the ground. I was watching the scene as a 5-year-old boy, living in a remote jungle settlement somewhere out there in the smothering heart of the Borneo rainforest.

The Catalina made a turn and lined up for a river landing. A great splash of white water sprayed along the hull. It all went so smoothly, and before I knew it, the flying boat had shut its engines and moored on a buoy, close to the riverbank. My father had come after me, and together we stepped into a small rowboat and boarded the aircraft for a flight to Balikpapan. It was not far away, but for me, it was like traveling into outer space.

I met that plane some 60 years ago and shall never forget the excitement that mesmerized me for a lifetime.

In 1993 and 1994, I had the incredible luck of flying again in a Catalina, this time over the Atlantic and the Americas. My passion for that plane had made me conceptualize a TV documentary script for three European Networks. As a creative director, I was participating in a bid for an original Global Travel TV series concept, in the spirit of Jules Verne's *Around the World in 80 Days*.

My proposal, named 'The Catalina Odyssey', was the outright winner in the contest. It was a pure and simple idea, based on my first flight experiences with that Cat, way back in 1952.

This book is the ultimate reflection of what the Catalina means to me. It is also about the realization of my dream to fly that aircraft again – low and slow over endless oceans and coasts – in search of my lost Borneo hero, the Catalina – our 'transport to heaven' and in French: 'a la recherche du temps perdu'.

View the 400 photos that I have selected for this idyllic book, which cover the PBY Catalina in its career from 1937 to 2017 – a lifespan of 80 years of that flying boat and still counting as there are a number of operational survivors around the world that we can still admire at air shows and in museums. They are all in this unique photo album about the best flying boat ever made, a book like none other you have seen before.

Hans Wiesman

(Photo Frans Lemmens)

Foreword

I HAVE HAD an interest in – some would say an obsession with – the Catalina flying boat for almost forty years. In that time I have met and corresponded with many people who appreciate the type and amongst them have been a few fellow obsessives! One of those is Hans Wiesman. As you enjoy this book you will discover that his interest was started through boyhood flights in oil company Catalinas in Borneo – later, he also became obsessed with the Douglas Dakota and Harley-Davidson motorcycles! But despite these distractions, his love of Catalinas extended to organizing two epic 'Catalina Odysseys' from Europe to South America and back in the mid-1990s in what were by then fifty-year old Cats'. Hans is anything but an 'armchair' enthusiast!

Hans's latest project is this beautifully produced book, lovingly put together, and a tribute to both the world's most successful flying boat and his enthusiasm for the wonderful Catalina.

David Legg, Editor of *The Catalina News* magazine

I remember my first encounter with the PBY Catalina, which took place in Borneo 1952 on the Mahakam River. That memory is similar to the idyllic scene in this photo. The Shell and KLM/Garuda owned Catalinas landed on the river close to our house, and passengers were boarding/disembarking via the large waist hatch into a small boat that was rowed to the riverbank. The Catalina frequently visited our remote jungle settlement, Sanga Sanga, as part of its itinerary to Eastern Borneo from Surabaya, Java, via Balikpapan and Samarindah to Tarakan. It was all rather primitive, but many of us, myself included, have very special feelings of nostalgia when seeing such a scene. For me, it was one more reason to write this book; there is no better way to keep the passion for this aircraft alive.

(Photo of the Shell-operated Catalina PK-AKS in the Dutch East Indies courtesy of Prudent Staal)

Introduction

I TRACE MY passion for the DC-3/C-47/Dakota and the PBY Catalina back to the age of five when I lived in the Borneo Jungle. Along with my father (an oil exploring engineer), I flew frequently in both aircraft in the years between 1950 and 1956.

Shortly after the war, my father was engaged by Shell to become a 'lifetime expat'. In 1947 he took the family from Holland to Curacao, and a year later to Trinidad. It was there that I, along with my family, made my first flight on board a DC-3 from Linea Aeropostal Venezolana (LAV). From there, we sailed back to Holland over the Atlantic and on to the Republic of Indonesia. In January 1950, Indonesia had just received its independence after 350 years of Colonial Dutch rule. Less than five years earlier, the Pacific War had come to an end but had left many scars in Eastern Borneo.

The omnipresent oil fields, exploited by Shell before the outbreak of the war in early 1942, were a key target for the Japanese invaders. Towards the end of the war, after more than three years of occupation by Japanese forces, eastern Borneo came under heavy Allied attack as a strategic fuel station for the Japanese Navy. By September 1944, the USAAF had launched bombing raids from the Biak Islands in western New Guinea. Those raids inflicted fatal damage to the oil refinery installations and storage tanks, cutting off more than 60% of the Japanese fuel supply so badly needed for their desperate naval war effort in the Philippines. In July 1945, Australian troops, with the support of American forces, started the invasion of the beaches in Balikpapan and Tarakan, the most important oil refineries on the east coast of that huge pacific island.

Catalinas were engaged in that assault (named Operation OBOE II), and one of them was left behind on the Balikpapan invasion beach after a crash landing. It was exposed to the elements for years, along with a couple of LCM Landing Craft (a photo of this wrecked Catalina on Balikpapan beach has been discovered, see page 67). Masses of military road transports such as trucks and Jeeps were also left behind by the Australian and American troops.

The ravages of that war were still fully present when I came to Borneo in 1950 on a DC-3 flight from Jakarta to the city of Banjarmasin. There were bombed-out storage tank parks, devastated oil drilling and pump installations, crashed landing craft, huge bunkers with smelly, charred interiors, and even a half-sunken submarine whose conning tower protruded from the bay water as a marker buoy for the shallow waters. It was all ubiquitous evidence of a ferocious war that had raged there for years.

For the Japanese military forces it must have been hell since July 1944, as many of the soldiers refused to surrender and were burnt to death inside their bunkers with flamethrowers – a most effective, but cruel weapon. But, when I arrived with my family five years later, the island had returned to more peaceful circumstances. Actually, it was paradise on Earth for me as a curious and inquisitive boy. A playground such as few kids of that age will have encountered, it added an unforgettable thrill, albeit with a few setbacks. The frequent encounters with jungle animals – snakes, crocodiles, spiders, foot-long purple centipedes, and aggressive monkeys – were very exciting, but occasionally left a few scars. The jungle started where the back garden ended and many of those animals came to the backyard in search of food. They showed respect for the adults and the pet dogs, and usually ran away or were killed by the servants with their *parangs* (short swords). But for brazen 6- or 7-year-old kids who tried to stop the intruders, they showed no respect at all. Instead, the larger animals instantly attacked, resulting in a bite or two, followed by hospital, stitches and tears.

The military transports left behind by the Allied troops were rapidly seized by the Dutch Military and by Shell in 1946 who were soon back in business, re-establishing their oil production. My father drove a Willys Jeep, while the repair stations drove the Chevrolet 2.5-ton trucks, the Dodge trucks and command cars in all their versions. They kept the oil exploration and drilling industry going, out there in the jungle posts. The rebuilding of all damaged oil pump equipment and port facilities, plus the expansion of the oil drilling installations, were accomplished in an around-the-clock effort to supply oil to a new post-war world that craved fuel.

In that frenzy, Shell Oil Company decided that to efficiently supply their remote oil drilling stations with new staff, personnel, spare parts, food etc. they needed aircraft – amphibians to be more precise. The first batch of PBY Catalinas was bought and converted in the USA for its new combined passenger/cargo transport role. The Shell-owned aircraft flew, on a frequent basis, north from Java, travelling along the east coast of Borneo, visiting Tanjung, Sanga Sanga, Samarinda, Tarakan, and Balikpapan.

My family lived in a small oil pumping station, named Tanjung, and later in Sanga Sanga, a jungle outback post along the 1000-km-long Mahakam River, near the river city of Samarinda. It was here that the Cat landed, more or less in front of our house. In an era where there was no TV, no DVDs, no computer games, not even a cinema, this event was the thing to look forward to. As well as being a spectacular sight, the Catalina brought sweets, gifts, mail, news, magazines and new people from far away – from a world that I only knew from the family photo album, from stories and a couple of magazine pictures. Once a week, a space-shuttle-like aircraft came flying in from that other world. And that plane landed right there on the crocodile-infested river – a dangerous place to be.

Such an awe-inspiring spectacle made the Catalina ascend to almost mythical proportions for the young boy who stood there gazing on the riverbank. This Catalina was not only the link to that parallel world but it was, in fact, like a cartoon hero: what Batman was for normal Western kids, or what a sports or pop star is now for young boys. Without doubt, my flights over the Archipelago in the ex-KLM/Garuda Douglas DC-3s and in the Shell/Garuda-operated Catalina left an indelible impression on me.

These memories from Borneo were to last much longer than I could have ever imagined, back in 1957 – the year my family left Indonesia. We returned to Holland where I went to a Christian high school in The Hague, then went on to study sociology and economics at Rotterdam University. My parents moved to destinations new as Shell expats and lived for years in Yokohama, Japan, and Melbourne, Australia. I visited them every year and, on the way there and back, made sightseeing stopovers in Manila, Singapore, Bangkok, Jakarta, Hong Kong etc. Almost immediately, traveling the world became second nature for me and that propensity came in handy in my later professional career.

I was born in Holland, but started to wander around the world when I was a baby. Right after the war, my father began working for Shell Oil Company as an oil-exploring engineer. With my family, I traveled to Curacao and some time later to Trinidad. In this photo you see me as a toddler with my Mom and sister Corine (to my left) and Rita, just about to board a DC-3 operated by LAV (Linea Aeropostal Venezolana), flying back from Trinidad. It was probably my first flight on board a Dakota but definitely not my last, as we were about to travel from the West Indies to the East Indies. Borneo was our station for the next seven years. That was the beginning of an adventure-packed episode where I would meet and fly the iconic Catalina.

In 1976, I starting working for an International Marketing Corporation, and was soon responsible for the development of new advertising themes and mass media/TV coverage of sports-related events. I entered the world of rally and racing with powerboating, motorcycle racing, and Formula-1. Also, the Windsurfing Pro World Cups took me from Monaco to Maui, from Guadeloupe to New Caledonia, from the Virgin Islands to Cabo Verde and beyond. It was a hectic life that lasted for 24 years, with an average six months per year away from home. During all my travels, I frequently ran into vintage aircraft, and as an advertising executive, I created an image platform for a vintage clothing brand, with an advertising theme named 'Cargo Pilot.' Under my direction, the first photo/film sessions for the brand were shot in Alaska, later in the Caribbean, Venezuela, and Bolivia, with the legendary DC-3/C-47 and the Curtiss Commando C-46 as the 'props' or thematic focal points. The old passion for the aircraft from my Borneo youth flared up again and became more compelling.

By the year 2000, I had left the corporation and started a company that sold artifacts, furniture and interior objects made from recovered DC-3 parts. The best-selling object was the DC-3 wing desk, made from the 230cm-long detachable outer wing panel of that legendary aircraft. With a mirror-polished finish and four sleek aluminum legs underneath, this limited series genuine wing desk turned into a much-desired interior design object, becoming a collector's item for sale in London and Monaco's high-class antique and design shops. But they soon reached the limitations of war-made stuff: my major suppliers (including Air Atlantique, in Coventry, England) ran out of surplus scrap wing tips that were recovered from British barns, bone yards etc.

In order to cope with a growing demand, I started to make my first epic 'Dakota Hunter' expeditions overseas, in search of the Legendary DC-3. Arriving in the USA, I went to see suppliers in Miami, San Antonio, Reno, Tucson, Anchorage, and Oshkosh, i.e. all places where bone yards and the DC-3 surplus parts could still be found in numbers. But even in the USA, the supply of the scrap vintage aviation relics soon ran dry.

I have made well over 20 expeditions all over the globe from the Yukon to the High Andes, from the Caribbean to Madagascar, from the Amazon to Thailand – and during my trips I came across derelict Catalinas in Venezuela and Colombia. I started to write about my adventures in 'The Dakota Hunter' newsletter, published online on my Facebook page of the same name. With so many adventures and fascinating photos collected over the years, the writing of a blog and book seemed the obvious next step. In May 2015, my first book – *The Dakota Hunter* – was published worldwide by Casemate USA/UK, from Philadelphia, New Jersey, and Oxford, England.

The Catalina Photo Album

This book has been produced with the intention of making it, arguably, the most colorful tribute to the iconic Consolidated PBY Catalina flying boat. It covers the 80 years of its existence from 1937–2017 and contains a wealth of photographs of the aircraft from before, during and after World War II, and up to the present day – including recent photos of the PBY 'survivors'. With only a very few of these aircraft left in airworthy condition, this book offers the reader a fascinating visual record of this versatile aircraft in its multiple roles, during its full life span. It contains some 400 sublime photos, most in color, and many never previously published.

The Catalina flying boat was a contemporary of the Douglas DC-3/C-47/Dakota. Both legendary aircraft started their careers as prototypes in the mid-1930s and had a lot in common, although their silhouettes were markedly different. Both aircraft had more or less equal dimensions and used the same all-aluminum airframe construction with the novel riveting techniques, and the majority of both types used the same radial aero engines –Twin Wasp R-1830s (made by Pratt & Whitney). Developed from earlier models from 1933, this radial piston motor became one of the most successful and most built aeroengines of all time. Both planes had their maiden flights in the same year – the Catalina in March 1935, the Douglas DC-3 in December 1935 – while their mass production began in 1936.

The Douglas DC-3 got off to a flying start as a civil aircraft. Almost overnight, it came to dominate the commercial market for airliner passenger transport in Northern America. Meanwhile, the PBY was designed from scratch as a military aircraft in its intended role as a Patrol Bomber (hence the prefix PB). By 1939, the PBY was considered to be obsolete, nearing the end of its military service life due to rapid development towards more modern 4-engine Patrol Aircraft and Bombers. But, from September 1939, with war in Europe imminent, the Consolidated factory suddenly received mass orders from the US Navy, England, France, and the Netherlands. The PBY got its name 'Catalina' from the British in 1940 and the name was later adopted by other users, including the USAAF and the US Navy, while Royal Canadian Air Force versions were known as the Canso.

The 'Cat' had a highly successful military career in WWII in nearly all theatres of war, and, in sharp contrast to the DC-3, it only entered the civil transport market in numbers after the war, as a surplus aircraft from the military storage depots. In spite of this 'Military Purposed Design' handicap, the Catalina was destined to become the most versatile utility transport for passengers and cargo, and in the specialized roles as a firefighting aircraft and an aerial photography/survey aircraft. By late 1941, alongside the initial pure flying boat version (the PBY-5 had no wheels), an amphibian version had been developed with retractable tricycle landing gear, which added the capacity of an optional landing/takeoff from Terra Firma. It would render the aircraft even more versatile, and, ultimately, it was this model, the type PBY-5A and the later model PBY-6A (with A for Amphibian) that would contribute so much to the longevity of the aircraft's career and give her that second lease of life after 1945 that would last for another astounding 50 to 60 years.

With that phenomenal life extension, the PBY Catalina belongs to the very select league of WWII-built legendary planes that even up to today can still be

Nice photo of Plane Sailing's first Catalina G-BLSC in RAF colors. This picture was taken in the spring of 1994 while flying over Duxford Airfield, Cambridge, UK. It was my personal 'test flight' and was flown by Captain Paul Warren Wilson. I can be seen on board the aircraft, sitting in the blister. Later that year, this same Catalina, in its new livery, flew us over the Americas during the second Catalina Odyssey Transatlantic Tour. More photos of this tour and this Super Catalina can be seen in Chapter 4, The Catalina Odysseys.
(Photo Ronald Speyer)

found flying, albeit in limited numbers only. Those 'Icons of Victory' (comprising also the Douglas DC-3/C-47, the Curtiss Commando C-46s, the 'Twin' Beech C-45s, plus a handful of vintage Bombers and Fighters) are all part of the 'Jurassic Park of Aviation' – the last of the wartime-made flying dinosaurs that have survived for over half a century, while some even continue to fly to this day.

While the Catalina/Canso's active role as a firefighter has recently come to an end, there are still a few PBYs that fly passengers at air shows and special events with water landings. Plus, a number of flying Catalinas owned by museums, foundations or private operators fly on a frequent basis for entertainment purposes and for occasional Movie/TV productions. Their numbers have steadily come down over the years, but in a few remarkable cases, museums and private foundations or operators have started new projects to bring derelict Catalinas back into the museums as static displays. Some are even planning to bring them back in the air as operational aircraft!

During the war, the Catalina's reputation rose to an iconic level due to its role as a long-range Patrol Bomber aircraft; its effectiveness as an enemy ship/fleet spotter; and, in its Anti-submarine warfare (ASW) role, for defending Allied shipping lanes over the vast oceans of the Atlantic and Pacific, and the Indian Ocean. Moreover, the aircraft was much appreciated by all Allied Army and Navy services for its role as a 'Dumbo', a Search and Rescue (SAR) aircraft that had the unique capacity to fly long distances, helping crews of downed aircraft or torpedoed ships by throwing out dinghies, food and life jackets, while directing rescue boats to the drowned pilots/sailors. And, in quite a few cases, Catalinas have been able to make risky water landings on open seas (often a very challenging operation with high ocean swells) and pick up the survivors from ditched aircraft or sunken ships.

In the Pacific War, these versatile and rugged aircraft were developed into a specialty role that even the designers at Consolidated could never have foreseen. Under the name of the Black Cats, a night-raider version of the Catalina was born and inflicted tremendous damage on Japanese port facilities, submarines, and shipping lines with mine laying, depth charges, bombs and torpedo launches that were carried at under-wing hard points. It was the WWII forerunner of the Stealth Bomber, but it had also adapted Stuka-like dive-bombing techniques for attacking enemy submarines and ships at a steep angle.

The Catalina was built in lower numbers than the C-47. The DC-3/C-47 ended its entire production of all versions after ten years of continuous production, with a total of over 10,600 made (excluding the Russian and Japanese license-built C-47s), while the Catalina's production numbers in the same ten years of production was just over 3,300 (including the license-built Cansos/Catalinas in Canada and Russia). That is roughly 30% of the Douglas DC-3/C-47 combined production numbers. That number may seem low, but it is an all-time world record for the production of this specialty category of floating planes/flying boats. Actually more than the total production of all other types and makes of seaplanes/flying boats/amphibians in all countries together! Apart from that, it also is the longest-living type and, therefore, the claim 'best flying boat ever built' seems righteous and the type deserves a top-ranking position in the '100 Years of Aviation History's Hall of Fame'.

My gratitude to the album's contributors

The making of this photo album has been accomplished with the help of many people. Most of them, like myself, have a longstanding interest in, or even a passion for the Catalina that goes beyond the mere collecting of photographs and images of that plane. Often, such passions lead to networking on social media and the sharing of information, photographs, leads, finds – very useful when preparing for a book like this one. It is clear that my participation in forums, my blog-post writing (under the name The Dakota Hunter on Facebook and in the *War History Online* magazine) and years of networking have contributed to the overwhelming supply of photos from which I could select the very best 400 photos for this book.

Photos have come from the major museums, operators and (semi) professional photographers. Many of the largest aviation museums in the USA (including the Smithsonian Institution in Washington, DC) have given me their full support, and my requests for their cooperation were honored. They have sent me their best photos. Also, my Facebook friends and the audience reading my Dakota Hunter blog posts have responded generously to my requests to send photographs from their family albums of their fathers, uncles or grandfathers who once flew as Catalina/Canso crews. Others have sent me vintage photographs from bygone days with a post-war Catalina in the picture. They have all helped to make this book so outstanding, with such a unique variety of photos: over 400 different images, reflecting the PBY's full life span of eight decades.

More photos and assistance in my global search came from my long-time friend, photographer and aviation buff, Michael Prophet. I met him for the first time in 1993 when the Catalina Z-CAT landed in Holland for an 'undercover' re-spray job in the sponsor's colors, prior to its press presentation the next day. Out of the blue, he stood there at the gate, almost smelling the presence of Cat inside the closed hangar, and asked me if he could have a glimpse. I invited him to come in, and ever since we have had a special relationship as two dedicated aficionados of vintage aircraft.

Also, I would like to express my appreciation to the two owners of the Catalinas that I hired for making the epic Catalina Odyssey trips to America in the mid-1990s. They have both helped me in the creation of this book by granting permission to publish their photos. I feel very honored to have flown with them. In preparation for the first voyage, I met Frenchman Pierre Jaunet in Zimbabwe. Pierre was the owner of Z-CAT when we hired it in 1993 (since the mid-1990s, this Catalina has been flying in New Zealand). A year later, in 1994, the second Odyssey flight was done with Paul Warren Wilson, the owner of Plane Sailing Air Displays Ltd, and the captain who flew us with his Super

Catalina VR-BPS. Both Cats are extensively described and depicted in the Catalina Odysseys Chapter 4 of this book.

For the Odyssey flights, we needed a ton of landing permits all over Europe, America and NW Africa. That was no small job and needed a lot of preparation, with patience and diplomacy. The final flight plans were excellently prepared by my own sister, Corine Quaterman-Wiesman. Corine was a private pilot, flying her own Cessna from Vermont all over the USA and has the same global wandering DNA as I have. She was the perfect tour manager for this mission, even able to arrange a unique water landing with Z-CAT in New York City harbor – right in front of the Statue of Liberty. Thanks, Corine, I will never forget the fabulous trips that we made together. All permits arranged by you with the authorities for 25 or so water landings at the most idyllic places have contributed so much to the making of the most awesome photographs printed in chapter 4.

Finally, words of special gratitude go to David Legg, Editor of *The Catalina News* magazine (a publication of the Catalina Society, Duxford, England). The foreword to this book is from his hand and he has given me tremendous help with tips, clues, photos, and the text editing of this book. David has a reputation in the Catalina world for his encyclopedic knowledge of the historical facts of the Catalina and his support in the making of my book was more than instrumental. His book, titled *Consolidated PBY Catalina: The Peacetime Record* (published by Airlife, England) contains many Catalina facts, numbers and 'nomenclature'. It was for me a most helpful source of information about registration numbers and historical data of the PBY aircraft during and after the war.

Hans Wiesman

Note: For a more complete list of all museums, operators, owners, photographers and contributors, please see the Acknowledgements on page 287. Given the large amount of photographs that the author has collected for this album, there are many different sources used and extensive research has been done. Every effort has been made to locate and obtain permission from the copyright owners of the photographs in this book. For any errors or omissions, tips or clues, please contact the author via the website: www.catalinaphotoalbum.com.

Where passions meet. Every year since 2004, we have ridden out with our Vintage Harley Davidson Club on a pilgrimage tour to Normandy for the D-Day commemorations on the 6th of June. An avid Harley rider for 50 years, I met this immaculate Dutch Catalina PH-PBY at Cherbourg Airport, Normandy, France, in 2014. My friend Prudent Staal and his team of the 'Stichting Vrienden van de Catalina' had flown her in from Lelystad, Holland, to participate in the D-Day air shows and parades, along with eleven C-47s/DC-3s/Dakotas that came to celebrate the 70th anniversary of the Normandy Invasion. This Catalina is the oldest surviving flying PBY in the world.
(Photo courtesy of Onno Wieringa)

The Wartime Years

On 28 October 1933, the Consolidated Aircraft Corporation in Buffalo, NY, had finished its design for a maritime flying boat, in compliance with the specifications issued by the US Navy. The prototype XP3Y-1 was built in Buffalo, but was moved to Norfolk, Virginia, for flight testing; the maiden flight being accomplished on 21 March 1935. It was an outright success and some six months later, the prototype aircraft even broke a distance record. Soon after, the aircraft was flown to San Diego, CA, where the company opened a brand new factory that commenced production of the PBY series in 1937.

From the start, many modifications were made to the original design. First with an extended fuselage, while the redesigning of the tail section was to become an ongoing affair in order to resolve the persistent directional control problems and heavy controls on the rudder. Additionally, developments in the aero-engine technology took place so quickly, that almost every year stronger versions of Pratt & Whitney's Twin Wasp R-1830 with ever-increasing max. hp output came available. It started in 1936 with the 850 hp R-1830-64 version, which was soon up to 1,000 hp, and finally, in 1941, came the R-1830-82 versions with 1,200 hp output.

In the mid 1930s Consolidated won a US Navy contract for the PBY-1 and beat the competition design from Douglas, be it mainly due to a lower price offer. On 25 July 1936, the US Navy made its first order for 60 PBY-1 flying boats, with delivery taking place in 1937, now over 80 years ago. A second order followed soon after for the slightly modified model PBY-2. The next model PBY-3 had stronger engines at max 1,000 hp, and sliding hatches on the sides of the fuselages for the mounting of Machine guns on either side. The next model, PBY-4, was the first model to receive those peculiar bubbled frog's eyes, a small number of the production run receiving them. Those 'Blister' posts featured an eyelid style opening for the machine guns, yielding more reach and visibility for the gunners.

All those types were delivered before December 1941, the month that the USA entered the war right after the Pearl Harbor attack. While the type was considered by many to be obsolete, the threat of war in Europe had brought massive orders from the UK and France. Also, the Dutch showed interest and even the Russians bought three examples.

At the outbreak of the European war in September 1939, the British ordered 50 aircraft of the latest type, PBY-5, with (again) a redesigned tail and rudder, and the newest version of the P&W engine R-1830-82, rated at 1,200 max hp. It was on this order in that same year, 1939, that the name 'Catalina' was introduced by the British, while the US Navy did not adopt the name until 1 October 1941.

The French Ministry of War ordered 30 PBYs but due to the outbreak of the Blitzkrieg in May 1940, the capitulation and occupation of France obstructed the delivery of those aircraft. Australia ordered 18 PBYs and the Dutch made an order for 48 aircraft (36 pure flying boats and twelve amphibians) for use in their colony, the Dutch East Indies. At that time (1939–1940), the war was still considered remote, but it would turn out to be much closer than anyone could have foreseen. Both air arms were to receive more Catalinas in due course.

In order to cope with the huge wartime military orders for Catalinas of various models, the company had to make some drastic steps to expand the production capacity. Consolidated merged with Vultee in 1941, becoming Consolidated Vultee Aircraft, later abbreviated to Convair.

Their San Diego factory was soon supplemented by a brand-new manufacturing plant at Lake Pontchartrain, New Orleans, Louisiana. Additionally, wartime Catalina production was sub-contracted to two Canadian manufacturers whilst a Russian State-owned plant built examples under license:

- Boeing Aircraft of Canada Ltd, Vancouver, British Columbia
- Canadian Vickers Ltd, Montreal, Quebec – reformed in 1944 as Canadair Ltd, the later manufacturer of the famed Canadair firefighting amphibians
- The Russians received a license to build the Catalina but their production facility was soon overrun by the invading German troops and only 24 Soviet-engined examples were built
- Finally, in 1944–1945, the Naval Aircraft Factory at Philadelphia produced a substantially redesigned PBY variant, named the Nomad or PBN-1. Most of those aircraft went to Russia

The Consolidated PBY Catalina was beyond any doubt the most versatile and successful flying boat/amphibian ever built. It served in large numbers not just with the US Army, Navy and Coast Guard during the war, but also with the Air Forces of Britain, Canada, Australia and New Zealand, with the Danes, Free French Forces, and Norwegians, as well as in Brazil, Chile, and Indonesia under the Dutch Colonial Navy Air Force (Marine Luchtvaart Dienst, or MLD).

Supplied with the two most reliable 14-cylinder air-cooled piston engines, the aircraft was employed as a maritime reconnaissance aircraft, as a (torpedo) bomber, as an anti-submarine weapon, a mine-laying platform, and as a search-and-rescue aircraft for day and night. In special operations, it ferried mail, Military VIPs, and secret agents across the world's oceans.

Remarkably, the Catalina gained its first combat experience in British hands. After the first order of 50, the Air Ministry purchased around 700 more Catalinas, and they served with RAF squadrons all over the world, some being passed on to other allied air forces.

Catalinas of the RAF and RCAF over the Atlantic

Great Britain was at war with Germany and relied heavily on its supply lines from overseas, mainly from USA and Canada, for keeping up its war industry that was in dire need of strategic materials such as oil, aluminum, steel, copper and zinc, but also (semi-) assembled machines such as aircraft, guns and weapons. The German U-boat fleet was to become a very serious threat to British shipping lines, while there was at that time no aircraft capable of giving any long-distance coverage to the shipping convoys.

In order to resolve this gap in the Atlantic protective 'shield' against the marauding U-boats, the problem could only be tackled with a coverage established on both sides of the pond. The RAF operated types such as the Beaufort, Hudson and Stranraer aircraft, which had insufficient range to deter the marauding U-boats in the mid-Atlantic. But the Catalina's remarkable, long-range capacity came to the rescue in the all-new ocean-wide battle that was about to escalate into a disaster for the British in 1940–1941.

On top of the submarine threat, yet another potential 'convoy-killer' came onto the scene. The fastest battleship of all time, the *Bismarck*, made a daring breakout from the Baltic Sea into the Atlantic with the clear mission to join in the annihilation of the Allied supply lines to the United Kingdom. Being hunted by the Royal Navy, the superior battleship first downed HMS *Hood* and then disappeared for two days. On 26 May 1941, it was an RAF Catalina that spotted the battleship on its way to Brest, a major naval port in Western France. The Cat radioed the find to the fleet and the rest is Naval History. Operation 'Sink the Bismarck' was accomplished; a day later on 27 May 1941, the pride of the Kriegsmarine finally sank, taking 2,000 sailors with her into the abyss of the Atlantic.

The German submarine fleet became very successful in intercepting the maritime supply lines due to their ever-improving assault techniques, and due to the number of U-boats coming from a Kriegsmarine that could exclusively focus on the operation and construction of new submarines. The German occupation of French harbors from mid-1940 offered a free, unobstructed entry into the Atlantic for Hitler's 'wolf packs', while their re-arming and refueling took place in the bomb-free submarine pens in Lorient that were nearly impossible to be destroyed from the air and so offered shelter.

With that 'Cat on the prowl' from both sides of the ocean, soon the RAF and the RCAF became the biggest users of the PBYs. The Canadians operated no less than thirteen anti-submarine squadrons; five on the Canadian west coast, six on the east coast and two overseas (the first Catalina squadron, No. 413, later moved to Ceylon). The Canadians identified the RCAF version of the PBY flying boat as 'Canso' and the amphibian as 'Canso A'. That amphibian version was yet another brilliant extension of the basic and pure flying boat design, which could only land on water.

The first PBY-5A was introduced in mid-1941 as a modification on the previous PBY-4, in which a retractable tricycle landing gear was installed. It made the aircraft heavier by about a ton, hence slower in speed, but the greatest bonus was its versatility as a real amphibian that could also land on a strip of runway. The 'standard' PBY needed the mounting by hand of beaching gear in the water, and a tractor to pull the flying boat out of the water on a ramp for maintenance and re-loading. All that cumbersome and time-consuming handling was over with the arrival of the amphibian versions PBY-5A, Canso A, and the later model PBY-6A. They just crawled out of the water under their own power, with propellers running and landing gear lowered in the water – it was a piece of cake!

Catalinas in South Africa

In 1942, the war in North Africa was at its peak. Allied and Axis forces attacked and counter-attacked. All supplies to the Allied forces in Egypt had to pass round the Cape by sea. The antiquated aircraft operating in South Africa under RAF command could no longer provide adequate defense of the sea routes around the Cape. To help protect shipping against the U-boat threat, the RAF's 262 Sqn started operating from Durban's Congella Base, using Catalina flying boats for the long patrol flights over the Indian Ocean. Langebaan lagoon was used regularly by the Catalinas for patrols on the Atlantic side of South Africa. In 1943 a detachment of Dutch Navy Catalinas, that had escaped the Japanese invasion of the Dutch East Indies in early 1942, was also active in Saldanha Bay/Langebaan lagoon (West Coast Peninsula, North of Kaapstad, SA). As the RAF crews returned home after their tours of duty, more and more South Africans were absorbed into 262 Sqn. In February 1945, just before the end of the War, 35 Sqn (SAAF) was born out of 262 Sqn. The new squadron's Catalinas soldiered on, and anti-submarine warfare remained a priority until the end of the war.

By mid-1943, there was a remarkable turn of the tide in the Atlantic U-boat battles. The massive ordering of the Catalina at the start of the war had a lot to do with the U-boat threat, as it was virtually the only weapon available in sufficient numbers that was capable of making such long-range flights over the oceans carrying bombs, depth charges, and machine guns to attack a surfaced U-boat. With a crew of seven, there were two 0.30-inch (7.62-mm) machine guns (later versions carried .50 guns) in the nose turret, the side blister posts, and in the under-belly tail position. 1,800 kg of bombs and depth charges were normally carried at under-wing hard points. The Cat had a standard range of 4,100 km at 280 km/h top speed but flew at a max of 160 km/h (100 mph or 90 knots) on the long-range mission in order to save fuel.

With hundreds of Catalinas delivered by 1941/1942 and swarming about the Atlantic around the clock, the U-boats started to feel the heat of being hunted. After two years of being the superior hunters, it must have been an uncomfortable feeling that they now were at risk of attack by ships and aircraft as soon as they opened fire or had torpedoed ships in convoys, and later even from 'out of the blue'!

The Germans were unaware that their magical secret code, Enigma, (which allowed for encrypted radio traffic with the home base) was deciphered, giving the Allies a good insight into their itineraries. Replies from the U-boats enabled the Allies to use direction-finding HF/DF, to locate a submarine as soon as it was using its radio. Later in the war, radar tracking equipment arrived on the Catalinas and that gave the hunting aircraft the sharp eagle's eyes to trace a surfaced submarine in all weather conditions, by day and night. It was the beginning of the end of the U-boat's superiority over the Atlantic.

The combined Allied aerial and naval anti-submarine attacks became more and more effective, and the number of downed U-boats rose to such high levels that the Kriegsmarine's new Commander-in-Chief, Karl Dönitz, had no other choice than to temporarily suspend all operations in the Atlantic in May 1943. Dönitz had been appointed in January 1943 as 'Gross Admiral', being the genius behind the U-boats' successes, but only three months later, he took the drastic step to recall his 'wolf packs' back to their stations for a total reconsideration of their attack plans. The Catalina had become his worst nightmare. Sure, the U-boats were to return, but their superiority in the Atlantic never recovered from that blow. Ultimately, the PBY played a substantial part in winning the Battle of the Atlantic.

(Info via Buskruit Burger)

Catalinas in the Pacific War

The Pacific War had effectively started long before the Japanese attacked Pearl Harbor on 7 December 1941. In May 1940, when France lost its independence against Germany, Japan was the first to take advantage of that defeat by occupying French Indochina (Vietnam, Laos, Cambodia) and this rapid deployment was a sign of worse to come.

On the very same day that the US Navy was attacked in Hawaii, a Catalina of 205 Sqn, RAF spotted an invasion force that approached the Malayan shore near Kota Bahru. That Catalina was shot down by Japanese fighters, and, unfortunately, was not able to radio the planned invasion to Air Headquarters in Singapore. The Catalina's 7-men crew, under command of Flight Officer Patrick Bedell, was killed in the ensuing crash, the first non-American casualties of the Pacific War that had started that same day. Sadly, in the ensuing naval battle on 10 December, both HMS *Repulse* and HMS *Prince of Wales* were sunk when they attempted to stop the Japanese invasion of Malaya.

With the Pacific war now rapidly spreading over SE Asia, Catalina squadrons from the RAF, USAAF, RAAF and the Dutch East Indies MLD became engaged in the patrol flights in search of the Japanese Imperial Navy. They were preparing to take over all the existing Colonies from the British Empire and the Dutch East Indies.

By early 1942, just months after Pearl Harbor and faster than anybody could have imagined, the Japanese Navy and Army had attained their initial strategic goals, taking the Philippines, Malaya, Singapore and the Dutch East Indies. The latter, with its vital oil resources on the islands of Sumatra and Borneo, was particularly important to Japan as they suffered from an oil embargo that had been put in place by the USA before the outbreak of the war.

The Dutch East Indies military forces were surprised by the speed of the Japanese invasion in Singapore, Sumatra and Java. Some of their Catalinas, along with a couple of DC-3s and Dornier Do-24 flying boats, were able to escape at the last moment to Australia, while a couple of PBYs flew from Java to the West, and landed in Ceylon (now Sri-Lanka). Of those Dutch Catalinas some were transferred to South Africa, others to Ceylon and Australia.

On 4 April 1942, a Catalina that was flown by Canadian Squadron Leader L. J. Birchall spotted a Japanese Carrier fleet that was approaching Ceylon with the mission to destroy the Royal Navy's Indian Ocean fleet. This time, the Catalina's patrol flight worked wonders as an early warning system and the fleet could take its precautions. (Contrary to popular belief, the Catalina involved was on loan from the RAF and was therefore not a Canso.)

It was also a Catalina that, in early June 1942, spotted the Japanese fleet approaching the appropriately named Midway Island, a small atoll situated halfway between California and the Philippines, 1,300 miles west of Oahu, Hawaii. The US Navy was more or less aware of an imminent attack on the Midway Island with its strategically situated air force base. Catalinas and B-17s could fly to the base from Hawaii, and the aircraft were desperately needed there for their long-range ocean patrols over the central Pacific.

On 4 June 1942, the day the battle started, 11 PBYs were leaving Midway at daybreak to run their search patterns for the fleet, and their main targets were, evidently, the aircraft carriers. At 05:34, a PBY reported the sighting of two Japanese carriers, and another Cat spotted the inbound airstrike wave ten minutes later. This crucial information from the Catalinas, along with the early radar systems that the US Navy had developed, plus the deciphering of the enemy's secret navy code, all gave the Americans an edge with their spy eyes and ears wide open.

The final outcome of that battle was an outright victory for the US Navy, although they took a heavy beating from the Japanese aerial attacks and lost one of their three carriers, the USS *Yorktown*. During the first day, the Japanese Navy lost three aircraft carriers in what seemed one of the most disastrous four minutes of action in WWII.

Only the carrier *Hiryu* stayed operational for the day, albeit fatally damaged. She finally sunk the next day, annihilating the total Imperial carrier invasion fleet within 24 hours, while the rest of the 'invincible' Imperial fleet was in full retreat. One could say that 'The Rising Sun' had gone down early that day, and it was Japan's last major naval campaign against the USA.

Amazingly, only six months after the Imperial Japanese Navy had started the war against the USA with the attack on Pearl Harbor, Nippon's great Pacific War offensive was over. Their military mission – to push the Japanese sphere of control to the East (and to the West, South and North) – ultimately failed completely.

Their planned invasion of Midway and the Hawaiian Islands never took place. The battle in the Coral Sea and Midway were the ultimate revenge for that infamy of Dec 7th the previous year, when Japanese leaders made their fatal miscalculation of what the USA could deploy in military and industrial power, and in the nation's determination to strike back with the annihilation of the aggressor.

Around the same time that the Midway campaign started, the Japanese Imperial Army occupied the minuscule islands of Attu and Kiska, the USA's westernmost Pacific territory at the very end of the string of Aleutian Islands in Alaska. During that same campaign two Japanese carriers made a surprise move by attacking the Dutch Harbor Naval Operating Base on the nearby Amaknak Island with their Val, Kate and Zero fighter/bombers. The base was much closer to the Alaskan mainland than Attu and felt like a serious attempt to invade Alaska. Again, the approaching fleet was detected by Catalinas, and, thanks to that early warning, the ensuing air raids on the harbor installations on 3 and 4 June only inflicted moderate damages. The Japanese had overlooked a new United States Army Air Force base at Fort Glenn on the adjacent island of Umnak from where P-40 fighters could be scrambled for a counter-attack.

In the end, two P-40s were shot down against four Vals, and one Zero crash-landed intact as a 'bonus catch'. In US hands, that first Zero was used for detailed analysis of the enemy's most advanced fighter. The carriers disappeared after the two-day attack, recalled in the wake of the defeat at Midway, only leaving behind that premium gift of their best fighter.

Most probably, the attack was planned as a diversion to lure the US Navy away from Midway. That ruse did not work but it must have worried the US Military as the island chain could be used in a hopping invasion plan from the West to eventually attack Alaska via the island chain 'panhandle'. Catalinas were deployed to keep a keen eye on the enemy fleet movements, flying day and night patrol flights over the most inhospitable islands with the notoriously adverse weather and fog between the cold Barents Sea on the north side and the warmer Pacific Ocean at the south side.

Catalina operations from RAAF & RZNAF

The Royal Australian Air Force (RAAF) and Royal New Zealand Air Force (RNZAF) also operated Catalinas over the SW Pacific, along with the US Navy squadrons. The RAAF began the legendary Black Cat operations, i.e. Catalinas deployed in all-black camouflage as night raiders against Japanese ports, shipping lines and submarines. With four squadrons – Nrs. 11, 20, 42 and 43 – they were engaged in all sorts of war operations. From April 1943 until July 1945, the Cats penetrated deeply into Japanese-held waters, dropping mines right in front of ports and along busy shipping routes, and inflicting damage to ships and supplies.

The Black Cat marauders came in by night, flying low and slow, skimming at 50 ft over the vast ocean waters in their black camouflage. Where the Japanese had no radar yet, the 'Cats' descended on the enemy ports and ships, creeping in from their secret daytime hideouts on rivers and in lagoons. They were closer to the enemy territory than the Japanese could ever have imagined. Hence, they could strike in total surprise at night. Before the Japsanese realized what had happened, the Black Cats had made their assaults with bombs, or had dropped mines near harbors and returned to their home base leaving no trace. The crews of many enemy ships that ran into mines or were attacked near Japanese-held ports or shipping lines must have wondered where the hell those explosives had come from.

Black Cats tied up the major strategic ports such as Balikpapan and Tarakan in Eastern Borneo, which shipped over 60% of Japanese oil supplies. By late 1944, their mining missions sometimes involved more than 24 continuous hours of flight and were carried out, in the dark, from as low as 150 ft. Their operations went further north as the Japanese were forced to leave their southern positions in and around Papua New Guinea.

By assisting in the landing of the Americans at Mindoro in the Philippines, the Cats helped with the blockade of the Japanese Navy in Manilla Bay. Later, Australian Catalinas also operated out of the Leyte Gulf in the Philippines and even flew all the way to the Chinese coast, from Hong Kong to as far north as Wenchow, to trap Japanese held ports with mine droppings. Both the US Navy and RAAF Catalinas operated in the night bombing raids on Japanese bases, with the RAAF claiming the slogan 'The First and the Furthest'. Targets of these night raids also included ships and surfaced submarines that could be traced with the arrival of radar aboard the PBYs.

51-P-1
51-P-3

Left: US Navy Model PBY-3. An early model US Navy PBY of Patrol Squadron VP-5. The longest recorded military flight made by a Class C seaplane left from the Norfolk Virginia Naval Air Station on 10 October 1935. Lieutenant Commander Knefler McGinnis, Lieutenant James K. Averill, Lieutenant Thomas P. Wilkinson, and a crew of three flew the XP3Y-1 – the prototype for the whole PBY series. Their flight covered 2,060 miles to Cristobal Harbor, Coco Solo Naval Air Station, Panama Canal Zone, in 17 hours, 33 min.

On 14 October 1935 they departed Coco Solo Naval Air Station and flew a record 3,387 miles nonstop arriving at San Francisco, California on 15 October after 34 hours 51 minutes, setting a record for the longest distance flown by a class C seaplane.

This photo of 5-P-1 was taken in 1939 and sent to me by Ken Berner, whose father flew this aircraft before the war. See next two photos for the full story.

Above: The text written on this postcard reads: 'Crew of nr 1, San Diego to Coco Solo, Canal Zone (one stop Gulf of Fonseca). Taken upon arrival Coco Solo. Flying time 27 hrs. Aug 31–Sept 1, 1939.' The captain of the Catalina was Lieutenant Warren Kenneth Berner, USN.

It gives a good impression of how, even before the war, the Catalina was engaged in executing long distance flights of over 24 hours. Through these frequent long-distance flights with PBYs the USAAF gained unique experience and pilot skills that would later prove very useful during the war with the anti-submarine warfare (ASW) patrol flights over the Oceans. Note the special logo under the cockpit.

(Photo courtesy of Ken Berner, from his father's photo album)

Above: Ken Berner's father, Captain Warren Kenneth Berner, USN (31 May 1898–20 August 1997) is seen here on the far right. He was a very skilled pilot who flew the PBY-3 Catalina many times from the Panama Canal Zone back to the USA and even flew its predecessor the P2Y.

In 1937 he was ordered to Coco Solo, Panama Canal Zone, as Commanding Officer of Patrol Squadron VP-5F, flying PBY-3 aircraft on anti-submarine warfare patrols. During this tour of duty he was promoted to Lieutenant Commander, also TAD to USS *Wright* (AV-1) flagship for Commander Patrol Wing 1, Aircraft Scouting Force.

In 1942 he was promoted to the rank of Captain and in 1943 was commissioned into the Great Lakes training carrier USS *Sable* (IX-81) as Commanding Officer, until 1944. He then commissioned USS *Makassar Strait* (CVE-91) as Commanding Officer in Bremerton, WA and participated in the war effort.

In 1947, he took command of USS *Wright* (CVL-49) in Pensacola, FL, training student pilots in carrier qualifications.

From 1950 until his June 1952 retirement, he served as Commanding Officer of Pre-Flight School at NAS Pensacola, Florida. He also served as interim Chief of Naval Air Training at that duty station.

(Photos and info Ken Berner)

Above: During 1938 and 1939, Dr Richard Archbold and his crew would complete the first flight around the world at its widest diameter, approximately at the equator. This private enterprise flight, in a Consolidated Model 28 NC 777 named 'Guba', included three firsts:

- The first flight across Australia by a seaplane
- The first flight across the Indian Ocean by any airplane
- The first flight across Equatorial Africa by a seaplane

The performance of 'Guba' heralded the genesis of an aircraft icon, with its very peculiar

aircraft that could fly further than any existing plane could ever do in that pre-war era. It was the combo of its novel all-metal, but lightweight airframe with the most reliable radial engines that made it possible to fly for over 24 hours non stop. A decade earlier such machine was unthinkable to produce.

Lindbergh's epic first Atlantic crossing in 1927 was the first proof of an engine that could hold that long. From there, it was a matter of time, to develop new streamlined airframes to achieve 24+ hours continuous flight with multiple engines and big fuel tanks.

Here is the first one built in large series that did just that. Bravo Consolidated!

(Photo credit: Consolidated Aircraft Corporation)

Above: NC 777 'Guba' at Rose Bay flying boat base, Sydney Harbour, Australia, in November 1938. The large Qantas Empire Airways hangar for their Short C-Class flying boats is under construction behind.
(Courtesy of Ben Dannecker collection)

Above: American Export Airlines, a subsidiary of the shipping company American Export Lines, acquired a commercial Model 28 in order to carry out trial flights across the Atlantic to Europe. Here, Mrs Towers, wife of Admiral Towers, Chief of the Bureau of Aeronautics, christens the aircraft 'Transatlantic' on 21 June 1939 at the Floyd Bennett Field's seaplane ramp (near JFK International Airport, NY). Just to be sure that she did not flip overboard, her ankles were gripped by the man behind as she bends over in style to strike a bottle of bubbly against the flying boat's mooring board.

Above: American Export Airlines Catalina model 28 named 'Transatlantic' (see also the previous photo) overflying the NY harbor and the Statue of Liberty in June 1939. Note the elliptical shape of the rudder's rear end, a feature that disappeared with the newly designed rudder of the PBY-5 which had a straight vertical trailing edge on its the rudder.

Right: Although it had had a successful career with the US Navy since 1937, the PBY Catalina design was considered obsolete by 1939. But the looming war dramatically changed the situation for the factory. Suddenly, the British and French Military placed big orders, followed by the Russians, the Dutch Naval Air arm, the Canadians and Australians.

The factory could barely cope with the surge and a new factory was opened in New Orleans. Additionally, Consolidated licensed the production of the PBY to Russia and Canada. Overnight, the PBY was *the* aircraft to have for protecting the Atlantic shipping lines against the U-boat raiders, from September 1939; and later, by the end of 1941, against the Japanese Naval forces that invaded SE Asia and the Pacific islands.

Total production at the close of the PBY assembly lines in 1945 included 2,160 aircraft from San Diego, 235 from New Orleans, 731 from Canada (Cansos, and other variants for the USAAF and other air forces: the RCAF, RAAF and RNZAF) and 155 PBN-1 Nomads from the Naval Aircraft Factory in Philadelphia. Plus 24 aircraft built under license in the Soviet Union, making a total of 3,305 aircraft delivered under the various designations of Catalinas, Cansos and Nomads. That number is more than the total of all other flying boats ever produced!

Above: In the pre-war days, US Navy PBYs came in flocks. Seen here flying in formations over the San Francisco Golden Gate Bridge, there are 33 Catalinas in this picture.

Above: From a restricted WWII Aircraft Recognition Manual, the bible for the gunners on board navy boats and aircraft in order to recognize the incoming aircraft instantly by their silhouette as 'Friend or Foe'. The Catalina has such a peculiar shape and easy-to-discern features, such as the parasol wing that any confusion with enemy aircraft seemed nearly impossible.

Above: Consolidated Aircraft Corporation logo

Opposite: The US Coast Guard's first PBY-5 V-189 over San Diego Harbor in 1940. Clearly visible in this classic photo are two rather 'archaic' features of the Catalina design. First, the under-wing struts: they were needed to support the weight of the long parasol wing (including the internal fuel tanks), plus two engines, while all that mass had only a narrow pylon in the centre to lean upon. By 1934, wing struts were considered old-fashioned, reducing the clean airflow and cruising speed.

Secondly, about 35% of the main wing area near the trailing edges were fabric clad (as were the ailerons, elevators and rudder), while in all contemporary designs of the early 1930s (DC-2/3 etc.) the main wings were all-metalized (aluminum clad). Worse, wing flaps that could greatly reduce the landing/approach speed of an aircraft were 'missing' in the Cat's wing design.

However, those 'old school' elements were compensated for by its extremely long flight range combined with a very rugged construction and proven reliable technology.

U.S.C.G.
U.S.C.G.
A-297 10-22-40
CONSOLIDATED AIRCRAFT CORP
PBY-5 AIRPLANE.

NO STEP

Opposite, top left: A 'posed' photo of a US Navy crew member boarding a PBY-5 Catalina via the waist blister, which was also one of the machine gun posts. The PBY had a reputation for its exceptional flight range but the downside was a slow cruising speed of some 110 knots (200 km/h), which made the aircraft very vulnerable to attack from much faster enemy fighters. The machine guns in the bow turret, in the side blisters and in the lower tail could barely deter enemy fighters as they came in at double the speed of the Catalina. Its board weapons were the bare minimum required for the Catalina to survive on long patrol missions.

Opposite, top right: Waist Gunner with .50 machine gun. The teardrop-shaped blister opened like an eyelid with the lower half being pushed upward and sliding under the higher part. Even with some protection from the 'closed' front of the blister, when they are opened it can be extremely windy at a speed of 100 knots. The goggles were no luxury item.

Opposite below: The Dutch Government ordered its first series of PBY-5s just before the outbreak of the War in Europe. As was the case with the French orders, those Catalinas could no longer be delivered in 1940–1941 in Europe, and the Dutch order was being diverted to the Dutch East Indies. In 1941, just before the outbreak of the Pacific War, the first batch was delivered in San Diego with an official handover that can be seen in this still, taken from a film. Note the odd orange triangle on the wing and the orange rudder. The Dutch insignia was later replaced by a Dutch flag and post-war by a more common tri-colored roundel.

Below: Row upon row of PBY-5s in use as training aircraft at Jacksonville Naval Air Station, Florida, illustrate the extent of the training requirement during WWII. All these aircraft have been picketed on the ramp on their beaching gear, with floats down ready to re-enter the water. Note the number of cables needed to anchor the aircraft to the ground. This was no luxury in Florida where gales and typhoons can seriously hamper the coastal areas.

Above: Beautiful shot of a PBY-5 on its beaching gear. This photo has been supplied by the Smithsonian Institution, Washington, DC. The so-called 'meatball' insignia below the cockpit probably dates the photo to before May 1942 as from that point orders were issued to remove the red dot from the white star.

Above: A PBY-5 is launched from the slipway at Naval Air Station Corpus Christi, TX whilst another taxies post from left for the open sea. Note the number of crew needed to do the job properly. Despite the US insignia, the camouflage and serial is visible under the tail shows that this is a RAF Catalina that was retained in the USA for training.

Above: A fascinating second photo supplied by the Smithsonian Institution, Washington, DC. A PBY-5 has just rolled off the ramp of Naval Air Station Miramar with the help of the tractor. The beaching gear has been removed and is on the slipway (at right in front) while the aircraft is now being readied for a takeoff with its crew of 6–7.

Above: Famous US Navy photo taken during the Japanese air attack on Pearl Harbor, 7 December 1941. There was carnage not only in the harbor but also on the surrounding airfields. Here we see explosions with a burnt out PBY in the front and another PBY on the left, more or less intact but with damaged elevators.

Above: Brave sailors desperately try to pull a damaged PBY Catalina ashore from the water at the Naval Air Station (NAS) Kaneohe Bay, Hawaii, during the Pearl Harbor air attack. Note that the rear part of the main wing's skin was burnt by the fire. That section of the wing was not metalized (as was the front and central section) but canvas clad and more vulnerable for damage.

Right: 205 Sqn, RAF Catalina Mk I W8411/FV-Y at rest off Seletar, Singapore, in 1941. This Catalina escaped from the invading Japanese troops during the withdrawal from Singapore, but was lost whilst on patrol from Diego Garcia in the Indian Ocean on 21 September 1941 with the loss of nine crew memb

An amphibious US Navy PBY-5A at Cold Bay, Aleutians. The crew, dressed in dry suits, stand by in icy water to assist in maneuvering the aircraft in the water: a cumbersome and chilly job. The amphibian PBY-5A version was supplied with a tricycle landing gear and would normally 'climb' out of the water under its own power, while mounting a ramp with its wheels down. The arrival of the amphibious version in late 1941 must have been some relief for the ground personnel.

Classic shot of a US Navy PBY-5 or -5A. This example is fitted with long shrouds running over the engine nacelles to feed the de-icing equipment in the wing's leading edges with hot air tapped from the engine's exhaust stacks. They were mainly used in the colder climate operations over the Northern Atlantic, in Alaska and the Aleutian Islands.

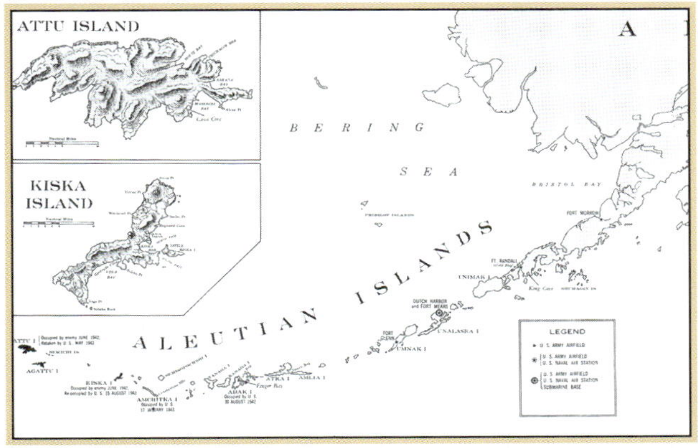

Above: Map of the Aleutian Islands with Attu and Kiska Islands highlighted – the only US territory occupied during WWII by Japanese forces. These are the tiny islands that almost drop off the map on the far left, between the Bering Sea in the north and the Pacific Ocean in the south. But, from there the Japanese Imperial Navy launched a far more threatening assault on Dutch Harbor on Unalaska Island with the help of two aircraft carriers that stealthily came within a few hundred miles of Fort Mears/Dutch Harbor. Japanese fighters and bombers attacked the port facilities and shot up the fuel depots.

The reason behind the Japanese occupation was to prevent the USAAF from building up air force bases on the remote islands, from where they could raid the Japanese Islands. But, the US Military went after the Marianas Islands (south east of Japan) to do exactly what the Japanese feared so much: raiding Tokyo with their long distance bombers, the B-29 Super Fortresses. For more information on this attack see my Dakota Hunter blog at https://www.dc3dakotahunter.com/blog/nippons-2nd-attack-plan-on-us-genesis-of-alaska-highway-1942.

Above: Magnificent shot of a US Navy PBY-5A on patrol on the Aleutian Islands, 1944. The island chain separates the Barents Sea from the Pacific and on that borderline of clashing extremities of cold and warm seas storms, mist, fog and cloud are common. Not the ideal flying conditions for a non-heated sea-patrolling aircraft that operates best as an airborne scout at lower altitudes between 1,500–5,000 feet.

Left: RAF PB2B-1 Catalina JX431/A of 205 Sqn from Koggala, Ceylon on a test flight over the beaches in 1944. Ceylon was the easternmost station that remained in British hands throughout the war against the Japanese military forces that had occupied most of SE Asia, including Malaya, Thailand and Burma.

Right: The Norwegian pilot Bernt Balchen landed this US Navy PBY-5A BuNo 7277 wheels-up on the Greenland ice cap several times in the early-Spring of 1943 during the rescue of a downed B-17 Flying Fortress crew. He also successfully took off in the same configuration.

It was proof of the very sturdy construction of the aircraft that it could land even on frozen water! In any case, the landing and takeoff required a tricky long run with direct contact between the snow-covered surface and the keel. One single block of solid frozen ice protruding from the snow could have ripped the fuselage open like a sardine can.

Above: Despite the beaching gear, this is a US Navy PBY-5A amphibian. It is being 'bombed up' with bombs and/or depth charges (see photo) but even large torpedoes were used. This was achieved by the use of removable winches that were fixed onto the upper surfaces of the wing for that purpose.

Above: Rare color view of a Royal Air Force Catalina. Coded AX-L, it belongs to 202 Squadron and is flying close to Gibraltar, its base for part of WWII. 'The Rock' remained in British hands throughout the war and played (as Ceylon did in SE Asia) a very strategic role as a forward positioned station for the airborne spy-eye Catalina that, from there, attacked enemy ports, executed mine droppings, hampered shipping lines and carried out its far reaching anti-submarine patrols.

Left: US Navy PBY-5s in formation over snow-covered terrain, possibly the Aleutians or Alaska. The big, strut-supported wing is evident, as is the very prominent bow turret on top of the narrow bomber-aiming window with shutter in the lower front. From the beginning in 1936, the PBY had a minor design flaw with its directional stability and the poor streamlining of that stubby nose. She was one of the slowest aircraft in a combat role and could use every extra mile per hour in speed gain.

Hence, few WWII aircraft will have seen in 10 years of production so many modifications in tail design and bow/turret re-shaping as the Catalina. But it all helped to form the legend of the PBY.

Right: RAF Catalinas off Malaya, early 1941. This photo was taken just before the Japanese invasion of Singapore and the Dutch East Indies between February and March 1942.

Above: The Soviets received PBN-1 Nomads from the USA under Lend-Lease. The Nomad was a modified PBY design with extended bow and keel, modified bow turret, extended hull, and taller tail and rudder. This one appears to be beached without beaching gear but with engines running! How did that Catalina get there with no wheels, and how did they plan the start of their flight? The cables in front suggest some serious towing work to be done to a lower lake or sea nearby, with a tractor or maybe the crew doing the job?

Above: A US Navy PBY-5 'on the step' during its takeoff run. As was normal practice, the wings are perfectly level so that the stabilizing floats on the wing tips are well above the water surface. From this photo, one can easily imagine that if the Catalina reached its near-takeoff speed, then there was a sudden windshift or downdraft, one wing would inadvertently drop to such an extent that a float would hit the water. A situation such as this would have been extremely dangerous. The float could 'dig in', resulting in a very fierce swing of the aircraft at high speed – the water equivalent of the much feared 'ground loop' that could destroy an aircraft in a matter of seconds.

Above: The sinking of the *Bismarck*. Lough Erne-based Catalina I AH545/WQ-Z of 209 Squadron, RAF, was the aircraft that famously first spotted the *Bismarck* in the epic ship hunt that took place after the German battleship left Norway for France in late May, 1941. It was to become a dramatic first and final battle trip. In its first confrontation with the Royal Navy on 24 May 1941, the *Bismarck* sunk the HMS *Hood* in less than ten minutes after the British opened fire. A shell from the *Bismarck* struck *Hood* near her aft ammunition magazines. HMS *Hood* exploded and sank within three minutes, with the loss of all but three of her crew.

There followed an unparalleled air and sea hunt by the Royal Navy and RAF, in search of that deadly battleship on the run over a vast ocean. It ended in the *Bismarck*'s destruction in the Atlantic, halfway between Ireland and the Azores. In the detection of the ship, this Catalina had an instrumental role, flying over the oceans as the airborne spy-eye with unrivaled flight endurance, surprising friend and foe with its capacity. Sadly, the Catalina that performed the legendary search for the *Bismarck* went missing during a ferry flight in July 1942.

Right: The Royal New Zealand Air Force operated a mixed fleet of Consolidated and Boeing of Canada-built Catalinas, both during and after WWII. NZ4003/XX-C, seen here, flew with 6 Squadron and was lost in a landing accident at Second Channel, Espiritu Santo on the last day of October 1943. Note the collapsible work platforms attached to the wing and engine cowlings.

Between 1943 and 1953, 56 Catalinas (NZ4001-NZ4056) were operated by the Royal New Zealand Air Force in the amphibian and pure flying boat version. The Catalinas operated with No 5 and No 6 SQNs and No 3 OTU, based at Hobsonville and various points in the Pacific. Their duties were in the anti-submarine patrols, shipping escorts, air-sea-rescue (ASR) and transport roles. The Catalinas continued their operations after the war, having a vital role in transport and communications in the South Pacific, which largely lacked land-based airports on the smaller islands.

Above: An excellent shot of an RAF Catalina showing lots of details. Note the bow turret and bombardier's window in the nose. The latter is covered with its protective 'shield'. The props are neatly 'dressed' to give maximum room for boats to get in close to the hull. However, the Anti Surface Vessel (ASV) radar aerials on the side of the hull, just under the props and below the wings, are a hazard! The port engine has its collapsible work platform in place, attached to the wing leading edge and cowling. Also visible are depth charge mounts under the wing and 'fishtail' type flame dampers on the engine exhausts.

Above: The Double Sunrise flight. During the war, Qantas Empire Airways operated secret flights with five Catalinas between Ceylon (Sri Lanka) and Perth, Western Australia – the only remaining westbound flight from Australia between 1943 and July 1945.

'Altair Star' G-AGFM was one of five Qantas Empire Airways-operated Catalinas – a nonstop flight of 26–30 hours over the Indian Ocean in total radio silence, partly crossing enemy airspace.

Throughout the service some 271 crossings were made, with 860 passengers carried, as well as about 1,000 lbs of very secret mail. The Catalinas that flew this route had an all-up weight of between 35,100 to 35,300 lbs, indicating an over-weight of 4 tons that came primarily from the extra gas! This flying fuel bomb was supposed to never meet a Zero during its long flights over the ocean. One single stray bullet would have been enough to create a fatal hell fire.

Left: During the war, the Norwegians operated two squadrons of Catalinas within the Royal Air Force. Mk I W8424 'Vingtor' served with 333 Squadron, based at Woodhaven on the River Tay in Scotland. Radial engines, such as the Catalina's Pratt & Whitney R-1830s, have a reputation for poor cold starts and were well covered during harsh winter nights to protect against the cold. The job to remove the insulated engine covers, as can be seen here, was not without risk. Balancing on an icy fuselage, turning the props and removing the blankets – quite surely once in a while a crew member must have ended in the freezing water six feet below him.

Right: A photo of a French 6 FE Catalina 'F34' that operated from Agadir, Southern Morocco, and was used for long distance Atlantic Ocean patrols in 1944. Note the flat/half-buried tire that stands off the wheel rim. A crew member puzzles how to solve this problem in that typical posture of 'Oh S ... no, not this now'.

34

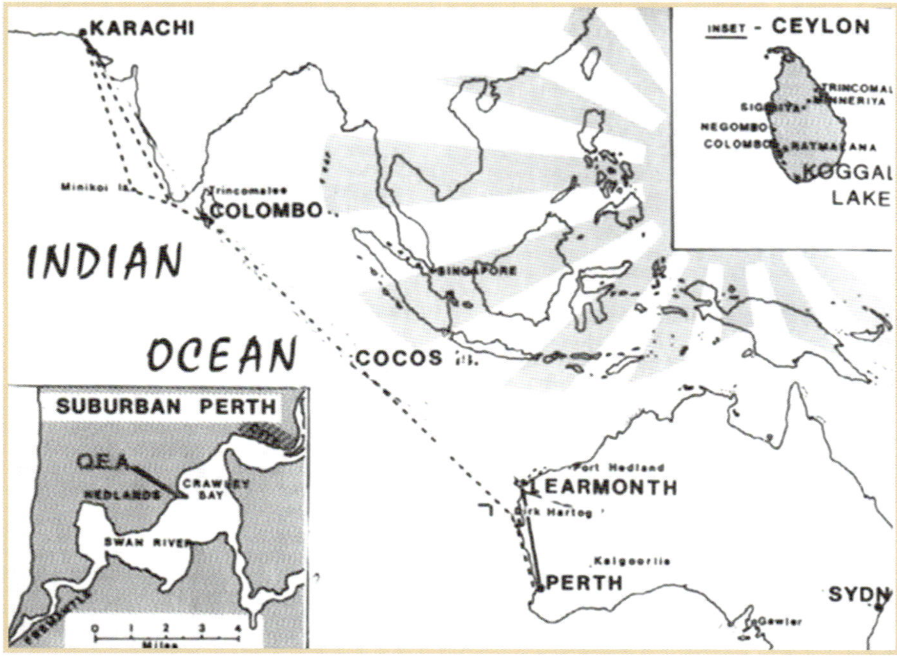

Above: Map of the Indian Ocean, showing the route flown between Koggala Lake near Colombo, Ceylon, and Perth, Australia – the longest stretch flown in hours aloft that existed during the wartime. This non-stop service between Perth and Colombo covered a distance of 3,592 nm (5,652 km). As the PBY typically cruised at 100–110 knots, this took between 28 to 32 hours and was called the 'flight of the double sunrise', since the passengers saw two sunrises during their long journey.

The long flight required extra fuel tanks on board and had a maximum payload of 1,000 lbs, or three VIP passengers plus 65 kg of military cargo and diplomatic mail. For the extra fuel required, inboard tanks were installed in the cabin, which were able to carry a total of nearly 2,000 gallons, weighing about 7 tons.
(Map courtesy of Rex Clifton Seniorhttp://pbycatalina.com/pby-facts/)

Above: Jungle Air Force patch. This patch indicated the 2nd Emergency Rescue Squadron of the 13th Air Force, USAAF, which operated in the Far East.

Right: Very nice and sharp photo of a bunch of PBY-5s. They are all 6 Sqn, RNZAF Catalinas, and the photo was taken at Halavo Bay, Solomon Islands. The precise date is unknown but it must have been taken in 1945.
(Info David Legg)

Above: Catalinas from Lake St Lucia. This South African wartime Naval Air base near Natal was the home of the RAF Catalina squadrons that flew long anti-submarine patrols over the SW part of the Indian Ocean.

Above: US Navy PBY-5A with Lockheed PV-1 Venturas in the background, Aleutian Islands, December 1943. Note the style of USAAF insignia with red outline, briefly used in 1943.

Right: USAAF OA-10A Catalina 44-33879 'Snafu Snatchers' in New Guinea whilst with the 2nd Emergency Rescue Squadron. The USAAF had its own designation system and called the amphibious Catalina the OA-10A rather than use the US Navy designation PBY-5A or the British name Catalina. One of my favorite Aviation Museums, the National Museum of the USAF in Dayton OH, has a restored Catalina painted to represent those original 'Snafu Snatchers'. (See Chapter 5, The Survivors)

Above left: Dramatic photo of a surfaced submarine, detected, and engaged in a fierce shoot-out with a PBY Catalina flown by L.T.J.G. Rowland. Note the high speed that this *U-662* is reaching while trying to avoid being bombed by the low-flying Catalina overhead. Possibly, the German sub is making a scramble for a dive or taking evasive action? The Cat was under heavy fire from the sub's AA guns at short range and was hit by bullets several times.

Many a Catalina crew must have faced a similar scene. Hours of boredom while flying over the endless ocean, suddenly broken by the horror of a sub encounter, followed by an attack, in this case, with an enemy willing and capable of dueling.

Above right: In this photo taken from the Catalina's RH waist blister, we can see that depth charges are being released and exploding next to the German submarine *U-662*. The boat made evasive maneuvers, trying to prevent the attacking Catalina from lining up for yet another bombing/strafing run. Meanwhile, the sub is operating its twin anti-aircraft machine guns against the raiding Cat and hits the aircraft several times. One projectile slams into the radio compartment, wounding radioman ARM2c, J. H. Watson.

By the end of this assault, the sub is deadly wounded and starts to sink rapidly. A few sailors (probably those on deck and in the conning tower) barely managed to escape from the sinking ship, which took all the other sailors into the depths of the ocean.

Left: The *U-662* survivors in life rafts. After a fierce shoot-out, the German sub was sunk on 21 July 1943 in the North Atlantic, in position 03°56..N 48°46..W, by depth charges from the US Catalina from Patrol Squadron VP-94.

L.T.J.G. Rowland's plane sighted five survivors and dropped two dinghies before departing. One survivor died immediately and four, including the C.O., Kapitänleutnant Heinz Müller, who was severely injured, climbed into the rafts. They were adrift for 16 days before being rescued by the USS *Siren*. The German captain, Heinz Müller, was so severely injured that he was repatriated to Germany in March 1944, as he was no longer fit for combat.

Above: Fabulous color photo of the USAAF OA-10A '83' with Flight Officer Jack Leonard returning from a search mission in 1945. There is one wounded crew member on board, evacuated via the LH blister (see the photo on page 45). 44-33883 served with 2 ERS in the Far East and was condemned in June 1945, in Manila, Philippines.

Above: Flight Officer Jack Leonard (in co-pilot's seat) and Catalina 44-33883 readies for takeoff on a search mission in 1945. Note the C-47 to the right with LH engine in maintenance and the wingtip floats of the Cat being cranked up (or down) with electric motors to their up (or down) position.

Above: PBYs on an Aleutian Airfield around 1942, with bombs and anti-submarine depth charges waiting on a trolley to be mounted under the wings of another PBY-5A Catalina.

Above: An interesting sign somewhere at Keesler Field, MS, 1944, depicting the parachute drop of a lifesaving boat that was carried under the wing of a OA-10A Catalina (seen on the left of the picture), or a B-17 Flying Fortress (right) on Ocean Patrol.

Above: Stall landing of an RAF Catalina on Lake St Lucia, South Africa. Note the sharp angle with aft part of the keel first touching the water. Landings on open seas were generally avoided, but for fast reduction of the landing speed of the Cat such tricky landings could be effective as an 'emergency brake'.

Catalinas had no wing flaps (as the contemporary DC-3/C-47 had). Therefore, their approach speed for landings was high, with little room for errors. With no wheel brakes in effect while landing on water, this was a method to instantly kill the speed and the floating effect of the large wing area just above the water.

But, with high ocean swell coming in, the bumps on the water could be very harsh, sometimes leading to buckled skin plates at the keel or worse! When thrown back into the air by a big wave, the landing could sometimes end in a disaster, with a sudden nosedive caused by a hard upward 'kick' under the tail-end that pushed the aircraft's nose into a sharp pitch down. Overall, water landings and takeoffs had more risks and were more accident prone than landings on terra firma. It required more skills and experience in a larger variety of conditions of wind, water and waves.

Above: Color photo taken from a slide of a wounded Sgt Roznovsky disembarking via the blister from OA-10A 44-33883 (see other photos of '83). This Catalina was badly damaged by flak during a mission to rescue the crew of a downed B-25 six miles SW of Tarakan, Borneo on 8 April 1945. Note the B-25 Mitchell and the 2.5-ton CCKW 'Deuce' fuel truck in the background.

Left: Dramatic photo of a splash landing of a Catalina, Aleutian Islands, early 1944. A bit more water on that track and the pilot could have opted for a wheels-up landing with floats down! Note the ambulance parked to the side and a fighter plane with a bend prop blade behind the ambulance. Maybe caused by a nosedive in the mud? This is not unthinkable for a tail dragger landing in a pool of slush.

Above: Interesting wartime map of the Pacific. The extent of the Japanese Army and Navy expansion is marked by the August 1942 red line, and the sites of the Battles of the Coral Sea and Midway are in view. Also note the small island of Attu at the westernmost end of the Aleutian Island chain, in the north. In the center are the Mariana Islands and Iwo Jima, from where the B-29 Superfortresses attacked Japan's main islands until Japan's surrender in August 1945 – three years after the 'Empire of the Sun' had reached its most advanced limits in SE Asia.

See my Dakota Hunter blog for more information about the Mariana Islands' role as a fixed aircraft carrier: www.dc3dakotahunter.com/blog/marianas-the-b-29s-fixed-aircraft-carrier/

(Map courtesy of the US Army Center of Military History)

Above: Aleutian Islands, 1943. Remarkable photo taken from another Catalina. In the background is the USS *Casco* (AVP-12), a seaplane tender commissioned in 1941.

On 5 May 1942, USS *Casco* arrived at Sitka, Alaska, for duty surveying Aleutian waters, laying moorings for seaplanes and providing seaplane tender services. Based at Cold Bay, Alaska, she operated at Dutch Harbor, Chernofski Harbor, Kodiak, and Nazan Bay. It was there, on 30 August 1942 that the ship was torpedoed by the Japanese submarine *RO-61*. The resulting explosion killed five of her men and wounded 20, but she could be beached and later salvaged. The ship underwent emergency repairs at Dutch Harbor and Kodiak in September 1942.

USS *Casco* returned to the Aleutian Islands in March 1943, operating at Constantine Harbor, Amchitka, as tender to Fleet Air Wing Four (FAW-4). In May 1943 (photo), she sailed west to Attu, in order to supply the Catalinas and OS2U Kingfishers that were involved in anti-submarine patrols, search missions and forward air control flights.

Right: Fabulous counterlight photo during the Aleutian Islands Campaign, June 1942–August 1943: a Consolidated PBY Catalina returns from a patrol flight to the harbor at Attu in the Aleutians where its mother ship USS *Casco* was anchored (see photo on this page).

The ship and its aircraft gave support to the US invasion of Attu, the only US-owned territory ever occupied by the Japanese. Attu and Kiska, two tiny islands at the westernmost chain of the Aleutians had come into their hands. Attu was fiercely defended, demonstrating to the US Military the formidable resistance that the Japanese Army could deploy, an experience to learn from for the future conquering of the Japanese-held Pacific islands. While the battle of Attu was a lesson for the USA it was the writing on the wall for the Japanese Army. With very heavy losses sustained in Attu, they secretly evacuated their remaining garrison from nearby Kiska, ending the Japanese occupation in the Aleutian Islands on 28 July 1943.

bove: This photo depicts a PBY-5 'Black Cat', moored on a riverbank in Papua New Guinea PNG) for refueling. It's a very sharp photo with amazing details: fuel cans, ammo boxes, arps, and food, all loaded aboard with help of the local tribesmen. It perfectly reflects the ersatility of the Catalina, the aircraft that could penetrate, at night, deep into Japanese-eld territory and attack harbors, ships, submarines, enemy oil-tanker facilities, and drop mines for hampering shipping/supply lines. With no Allied airfields close enough to the Enemy, only the Catalina could do the trick in such primitive conditions. With hardly any basic ground facilities available, they could launch attacks from their daytime hideouts at hard-to-detect rivers and lagoons, sometimes in cooperation with PT boats. Striking at night, as rogue sharks from the deep of the ocean, the Japanese hardly found an answer to the surprise night attacks of the Black Cats. Both the USAAF and the RAAF operated their Black Cats from Northern Australia and New Guinea to attack the Solomon Islands and the Borneo based oil-harbors. Later they moved to Morotai and Borneo for attacks on the Japanese Navy in the Philippines and beyond.

Above: RAF Catalina crew of XJ202 just returning from a long-distance patrol mission over the Atlantic or the Gulf of Biscay in 1945. Their Catalina shows very visible traces of oil spills over the wings. Note the Short Sunderland in the background.

The U-boat war may well have been 'won' by the second half of 1943 but the endeavor of hunting them down remained no less dangerous. The battle became particularly intense over the Bay of Biscay; the wedge shaped entry to the U-boat harbors. A large percentage of U-boats transited the 300 by 120 mile Bay of Biscay en route to, or returning from, their Atlantic patrol areas. Soon, Coastal Command would launch an air-patrol campaign to intercept them as they moved across this bottleneck sea corridor.

Enemy submarines surfaced often at night to recharge their batteries; it was then that the U-boats were most vulnerable to attack. Every effort was made by the Germans to keep the route open for their U-boats to leave or enter their U-boat bunkers that seemed indestructible.

Lorient in Brittany, France, houses the biggest bunker complex ever built. The Keroman U-boat shelter numbers 1, 2 and 3 had multi-layer roofs some 25-feet thick and survived all bombing raids that were executed. In May 1945, there were still hundreds of German U-boats operational and the Keroman bunker remained intact throughout the war; it was even used by the French Navy until 1969. It is now partly open for the public. Amazingly, it still looks as if not even a scratch was ever made by the hundreds of tons of Allied bombs dropped on the complex!

Above: Phil Hougland sent me this awesome photo. His father, Herman Hougland, was a PBY pilot in the Pacific War in 1943 and 1944. You can see him sitting on top of the cockpit hatch without a hat. His squadron VP 101 was awarded a Presidential Citation for actions in the battle of the Bismarck Sea.

The Allied Forces detected a Japanese troop convoy, on its way from Rabaul to New Guinea, which came under sustained air attack on 2–3 March 1943. On 4 March, follow-up attacks by PT boats and Catalinas were made. Herman Hougland, his crew and the other Cats and ships were able to knock out all eight transport ships and four of the escorting destroyers were sunk. Out of 6,900 Japanese troops, only about 1,200 made it to Lae, PNG. With this outright victory, the Japanese made no further attempts to reinforce Lae by ship.

Herman and his crew also rescued a downed F4U Corsair pilot in very heavy seas; and yet another air medal was awarded to Herman after he spent three nights adrift in the Pacific on open rafts. During a bombing run on a Japanese submarine, their Cat suffered from the premature detonation of a bomb that blew off part of the tail of the aircraft! Later, a stunning adventure-packed report about this incident was written by Thomas I. Hine, USN (Retired):

Flew 12–14 hour patrols every third nite.
Oct 11, 1943 flying BuNo 08328, armed with 2 x 325lb bombs, and 2 x 650lb depth bombs.
One mile south of Gasmata sighted I class Japanese sub.
9:30 pm made a glide for bombing the sub with release at 150 feet.
Dropped one bomb, one depth charge.
One must have been armed for immediate detonation, damaged our port horizontal stabilizer hanging down vertically, foot-wide holes in hull. Sank in about 10 min.
Landed in sea, crew got out in two seven-man rafts with provisions.
Voted to go ashore at Gasmata (Japanese held) or head toward Trobriand Islands about 160 nautical miles away. Vote unanimous to head to Trobriand.
Two men paddled and two steered in each raft, navigated by stars and compass.
Whenever B-24's flew over, signaled with smoke and mirrors.
Made about 100 nautical miles in 3 days.
Finally sighted by army Dumbo PBY-5A and picked up.
Navy gave them 30 day r and r on palm island.

(Info and photo courtesy of Phil Hougland)

Above: RAF Catalina, serial AM269/BN-K of 240 Squadron at its mooring in a UK harbor. This Cat was involved in the anti-submarine warfare on the Atlantic and in the Gulf of Biscay, known as the 'Wolfpack's Den'.

Germany's major submarine stations were operating from bases along the Biscayan coast after the fall of France in 1940. As the naval war on the Atlantic intensified, their U-boats sailed to and from massive concrete-fortified pens at Brest, Lorient, St Nazaire, Cherbourg, and Bordeaux every month. Operating in wolf packs, this submerged fleet proved most difficult to defeat and were soon responsible for the sinking of a large percentage of war supplies – fuel, ammo and food – that Great Britain needed so urgently to survive the war.

It was Royal Air Force (RAF) Coastal Command with its Operational Research Section (ORS) that tackled the problem and developed a reliable magnetic detonator fitted to depth charges, plus a 'killer-device' known as the Leigh Light.

The detection of a U-boat by MAD (Magnetic Anomaly Detection) or radar was one thing; the precise attack run and knockout was yet another thing to do. To ease the exact position and tracking of the U-boat, a strong searchlight was needed and became known as the 'Leigh Light'. This super-strong torch lamp came in a variety of forms. This photo shows two of them, slung under each wing.

The Leigh Light was a powerful (22 million candela) carbon arc searchlight with a 24-inch (610-mm) diameter. The new Air-to-Surface Vessel radar (ASV) demonstrated that the radar's minimum range of about 1 km meant that the target was still not visible when it disappeared off the radar display; a very confusing gap.

Wing Commander Humphrey de Verd Leigh hit upon the idea of using a searchlight that would be switched on just when the target was about to disappear on radar. The U-boat, mostly not aware of the Cat homing in, had insufficient time to dive and the aircraft's bombardier in the nose compartment had a clear, spotlighted view of the target. Introduced in June 1942, it was so successful that for a time German submarines were forced to switch to charging their batteries during the daytime, when they could at least see aircraft approaching.

Later in the war, the Germans also developed a new device – the schnorkel. Mounted on their U-boats, this air-duct allowed them to stay just under the surface of the sea while 'breathing' and running their diesel engines via the floating air hose. It gave them the opportunity to recharge their batteries while still submerged. (See also the photos at the end of this chapter.)

Right: Ben Mathis (back turned) looks at the shore as a crew member sets the anchor. Jarvis Yagla looks on. This Aircraft 44-33877 was lost in a forced landing NNW of Morotai after running out of fuel whilst evading enemy action during a courier flight to the Philippines on 26 October 1944, with the loss of five crew.

Above: Photo of K-5 airship and PBY-5A in flight during WWII (Photo US Navy). As of August 1941, a novel AI-10 microwave radar was tested for airborne application. The radar was developed by the Radiation Laboratory at the Massachusetts Institute of Technology (MIT), in Cambridge, MA. The radar included a Plan Position Indicator for display. Aircraft were detected at a range of 3.5 miles and ships at 40 miles. From October 1941 the tests results were used in developing operational radars such as the ASG for K-type airships and the AN/APS 2 for patrol aircraft like the PBY-5 Catalina. The PBY was one of the first US aircraft to carry radar. At first this was a metric wave radar with arrays of dipole antennas on the wings, and later came a centimetric radar in a teardrop shaped fairing on top of the cockpit. A Leigh light was installed under the wing.

The arrival of this radar, along with the MAD boom (Magnetic Anomaly Detection device in the tail), plus the cracked secret Navy codes used by the Germans and Japanese, were to become the death knell for the Kriegsmarine and the Japanese Imperial Navy submarines. The age of radio, sonar and radar tracking had just started and gave the Allies an immense cutting edge in their naval warfare.

What MIT had developed in advanced radar technology, and what the British Government Code and Cipher School in Bletchley Park had done with its 'Ultra' project to break the secret German 'Enigma' codes, may remain out of the spotlight, but they were both phenomenal steps towards the final defeat of the German and Japanese sub and surface fleets.

The Catalina was able to perform so well due to its unique design and durability, but with the help of radar and Ultra (plus sonar, MAD and the Leigh Light), the PBY matured far beyond its own speed and design limitations into an intelligent airborne spy platform, with a formidable reputation as the most efficient ship- and sub hunter killer, and spy eye, of the Navy.

Left: Fabulous shot of two Catalinas on anti-submarine patrol over the South Atlantic. Rio de Janeiro's Ipanema Beach is right below, with Copacabana Beach in the center, and Sugarloaf Mountain in the distance.

On 31 July 1943, a raiding German U-boat, *U-199*, had sunk two ships off the Brazilian coast. The sub was found on the surface, off Rio de Janeiro by three aircraft: a PBY Catalina and a Lockheed Hudson (both Brazilian Air Force), and an American PBM Martin Mariner of VP-74. The Catalina, named Arará, hit *U-199* with depth charges, leaving the boat sinking. Forty-nine of the U-boat crew were killed, and only twelve Germans managed to escape the doomed sub, including the captain. Their lives were saved due to the actions of the Catalina crew, who threw a lifeboat to the survivors. They were rescued by the USS *Barnegat* and taken to Brazil, and then on to captivity in the United States.
(Source Wikipedia)

Right: Another magnificent photo of 'The Rock'. Consolidated RAF Catalina Mark I, Z2147 'AX-L', of No. 202 Squadron RAF, flies by the North Front of the Rock as it leaves Gibraltar on a patrol.
(CM 6238: Photo is Part of the Air Ministry Second World War Official Collection, Daventry, B.J.H. (Fg Off), Royal Air Force official photographer)

Above: Logo of the Black Cats as used by the USAAF in the Pacific War.

Left: Somewhere out there, on a Pacific Island, a rendezvous under idyllic palm trees.

Below: Three P-38 Lightnings overfly the crew of a PBY-5A Catalina practicing the recovery of downed airmen from a dinghy, Guadalcanal, Solomon Islands, 1942–43.

The Lockheed P-38 Lightning was a highly successful American Fighter aircraft. Much feared by the Japanese forces, they dubbed it the 'two planes, one pilot' aircraft due to its twin engine, twin tail configuration. The P-38 was used for interception, dive-bombing, level bombing, ground attack, night fighting, photo reconnaissance, radar and visual pathfinding for bombers, and, as seen in this photo, as air cover for the vulnerable Catalinas when moored.

In the Southwest Pacific theater, the P-38 was the primary long-range fighter of USAF until the appearance of large numbers of P-51D Mustangs toward the end of the war. The P-38 was the only American fighter aircraft in high-volume production (over 10,000 were manufactured!) throughout the war. Allegedly, the Lightning's wing design was used on the Lockheed Constellation.

(Source: Wikipedia)

Above: Dutch Catalina squadrons in diaspora. With the homeland, Holland, occupied by the German troops since May 1940, the first factory deliveries took place in 1941 and were flown over the Pacific to the Dutch East Indies, just prior to December 1941. With the rapidly approaching Japanese Invasion force, and the ensuing fall of Singapore and Java in February/March 1942, a number of RAF, and later Dutch, Cats were able to make a last-minute escape to Ceylon and Australia. The regrouped Dutch squadrons were dispersed and operated from South Africa (see photo, taken in Pretoria, October 1944), Walvis Bay (Namibia), Socotra (an island in the Gulf of Aden), Ceylon and Australia.

Right: Dutch squadron Catalina PBY-5 Y-45 in Rose Bay, Sydney, Australia, 1945. A simple red, white and blue flag is positioned behind the blister and note the Dutch lion and crown nose art under the cockpit. (Photo courtesy of Prudent Staal)

Above: Remarkable, but blurry, photo of an RAAF Catalina flying boat PBY-5 A24-42 (FJ-K) on the Marine Section tarmac, Doctor's Gully, Darwin, 1942. The GMC DUCKW amphibian truck in front most probably had a dual function as a vessel to tow the Cat in and as a land-based tractor to get her out of the water on to the ramp.

(Photo courtesy of Northern Territory Library)

Below: Stunning photo of the PBY-5 Catalina with Royal New Zealand Air Force roundels under the wing. There are some 135 soldiers on top of that PBY parasol wing. It may look overloaded, but with a total wing load of some 12 tons (28,000 lbs), this is what the aircraft wings also experienced when airborne. Catalinas are known to have taken off with over 32,000 lbs of total weight.

Above: Bay, Leyte Gulf, Philippines. On 3 December 1944, USS *Cooper* was struck by a torpedo while in a naval battle with Japanese ships. The torpedo downed the *Cooper*, which sank in less than a minute, with the terrible loss of 191 crew members and 168 survivors left struggling in the water.

This Catalina, flown by Lt Frederick J. Ball, was on its way back home from a long-range patrol mission when they spotted the survivors scattered all over the bay. Lt Ball landed his aircraft in the bay and rescued 56 sailors from drowning. With that hefty overload on board, he started an almost impossible takeoff run. It took him three miles to finally get airborne and he brought all passengers safely back home. There were another 112 sailors out there in the water, and they were picked up by yet another VPB-34 Catalina. Impossible to handle the load, this Catalina shuttled groups of survivors outside the bay, where US Navy ships were waiting to take them over, outside the range of the enemy fire. Lt Ball received the Navy Cross for his outstanding bravery.

Above: Night shot of an amphibious Catalina that has probably just returned from a mission. It has no armament and no bombs mounted under the wings. It could be the US Navy PBY-5A BuNo 48281.

Above: Australian Members of No. 20 Squadron RAAF, 1944, Darwin. Note the two mechanics working on the Nr 2 engine of their Catalina while sitting on their foldable decks, hooked up to either side of the engine. This factory-delivered equipment was a most practical device that made the Catalina maintenance relatively independent of external scaffolds and ramp installations.

In the remote outback where the Black Cats operated in PNG, this was a very handy piece of equipment indeed for engine repairs and checks, especially when hidden in lagoons and on jungle rivers etc.

Above: A very nice photo with a proud crew posing on the NZ4001. It was the first Catalina to be delivered to the RNZAF.

Below: Pearl Harbor: a Catalina PBY-5 taxiing along a cargo ship with AA-guns and a cannon on its front deck. Dated February 1942. Those were the days when many believed that Japan would attack California after its successful assault on Pearl Harbor only 3 months earlier. The Catalinas made around-the-clock patrols over the Pacific Ocean, but that dreaded invasion fleet was never spotted.

Above: A fine shot of the Dutch Catalina PBY-5 Y87, stationed in Australia or New Guinea, in what seems to be the final stage of an approach for a water landing, with floats down.

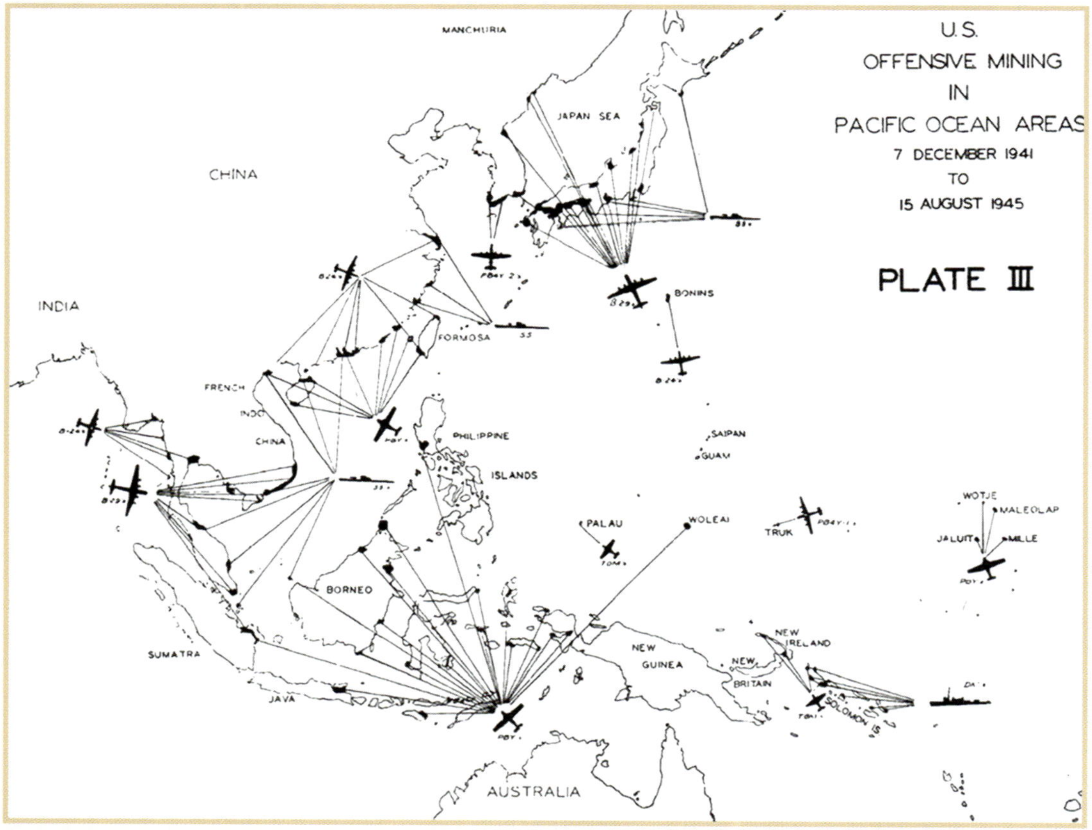

Left: This map depicts the offensive mining dropping operations of US Navy, USAAF, RAAF, RNZAF and Allies against the Japanese Imperial Navy during the full Pacific War, from December 1941 to 15 August 1945.

This is may be the lesser-known part of the naval war that raged over the Pacific, but while the Catalina had a predominantly ASW role in the Atlantic, the PBYs (and other aircraft types) in the Pacific executed primarily mine droppings on a large scale. It took place all over the Pacific West and SW rim, in order to hamper enemy port entries and their shipping and supply lines.

From the South Pacific islands of Wotje, Truk, Palau, the Solomon Islands, Western New Guinea, and far into the Dutch East Indies, the mine droppings were relentlessly executed. Later in the war, with the allied bases moving into New Guinea and Borneo, their dropping activities spread way up north, via the Philippines, into Formosa (Taiwan) and the Chinese coast. The B-29 Super Fortresses, departing from the Marianas, attacked the Japanese harbors with mining operations and bombing raids.

Opposite: A bad accident caused by a runaway propeller that flew the wrong way and seriously damaged the cockpit roof. Hopefully the pilots survived this nightmare. Note the under-wing pods: those are the auxiliary tanks with additional fuel for extra-long flights that could exceed 24 hours. Along with its versatility and independence from complex airfield installations, the Catalina could take the enemy by total surprise with its sudden appearance 'out of the blue' as an assault platform, with bombs, mines, depth charges and machine guns, for strafing ships, subs and harbor facilities.

Right: A PBY Catalina flying past the escort carrier USS *Sangamon*, at anchor in the Solomon Islands in the campaign of 1943. The Catalinas, with their ASW equipment, were an integral part of the security cover for such large ships against the ever-looming menace of a Japanese submarine. The subs were lured by eternal fame to sink a US Navy aircraft carrier loaded to the brim with airplanes.

During the successful Pearl Harbor attack on 7 December 1941, the US Navy Pacific fleet was wiped out, but, by sheer coincidence, all US aircraft carriers were out and escaped the carnage. That was an intelligence error by the Japanese – a monumental mistake that would cost them dearly in the forthcoming battles of the Coral Sea and Midway.

Every Japanese submarine captain knew of the huge threat that the US aircraft carrier fleet posed to their homeland, so they must all have dreamed to one day see this picture in their periscope. They could gain eternal fame by sinking such a ship, jam-packed with aircraft on its deck. But that single Catalina, flying low overhead, would become their nightmare, destroying their dreams long before they could even come close.

Above: A pre-delivery shot of a PB2B-2 Catalina built by Boeing of Canada for the Royal Australian Air Force. This version featured the redesigned higher tail rudder and full-span elevators also used on the PBN-1 Nomad and PBY-6A amphibian. It had a so-called 'eyeball' bow turret and radar teardrop (radome) atop the cockpit roof – all signs of a late version of the Catalina.
(Photo courtesy of Collins Family)

Above: A trial full-stall landing with the PB2B-2 Catalina built by Boeing of Canada. This type of landing was normally reserved for rough sea conditions. The first point of touchdown can be seen behind the aircraft so it had clearly bounced. The photos are likely to have been taken at the Naval Air Station, San Pedro, CA.
(Photo courtesy of Collins family)

Above: The RAAF Catalina test flight at NAS San Pedro, CA. Note the much higher tail of the PBY-6 model, now also featuring on this model built by Boeing of Canada. That redesigned tail with horn-balanced rudder was the final model that improved the directional stability of the aircraft.
(Photo courtesy of Martin Collins)

Above: PBY-5, A24-64, OX-D, 'The Dabster', from No. 43 Squadron above Lake Boga, Victoria, Australia, in 1944. A very blurry, yet remarkable photo. Note the unusual camouflage in matt black with very light grey patches above the wings.
(Courtesy of www.airpages.ru and Frank Smith)

Lake Boga is situated NW of Melbourne. This 'secret' lake was the hideout repair station for the RAAF flying boats, out of reach for the Japanese raiding fighters. On 19 February 1942, Darwin was attacked by a large fleet of 242 aircraft, which had come from the occupied Dutch East Indies island of Timor. This surprise assault killed 235 people and damaged the oil tanker depots, the port installation and parts of the town to such an extent that all flight operations of the Catalinas were 'withdrawn' down south to Lake Boga.

Less than two weeks later, on 3 March 1942, nine Mitsubishi Zero fighters bombed the Broome airport and Roebuck Bay in a devastating assault that destroyed 22 aircraft and killed 88 passengers and crew. Out in the bay, there were eight Catalinas, a Sunderland and five Dornier D0-24 Flying Boats moored. Not one of them survived the carnage, while many of the Dutch aircraft were jam-packed with passengers, waiting to be flown to the South of Australia.

Left: Aleutian Islands Campaign, June 1942–August 1943. PT boats lie alongside the tender ship in Attu Harbor. In the background is a PBY Catalina landing. Photographed by Lieutenant Horace Bristol, July 1943. US Navy photograph, now in the collections of the National Archives.

PT boats, as much as the Catalinas, had the role of the sneaky scouts and 'raiders in the dark' that could penetrate deeply into enemy territory. From out of the blue, they would launch torpedoes or gunning ships in hit-and-run raids, often by night, disappearing in the dark before the enemy could regroup for a counter-attack.

The PT boats were powered by three Packard engines 4M 2500 cu-in V12 for their high-speed attacks. This reliable engine was based on the 1925 Liberty aircraft engine, which was converted for marine use (racing boats) before the war. With 3,000 gallons in their tanks, they guzzled more fuel than the Catalina did at an average 100 gallons per flight hour.

In total some 600 PT boats were built in WWII. For more information see my Dakota Hunter blog at: www.dc3dakotahunter.com/blog/raiders-pacific-pt-boat-mosquitos-pby-catalina-black-cats-rogue-sharks-vol-1.

(Photo from the National Museum of the US Navy)

Left: French Catalina PBY-5A stationed at Agadir, Morocco in 1944 and 1945. The 6FE Free French Aeronavale of General de Gaulle was under American command and operated the Cats on behalf of anti-submarine patrols over the mid Atlantic and western Mediterranean. Note the 'Croix de Lorraine' sign painted on the fuselage, right behind the aerial under the engine. This was the Free French Army emblem that distinguished them from the Vichy French Army/Navy, which collaborated with the Germans.

Squadron Insignia and Nickname

The squadron's only known insignia was approved by CNO on 3 November 1944, after it had been redesignated VPB-63. The design was inspired by the squadron's MAD gear. It featured the face of a "mad" cat wearing a sailor hat, holding a broken submarine in its paws. Colors: field, yellow; border, dark blue; paws, jowls and hat, white; cat face blue; eyeball, yellow and green; pupil, dark blue with white iris; submarine, black; lettering, green with dark blue shadows.

The squadron's insignia.

Nickname: The Mad Cats, 1943–1945.

Above: Stunning photo of a late model RAAF Black Cat with two mechanics working on the fine tuning of the nr 1 engine, while sitting on their folding scaffolds – a windy and noisy job out there in the full prop wash. The dropping of tools or spares was not allowed! The man in the waist blister waits with a net to catch the wrench jocks in case they would drop off

Above: A Catalina 'MAD cat', a nickname used for the heavily armed Catalina with a rack of 2 x 12 retarding/retrograde rockets under the main wings. They were used in a combination with special devices developed for advanced anti-submarine warfare. The first one was this Magnetic Anomaly Detection (MAD) system, housed in the tail boom (see the 'tail' extension under the rudder in the above photo). This device detected the presence of a submerged submarine, assuming that the sub was not too deep and that the aircraft was flying at low altitude. The second device was the radar, which could only be used for detecting surfaced submarines/ships. Yet another, third detection device was the sonar buoy that could be dropped during flight, and, once in the water, the buoy transmitted by radio the grinding sound of the sub's screw, indicating its position under water.

Once the sub had been located by one or more of the electronic devices at hand, smoke markers could be dropped during the low (bombing) run over the sub in order to mark the last known position of the U-boat – very practical for a second attack after an orbit was made. For an instant attack right after detection by MAD, sonar or radar, these aircraft had only a short time slot to hit their target, which would try instantly to escape into the abyss.

The Cats came in with an in-air speed of some 110–120 mph or more and flew over a boat that reached a maximum of 20–24 mph (17–21 knots) under water. The bombs to be released had the same initial speed as the Cat's – six times faster than the targeted U-boat. In order to have a fair chance for a strike, a shorter gliding path would help in a more accurate aiming of the bombs/depth charges. So, the Cats were fitted with special 'retarding' bombs, to bring the release moment of the explosives very close to the target.

The idea was to make them fall straight down, instead of traveling in a long horizontal path driven by the speed of the aircraft. This retrorocket (or retrograde rocket) is a rocket engine that provides reverse thrust, i.e. opposing the motion of the aircraft, thereby causing it to decelerate quickly and preventing it from overshooting the targeted submarine. A second bomb run was only a 'Limited-Offer' option, as the sub would have soon disappeared out of reach of the bombs and even depth charges.

Right: Stranded 42 Squadron, RAAF Catalina that most probably had come loose from its mooring station during a storm and was beached by the high swell. In the process, the right-hand wing float had broken off and can be seen behind the Cat.

On open water, a river, lagoon or lake, the Catalina would be moored on a single anchor line or buoy. An incoming storm with a high swell was often reason for imminent problems caused by the fierce bobbing of 10 tons of aircraft. Acting like a giant wind vane with its large surfaces, and jerking hard on the anchor line with every wave that came in, it is not surprising that many a flying boat came loose from its mooring and ended up on a shore line or river bank, often damaged, sometimes beyond repair.
(Photo courtesy of Peter Dunn)

Above: Australian troops on Balikpapan Beach, Borneo. In August 1945, with all Japanese soldiers killed or driven into the jungle, the troops had some chill time for a swim and drove around in a captured Japanese Tankette Type 92. Seven years later, that very same beach became my playground. The wrecked Catalina was there to stay for a long time.

Left: Very nice shot of a PBY crew proudly posing on an airfield somewhere in the Aleutians – seven men flying long patrols every two or three days over the string of barren islands all the way to the west and back, monitoring the possible appearance of the Japanese Imperial Navy. This is not a fantastical scenario as, on 3–4 June 1942, Dutch Harbor, Alaska, came under aerial attack from Japanese bomber/fighters that were launched from two Japanese aircraft carriers. Luckily, the USAAF knew that an assault was underway due to intercepted radio messages, which could be deciphered thanks to the broken secret code. This Northern sea route was, from that time, under the heavy surveillance of the Catalinas and Harpoons.

Above: Surrender of German Submarine *U-899*, monitored by an overflying RCAF Canso.

After the German surrender on 8 May 1945, the German High Command ordered all U-boats to surrender. Many U-boat captains opted to scuttle their ships instead of handing them over. On the afternoon of 10 May, an RCAF Canso spotted *U-889* south of Newfoundland. The boat was flying a black flag of surrender. Royal Navy ships intercepted the submarine an hour later. *U-889* was ordered to head to Bay Bulls, Newfoundland. The sub was turned over to the frigates HMCS *Inch Arran* and HMCS *Buckingham* who escorted her to Shelburne Harbour, Nova Scotia. This photo was taken just before she was boarded for the surrender formalities. The German officers wait on the conning tower in their final minutes of commanding their ship, which, not long before this moment, had terrorized the Allied shipping lines on the Atlantic.

The capitulation of Germany was no guarantee yet for the immediate cessation of submarine war, and there was a widespread fear that many a U-boat captain would continue as a 'rogue shark' and attack ships at random up to the last torpedo. On 7 May, *U-2336* sank two British ships off the Firth of Forth, while an RAF Catalina attacked and destroyed the last U-boat (*U-320*), which had tried to escape from the Baltic to the Atlantic.

However, many captains did opt to surface and surrender to the Allied Forces, as seen in this fascinating photo. This was no small-scale operation as over 150 U-boats surrendered and more than 200 were scuttled by their own crews. Most of the surrendered U-boats were later sunk in the Atlantic off Northern Ireland, so there must be a huge submarine graveyard somewhere out there in the deep. You can watch dramatic footage of a submarine surrender to the US Navy at: https://www.youtube.com/watch?v=nFBMdtM-jEk&sns=fb

Above: Fabulous photo of the RCAF Canso in a low fly pass over the U-boat *U-889* that has just been taken over. A Canadian guard stands on the conning tower while the Kriegsmarine's commanding officer makes a formal surrender. The Royal Canadian Navy flag is shown now flying.

Note the big tube running along the right-hand side of the conning tower. This is the folded schnorkel mast. With this breathing device in an upright position, the sub was able to run its diesel engines for propulsion and the recharging of its batteries, while remaining submerged just under the surface of the water, out of sight of radar. But sonar, the MAD boom and the broken Kriegsmarine secret code were other indicators that helped the Allied hunter ships and aircraft to detect the sub's hidden position.

On 14 May 1945, *U-889* was commissioned in to the RC Navy and decommissioned in December 1945. Experiments were conducted on her special hydrophone equipment before she was scuttled at the end of 1947.

Opposite: USAAF Catalina, the first plane to land at Seppingan Aerodrome, Balikpapan, Borneo, July 1945. It landed smoothly only a few minutes after Australian engineers (in foreground) had filled the last bomb craters on the strip.

This was the final act of Operation OBOE II, the Allied conquering of the East Borneo oil refineries, which cut off the major Japanese oil supply lines from their war effort. The Japanese Navy was desperately engaged in the naval battles around the Philippines and in dire need of fuel for their aircraft and ships. The loss of Balikpapan and Tarakan oil supplies must have been a real disaster for the Military of the 'Empire of the Sun'.

The Post-war Years

After the war, most Allied bombers and fighters were decommissioned and trashed by the thousands, feeding the smelting ovens that ran overtime to recycle the precious aluminum, reshaping aircraft into solid ingots for industrial re-use. But the Douglas C-47, the Curtiss Commando C-46, the Beechcraft C-45 and the PBY Catalina (to a lesser extent) remained mostly intact. While large storage depots were filled to the brim in 1946 with surplus aircraft, soon the world would crave the air transport capacity that those ready-to-go aircraft offered for cargo and passengers. But also in the Military role, a huge export market opened up that could be filled with those cheap war-surplus machines, for Coast Guard duties and later, with the Cold War starting in 1948, for anti-submarine patrols against the Communist threat.

The ex-military transports were available, more or less for grabs, and could be fairly easily converted into cargo or passenger aircraft. With low prices per aircraft, and with spare parts and brand new engines available in vast stockpiles – sufficient for years of flying – the surplus aircraft sold well all over the globe and entered their second lease of life in a military or civil role. The C-47s and PBY Catalinas went to nearly all Military Forces of the Free World and to all operators, starting with passenger airlines in the rapidly expanding civil transportation market.

While many of the military surplus C-47s/Dakotas were quite simply converted into the civil DC-3 version, with sound insulation applied and rows of chairs mounted on rails on the reinforced floors, it took a bit more of an effort to convert the military PBY to a comfortable passenger transport aircraft. The Catalina not only had gun and bomb aimer positions that had to be removed first (which was quite a drastic intervention if thoroughly done), but it was also an aircraft with a typical boat hull and keels that limited interior space, especially in the rear end.

In addition, the Catalina was a rugged aircraft, designed to withstand hard water landings. To improve the structural strength of this peculiar non-tubular fuselage, the factory designed a number of serious bulkheads inside the cabin that split the fuselage into three 'living' compartments: the first in front (just behind the cockpit); the second one aft of the main wing pylon; and finally, the third one in the Blister area near the tail. Bulkheads are strongest when they have no orifices, but the Catalina had bulkhead openings, be it nothing more than large 'man holes' with a high threshold. This was not good for passenger loading, so in many cases the original openings had to be enlarged, to some detriment of the structural integrity. With no real big door to enter the aircraft, passenger comfort always remained awkward. Also, there was more limited seating than in the purpose-built passenger/land aircraft of that era that had no bulkheads in the cabin space. Consequently, the Catalina in its best passenger conversion could carry 16–20 seats at most, while the DC-3 had a capacity of 24–28 or even 30 seats.

Translated in the green stuff, the DC-3 – with lower risks, lower operational costs and more revenue potential per flight – was a better money-maker for its operator. But the Catalina had a cutting edge as a passenger transport in those more remote areas where there was no airstrip yet at the in-between or end destination. While she could take off from any 'hub' airport with a sandy, gravel or asphalt runway, the Cat could land right in the middle of nowhere, on any stretch of water, to deliver its passengers or cargo at an outback camp, remote settlement or an island in a matter of hours; a journey that otherwise would take days to get there by boat or a truck.

It is exactly this feature that gave the Cat a bright future right after the war, with an extended operational life in water-rich or ocean-surrounded countries like Alaska, Northern Canada, Brazil, The Caribbean, Australia, New Zealand, Indonesia, etc. Apart from this passenger transport role, we see the Catalina show up in many more roles as a revenue-making machine: as a water tanker/firefighter or as a photography/survey aircraft that skimmed the jungles and deserts with special magnetic field equipment, in search of exploration opportunities for precious metals, oil, and ore.

Opposite: Post-war rescue Catalina in Alaska. Note the long exhaust shrouds that divert hot engine exhaust air to the wing de-icing equipment. By this stage of the Catalina's history, the iconic US Star & Bar emblem reached its final post-war version. A red horizontal bar had been added to the blue and white nationality markings below the cockpit. Note in the background the M-29 Weasel tracked vehicles built by Studebaker for Arctic and mountainous rescue/transport operations.

RESCUE

Above: PBY-6A Catalina BuNo 46640 of the US Coast Guard at French Frigate Shoals in the central Pacific Ocean, NW of Hawaii in 1953. Before the war, French Frigate Shoals was nothing more than an obscure atoll acting as a huge bird's nest, but after the Pearl Harbor attack it was considered a potential hideout for Japanese submarine-tankers that could refuel flying boats on their way to attacking (again) the Hawaiian Islands. The shoals were occupied by the US Navy in 1942 and used as a patrol station for the Coast Guard Catalinas after the war. All three Catalinas shown on this page have ASV radar in a housing above the cockpit roof. This upgrade came late in WWII but remained a feature of many post-war Catalinas.

Above: This US Navy Catalina and the one depicted in the first photo have ASV radar in a housing above the cockpit roof. This upgrade came late in WWII but remained a feature of many post-war Catalinas. Unlike the others, the Catalina in this photo did not make the end of the war and can be seen dashed against rocks in the harsh conditions of Alaska. In 1948 – only a few years after the war came to an end – the Berlin Blockade led to the heightening of Cold War tensions and gave rise to the resurrection of certain anti-submarine patrol flights over the Northern Atlantic and the Baltic to counter the potential Russian sub threat. Denmark, the UK and the Netherlands all participated in this program.

Left: A spectacular photo of a post-war US Coast Guard Catalina PBY-5A using hull-mounted JATO bottles. This Jet-Assisted-Take-Off was used in circumstances when only a very short takeoff run was foreseen, for example from smaller bodies of water such as lakes, rivers, and bays, or from unsheltered seas with high swell that otherwise would prevent a long takeoff run over rough waters. The JATO bottles looked like a pack of giant firecrackers with their spectacular smoke trails.

Above: US Coast Guard PBY-5A in San Diego, CA. Note the droppable lifesaving boat, streamlined and neatly tucked away under the wing like an engine nacelle. If water landing was impossible, these boats could parachuted to help drowned sailors or aircraft crews.

USA

Right: An unidentified passenger-carrying Catalina belonging to Long Beach-based California Maritime Airlines (CMA) gets up 'onto the step' for takeoff from the bay at Avalon, Santa Catalina Island, off the US West Coast, in 1948.

Below: Dan Shirey, who grew up in Ketchikan, Alaska, sent this photo from his family photo album. It was taken on Annette Island in the mid-1950s and shows an aircraft owned by Ellis Airlines, which later became Alaska Airlines. Note the rather primitive platform facilities and equipment, wooden household stairs for the passengers and for the ground crew communicating with the pilots! This Cat has a number of big windows, including two in the XL-sized hatch.

Above: Rick Petersen has been working on his PBY-6A restoration project at Moses Lake, WA for many years. This Cat N9825Z, originally US Navy BuNo 64107, was the last Catalina to be built. The removal of the front gun turret was often the first job to do during the demilitarization of the Catalina. It improved the streamlining and gave a better forward view for pilots during water operations. The bulky turret was removed and covered with a lower longer needed. It was often covered with a plate, and in many cases a new clipper bow was mounted, with a more rounded shape and sometimes a black rubber nose cushion, acting like a bumper. This was very practical when maneuvering in waters where there was no launch to help with moorings on a buoy or pier. The clipper bow surely made the Cat's stubby nose appear more elegant.

Above: Originally built for the Royal Canadian Air Force as a Canso A, N68740 had a successful civilian career and traveled widely. It is now an exhibit at the Pima Air & Space Museum, Tucson, AZ.

Above: The Confederate Air Force has flown a number of Catalinas over the years – here are two of them. Closest to the camera is PBY-5A N68756 in pseudo RAAF colors, whilst behind it is the former Royal Danish Air Force PBY-6A N16KL before it was destroyed in a fatal crash in the Gulf of Mexico, TX on 13 October 1984.

Right: A number of commercially operated Catalinas were converted to so-called 'Super Cats' or 'Super Catalinas' by installing more powerful Wright R-2600 Cyclone engines of 1,700 hp each in place of the 1,200 P&W Twin Wasps of the original design. N2886D was used as a water bomber and was lost during a water pick-up run on a lake at Northport, Washington, on 29 July 1985.

Above: PBY-6A N4NC owned by Wilson 'Connie' Edwards of Big Springs, TX was painted in a special scheme to commemorate the 75th Anniversary of US naval aviation in 1986. It flew across the Atlantic to the UK in the same year to replicate the original flight, 67 years before, of a formation of US Navy NC-4 flying boats.
(Photo via Bill Bailey)

Left: This colorful Catalina – N68756 – was owned for a while by the US TV personality Herb Shriner before being acquired by the Confederate Air Force (CAF), stationed at Harlingen, Texas in October 1979.

It had been converted to a Landseaire luxury air yacht in 1952 and had a series of corporate owners before it traveled to Australia and back with the CAF. It then lapsed into unserviceability and, later, into dereliction in Texas. (Info courtesy David Legg)

Left: Tofino Canso crash site revisited.

The Last Flight of Canso A. RCAF Serial Number 11007
On 8 February 1945 the Canadian Vickers Canso A, RCAF serial number 11007, took off from Tofino airport with 12 personnel, its normal emergency gear and full tanks – about 750 gallons. The aircraft also carried four 250-pound depth charges as they were on a coastal night patrol, looking for Japanese submarines.

Right after takeoff, the port engine quit. The Canso was way too low to turn and did not have enough power to gain altitude with that load. The pilot, Ronnie Scholes, opted to land into the dense wood straight ahead. Just before first contact was made, he pulled the doomed aircraft into a full stall.

Navigator F/O Lace Knechtel was riding in the port blister. He felt the tail go up, then it crashed back down into a heavily wooded hillside. All the lights in the aircraft went out, and there was silence, but for the gushing sound of gasoline escaping from the ruptured left wing tank. Worse, the port engine was on fire. In the end, with the fire extinguished all 12 crew members survived the crash, with only two of them injured.

For more info and photos, see also:
https://villagephotographer.wordpress.com/tag/tofino/

Above: Special thanks go to Bill Bailey for this awesome photo. Wilson 'Connie' Edwards' PBY-6A N4NC leads a unique flying boat formation with a Grumman Albatross and a Grumman Widgeon, all US Coast Guard veterans.

The Grumman G-44 Widgeon was built from 1941–1955 in limited numbers (317 including the French license built Widgeons) for the United States Navy, the USAAF, the US Coast Guard as OA-14, and for the Royal Navy as the Gosling. The much larger Grumman Albatross HU-16 was built from 1949–1961 (in total, 466 aircraft of the various types). Primary users were the United States Air Force, the US Coast Guard and the US Navy. The Albatross also flew for 20 foreign coast guard and military services in the SAR role.

The Albatross was used by the US Air Force's Aerospace Rescue and Recovery Service and saw extensive combat service during the Vietnam War. Other examples of the HU-16 made their way into Air Force Reserve air rescue units prior to its retirement from USAF service. The final USCG HU-16 flight was at CGAS Cape Cod in March 1983.

To give these figures some scale: The PBY Catalina and Canso models were built between 1936–1945; in total just over 3,300 were built of the various types, a figure that, due to the war production, far exceeded the numbers of Albatross and Widgeons built.

Below: Nice photo of Canso A 11041 of the Royal Canadian Air Force overflying Vancouver, BC, in June 1956. After many years of service, its days were numbered as it was to be destroyed in a landing accident at Seal Cove, Prince Rupert, BC, on 30 June 1959. Note the plexiglass dome on the bow fairing, unique to some post-war RCAF Canso As.

Above: Two Convairs! Canadian Pacific Airlines operated both the Convair 240 and the Canso A. The latter was designed by the Consolidated Aircraft Corporation, which later became Convair. The two types are shown in this classic shot at Sandspit, BC, where passengers were transferred to the '240 for onward flight to Vancouver. Note the rear airstair on the Canso.
(Photo courtesy Dave O´Malley)

Right: Canadian Pacific's CF-CRR and crew at Prince Rupert, BC, in between flights. Captain Dennis Baxendale stands on the left. Next to him are agent Lou Burtsch and two of the CPAL mechanics. Kneeling in the front are First Officer Denny Denman and dispatcher Lou Burchell. In April 2017 Dave O'Malley wrote to me explaining: 'Sadly, the Canso Captain who poses in this photo, Dennis Baxendale, died last month of ALS. All of the images used in the story of CF-CRR in CP markings came from him. In honor of him, would you like to place this photo in your book as a tribute to Dennis.' Thank you Dave, hereby as promised, his unique photos placed with pride, in honor of Dennis.
(Photo courtesy of Dave O´Malley)

Above: CF-CRR prepares to alight at Prince Rupert, BC. This Canso was a real 'warbird', having one U-boat 'kill' to its credit.
(Photo courtesy of Dave O´Malley)

Above: CF-CRR 'on the step' and about to depart the water at Prince Rupert. This aircraft made a very eventful career after its operations with Canadian Pacific. More of that can be seen in Chapter 5, The Survivors.
(Photo courtesy of Dave O´Malley)

Above: Photo of Canso CF-IZO taken in 1966 at Brabant Lake, Saskatchewan by Canso pilot George Horne. Canso CF-IZO was owned and operated by North Canada Air Limited (Norcanair Ltd). This trip was made to move Nap Hanson and his family from Prince Albert to Brabant Lake in Northern Saskatchewan. (Nap Hanson was a radio communications operator at the new Brabant Lake key radio station for the Saskatchewan Department of Natural Resources.)

(Photo via Les Oystryk)

FOR IMMEDIATE SALE

CANSO PBY5A AIRCRAFT

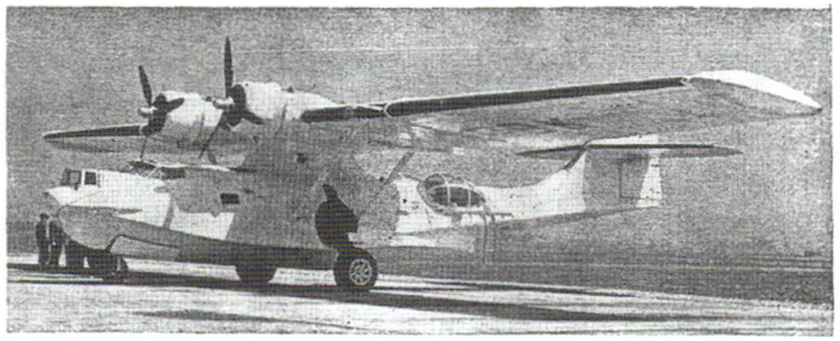

The Babb Company (Canada) Limited has for immediate disposal a number of Canso PBY5A aircraft, located at various points throughout the Dominion. Prices on these aircraft range from $9,000 to $15,000 depending on condition, total times, etc.

These aircraft are offered "as is, where is". The Babb Company (Canada) Limited will undertake to deliver them to any point on a cost-plus basis. Aircraft may be inspected by special arrangement only.

write or wire . . .

THE BABB COMPANY (CANADA)
LIMITED
The World's Largest Dealer in New and Used Aircraft and Components

THE BABB COMPANY
1007 Airway, Glendale, California
THE BABB COMPANY INC.
444 Madison Ave., New York, N.Y., and Mexico City

1477 Sherbrooke St. W.,
MONTREAL, CANADA

Left: Charles E. Babb was an established aircraft dealer in the USA, specializing in sales to overseas countries, including to the RAAF in Australia. His business grew during the post-war military disposal sales, selling bulk surplus aircraft to foreign Air Forces and civilian buyers. With offices in NY and California, the Babb Co established a Canadian company to handle large-scale purchases of RCAF disposal aircraft.

Right: Out of the blue the unlucky Catalina CF-HFL, which crashed in the woods (see next photo), got a second lease of life. In 1986, twenty-nine years after the accident, it was recovered by a helicopter and is now undergoing a rebuild with the Atlantic Canada Aviation Museum at Halifax, Nova Scotia, Canada.
(Photo from the David Legg collection)

Above: Having served with the US Navy, and then as a commercial airliner in the Caribbean, PBY-5A BuNo 05021 ended up with Eastern Provincial Airlines in Canada as CF-HFL. It was forced landed in trees by its pilot after an engine failure 50 miles from Goose Bay, Newfoundland, on 1 October 1957. Twenty-nine years later, in 1986, it was recovered by helicopter (see previous photo) and is now undergoing a rebuild with the Atlantic Canada Aviation Museum at Halifax, Nova Scotia.

Above: Canadian postage stamp, honoring the successful 1940–1945 anti-submarine warfare role of the RCAF Cansos against the German subs. The aircraft depicted is Canso A 9754 in which Flt Lt David Hornell earned his posthumous Victoria Cross.

Above: The harsh reality of flying post-war Catalinas on operations as a fish hauler in Beaver Lake, Ontario, Canada. Shown here is CF-SAT looking 'well used' – she went on to have a long civilian career, proving the ruggedness of the design. For more photos of the civil Canadian Catalina operations, see Chapter 3.
(Photo courtesy of Les Oystryk)

Left: Fabulous photo of a Bell-47 helicopter, landing with its inflatable floats on the main wing of an Austin Airways Catalina in Canada. Was this a show-off stunt or a 'daily routine'? The pilot was the legendary John Schulz: according to Con Campbell (who supplied me with this photo) the best chopper pilot in all of Canada.

The Bell-47 'Soap Bubble' helicopter flew with the US Army as the H-13 Sioux and earned its place in the hall of fame during the Korean War (1950–1953), then with the classic TV series M.A.S.H. with the theme song 'Suicide is Painless'. The series, starring Alan Alda and Loretta Swit, ran on TV networks all over the world from 1972–1983 and became a S-Mash hit.

More than 5,500 Bell-47s were built between 1946 and 1974. In 2011, there were still over a 1,000 registered in USA. Like with the Catalina, in those days, they built transports to last for decades or longer!

Above: Former RCAF Canso A CF-JCV of Austin Airways makes an evening departure from Moosonee (Ontario) as another Canso bobs at its moorings. Austin Airways was Canada's oldest airline and started service in 1934. Its home base was Timmins and it served isolated and remote airports in northern Ontario and Quebec provinces as well as in the Northwest Territories (NWT), Canada. Along with some larger airports across Ontario, it had Minneapolis–St Paul in the US as its only non-Canadian destination.

In June 1987, Austin Airways merged with Air Ontario Ltd (formerly Great Lakes Airlines, formed in 1958) to form Air Ontario Inc. In turn, Air Ontario became part of Air Canada Jazz in 2001.

(Photo courtesy of Larry Milberry)

Above: The photographer, Larry, wrote: 'As passengers await, an Austin Airways Canso arrives at a provincial Canadian settlement.' Or, considering the wing-tip floats are in retracted position, did they just miss their plane? Walking a mile from home and seeing the once-a-day-only flight depart like this, OMG, the ladies must have felt forlorn on the bank of that windy lake.

Larry's final remark under this photo is an understatement: 'Not the typical scene of today's modern terminal buildings!' It gives a good impression of how things in public transport have dramatically changed over the past 70 years, especially in the remote settlements of Northern Canada.

(Photo courtesy of Larry Milberry)

Above: A most interesting photo showing three legendary aircraft that were largely responsible for the opening up of the Canadian outback. In 1954, in Northern Saskatchewan, Waite Fisheries used two Cansos for transporting fish.

Note the floatplane Cessna 170 in the front, 5,000 of which were built between 1948 and 1956. In the second row, we see what seems to be an early type of the Noorduyn Norseman, the legendary Canadian-built bush plane that is now a much-desired museum piece/collector's item. More than 900 were built. Designed by Robert B.C. Noorduyn, the Norseman was produced from 1935 to 1959, originally by Noorduyn Aircraft Ltd and later by the Canada Car and Foundry (CC&F). The rugged plane was quickly adopted in 1940 by the RCAF, RCN, US Army Air Corps, USAAF and US Navy. An additional 14 more overseas air forces would go on to purchase this plane, as well as 16 civil operators from all over Canada and beyond (including Buffalo Airways).

The old truck in the photo has 'Albert Chalifour – Debden, Sask' written on the door. Debden is a very small community not too far from Big River and possibly Mr Chalifour was hauling either freight or fish to or from this dock and associated aircraft.

(Photo courtesy of Lance Reed)

Above: Yellowknife, NWT, Canada – the water-tanker base of Buffalo Airways, 1998. In the foreground is the mother of all flying firefighters, the PBY-5A Catalina and its successor, the Canadair CL-215, that arrived in the late 1960s. Ironically, Canadair is the successor of Canadian Vickers, which license-built the Catalina/Canso in wartime for such clients as the RCAF and USAAF. During that period, Canadair (later taken over by Bombardier) acquired the skills to build fine flying boats. With that, they focused on the specialty production of purpose-built water bomber aircraft. In 1968, the first CL-215 came out with the P & W R-2800 radial engine of 2100 hp (see photo). This was followed, in 1989, by the model CL-215 T, a highly successful model with turboprop engines.

AUSTRALIA

Right: RAAF Catalina PB2B-2 over Rose Bay, Sydney Harbour, Australia.

In 1934 the British Government decided to instigate an airmail service for the whole Commonwealth at fixed rates. For this purpose, Imperial Airways contracted Short Brothers to create a new format of flying boat. They were known as the 'Short Empire' and were called 'C' class because all had names starting with C, such as Cleopatra and Coogee.

Sydney's first international airport was in its harbor, at Rose Bay, to the east of Sydney Harbour Bridge. From 1938, the flying boat mail and passenger services from Rose Bay connected the city more closely than ever to the rest of the world. Rose Bay was part of a world network of water airports, including those at Singapore, Calcutta, Cairo, Southampton, Lisbon, New York (La Guardia), Auckland (Mechanics Bay), Rio de Janeiro (Santos Dumont), Honolulu/Hawaii and locations all over the Pacific.

By 1947, more than 270 people were working at the base: maintenance and engine mechanics, employees of Qantas Empire Airways and Trans Oceanic Airways, the Department of Civil Aviation, Shell Oil, and the Bureau of Meteorology. Military surplus Catalinas were waiting in large rows to be taken away for grabs, out of which a new industry would emerge in the late 1940s: tourist flights to remote fantasy Islands, off the east and northeast coast of Australia (Great Barrier Reef).

After the war, flying boats helped to increase access to the South Pacific and appeared in a great array of private ventures, but their place gradually diminished due to the wartime and post-war construction of land-based airports. In 1974, the last regular Australian flying boat passenger service between Sydney Harbour and Lord Howe Island finished, and the 50-year era of the Australian flying boats was over. Rose Bay, the last major flying boat terminal in the world, closed.

(Info courtesy of www.australia.gov.au/about-australia/australian-story/flying-boats-of-australia)

Right: The Royal Australian Air Force flying boat base at Rathmines, NSW (near Newcastle), was a notable base for Catalinas and many were stored there awaiting disposal following the end of the hostilities. By the end of WWII, the Royal Australian Air Force had received a total of 168 Catalinas in a variety of models. Soon after the war, RAAF retired most of their Catalinas; only a few were kept operational for SAR duties and special missions.

In 1946 the remaining Catalinas were stored at either the Flying Boat Repair Depot at Lake Boga, Victoria, or, the Repair Depot at Rathmines, NSW, where they awaited their disposal (see photo). Exposed to the elements, some Catalinas at Rathmines were damaged by hailstones in a storm in 1946, causing dented skins, shattered Perspex, and torn fabric control surfaces and wings.

In October 1946, the Commonwealth Disposals Commission started the public sales of surplus aircraft for a total of 60 Catalinas located at Lake Boga and Rathmines. With some aircraft in 'as new' condition, most Cats were sold for £1,000 each, while lower prices were paid for those in poor condition or with high running hours since their last engine overhaul. Initially, there were operators with plans to fly them as civil aircraft with airlines. Others were acquired by parts dealers to remove the P&WR 1830 Twin Wasp engines, instruments, fuel tanks and other parts to be held as DC-3/PBY spares stock.

See also this interesting link at: http://www.goodall.com.au/australian-aviation.htm

Above: Photographed from a native canoe, passengers are about to disembark from Qantas Empire Airways' VH-EBC named 'Island Chieftain' in New Guinea, 1949. Captain Hugh Birch is standing between the engines. The final New Guinea Catalina revenue flight was made on 24 July 1958. The two Catalinas were retired, replaced by Qantas floatplane Beavers and Otters. During nine years of New Guinea service, they had carried a total of 54,259 passengers and logged 12,427 flying hours.

Qantas operated the largest number of civil Catalinas in Australia. Their operations were based at Rose Bay flying boat base at Sydney Harbour. Right after the war, Qantas was keen to create new routes to Pacific island nations and ex-RAAF Catalinas were perfect for the task. Their aircraft flew services to Lord Howe Island, New Caledonia, Fiji, Port Vila and Espiritu Santo.

The initial interior conversion of RAAF Catalinas to a 15-seat passenger airliner at Rose Bay used luxury passenger seats salvaged from scrapped Qantas Short C Class Empire flying boats. From April 1951 Qantas Catalinas on these Pacific islands were replaced by Short Sandringhams.

(Photo: Qantas via Greg Banfield collection)

Above: 'Triste Finale' for many surplus war birds, about to be trashed by the cutting torch. Such a sad view was a reality often seen. As for many of the 2,000 or so war-weary Catalinas, many were redundant, with no more employment to be found. Even with hundreds of PBYs being exported to over 30 nations for military services, coast guard duties, firefighting and aerial survey duties, corporate/commercial transports for pax/cargo and a small number of private luxury yachts, there was still a numerical surplus that resulted in sad scenes like this one.

Those aero engines had a value that exceeded the price paid for the total Cat. The radial piston engines P & W R-1830s were dismantled and went straight to the dozens of DC-3 operators that had popped up worldwide, using the same engines. There was a much bigger market for a rugged aircraft that had never seen salt water and were therefore mostly better conserved than the war- and seawater-ridden airframes of the PBY.

Note, the Catalina A24-112 in the foreground was lucky to escape the ever-looming fate of 'Death by the Torch' and actually went on to have a second career with the Dutch MLD. (Marine Luchtvaart Dienst; see photos of MLD in this chapter)

Above right: As VR-HDH, this Catalina flew with Cathay Pacific Airlines in the Far East before being sold to Trans Australia Airlines (TAA), for whom it was refurbished by Bristol Aviation at Bankstown, near Sydney, NSW. It is seen here before the application of its Australian registration VH-SBV.

Above: An excellent shot of VH-SBV at NSW Australia in October 1962. Trans Australian Airways operated this Catalina VH-SBV in New Guinea between 1962 and 1966. Its last flight in 1966 was to Port Moresby where it went into storage, minus its engines, and was used for the Airport Fire Brigade trainings.

TAA was founded by the Commonwealth Government. On the 1 September 1960, TAA took over the internal network of PNG routes from Qantas and introduced the TAA Sunbird Services logo for all their internal aircraft. They flew DC-3s, DC-6Bs PBYs and smaller aircraft. Services to PNG were begun by TAA and Ansett-ANA on 9 July 1960, along the Sydney-Brisbane-Port Moresby-Lae route, using DC-6B aircraft.

This Catalina is now under restoration at the Royal New Zealand Air Force Museum, Wigram, Christchurch, New Zealand. (Photo courtesy of Eric Allen)

Above: Sad sight of VH-BDY being scrapped at Lake Boga, Australia, in 1950. The ex-RAAF Catalinas had a very limited chance of surviving after 1945, especially the non-amphibian version (as seen in this photo), as it was more cumbersome to handle and therefore less desirable for civil use, and maintenance always required the beaching gear to be mounted. The types came for sale for grabs as their condition deteriorated quickly under the scorching Australian sun. Note how the wing's fabric is torn and the overall decrepit state of the aircraft. The only real value was in the Pratt & Whitney engines – the first parts to be taken off, while the airframe was often discarded for scrapping and ended in the smelting oven, only to reappear in the shape of aluminum ingots for industrial recycling.

Above: This photo shows the Catalina VH-AGB, operated by Adastra-Hunting Geophysics in Australia, Europe, Africa and the Americas. This London-based company, founded in 1954, went in search of areas of minerals based on the earth's magnetic field. The most commonly used geophysical instruments included:

- A magnetometer to measure the distortions and additions to the magnetic field of the Earth due to the rocks and minerals
- An electromagnetic (EM) sounding system to measure the effects of the electrical conductivities of the rocks
- A radiometric survey system to measure the radioactive emanations from the radioactive isotopes of the elements that are the constituent components of the rocks and earth below the aircraft.

(Photo and info courtesy of G. Goodall/Ben Dannecker collection)

Left: Catalina fuselage re-purposed as a houseboat in Moira Forest, NSW, in 1976. A former RAAF Black Cat that in December 1944 operated over Manilla Harbour executing mine droppings to hamper Japanese shipping transport, she is now to be found under restoration with the Australian National Aviation Museum at Moorabbin Airport, Melbourne

(Photo courtesy of G. Goodall)

Above: Geophysical survey equipped 'Super Cat' VH-UMS with Wright R-2600 Cyclone engines and non-standard prop' spinners. The various aerial arrays around the hull and wing were feeding the magnetic field gauges that mapped an area for the presence of metals or oil. This particular aircraft, with Australian registration of Selco Exploration Co. is seen here on public display in August 1964, most probably in Meekatharra, Western Australia. Note how it retained its rare RCAF glass dome on the 'clipper' bow.
(Photo courtesy Graydon West, via Jim Leppitt)

BRAZIL

Below: Panair do Brasil was a joint operation with PAA (Pan Am). The Company was an avid operator of the Consolidated flying boats, even before the Catalinas arrived. Its forerunner, the Consolidated Commodore Model-16, can be seen here under maintenance in 1935. The Commodore was 'Old School' in 1935, but had distant features of the Catalina with its parasol wing. It was clearly a less graceful and streamlined design with its struts and bracings, and only rudimentary engine cowlings. But the type surely established the reputation of Consolidated as a top-class manufacturer of reliable land and sea aircraft.

Above: Panair do Brasil Canso PP-PCX. The Cats were used in the Amazon territory, where the huge river offered an ideal 'runway' to land in the heart of the Green Hell, which was otherwise nearly impenetrable, taking days by steamboat to get there. Their frequent arrival on the outback posts must have dramatically changed the isolated lifestyle of some jungle settlements in the Amazon.
(Photo courtesy Michael Prophet)

Left: Moored to its buoy on a placid stretch of water is PP-PCX of Brazilian airline Panair do Brasil. Note the twin cargo doors on the port side of the hull where the rear gun 'blister' originally would have been.

Above: With 'luxury' airline stairs in position, ready to receive its passengers through the rear cargo doors, Panair do Brasil's PP-PDB awaits its next service.

Above: Brazilian Catalinas PP-PDB/PCW/PEC. A large number of Catalinas were operated in Brazil, both by the Air Force and with civilian operators. Here, three examples belonging to Panair do Brasil S.A. are lined up ready for flight.

Above: Panair do Brasil Catalina PP-PCY. I remember similar situations very well from my childhood years in the Borneo jungle in the early 1950s. In remote stations and outbacks, the arrival of the Catalina by a water landing on the river was often a good reason for a social party for the local community. The Cat brought news, magazines, food, beer, friends, and mail. In a time when there was no (satellite) TV, no mobile telephone, and only scarce radio contact with the outside world, this was surely the place to be when the Silver Bird had landed.

Right: By mid-1949, six Catalinas were stationed by the Brazilian Air Force (FAB) in Belem on the north shore of Brazil, near the Amazon delta. The aircraft were modernized with radar APS-1 and also flew for the government on administrative missions, with army support, in order to patrol and protect the remote borders.

A Frontier Mail service was provided by the end of WWII, at the time that the FAB shore patrols and anti-submarine flights were ended. The FAB Catalina service soon also transported civil passengers and cargo to isolated places, a typical South American phenomenon that I encountered also in Ecuador and Bolivia, and which lasted until the 1990s with the Hercules C-130s.

The Catalina in the photo is FAB 6525. The very last FAB Cat services in Brazil ended on 12 June 1982. A reliable service that had lasted for 23 years, often in very primitive circumstances, had come to an end.

(Courtesy of www.pilotesdufeu.com/cansonet/Operateurs/aeronavale/aeronavale.html)

Above: This beautiful shot shows a Brazilian CAM (Correio Aéreo Nacional) Catalina based n Tapaua, at the heart of the impenetrable Amazon, south west of Manaus. Brazil had the

distances and no infrastructure of roads or airfields but gifted with huge rivers, lakes and bays. Notably in the Amazon region, the Catalina could land at choice, with huge water

Above: Both the military and civil operators had the Cats in numbers and operated them for many years. After the Força Aérea Brasileira (FAB) retired its Catalina fleet in the early-1980s, a number were acquired by American owners and flown to the USA. This one still wears its FAB bow code and tail colors, and sports a suitable message on the hull: 'Adeus FAB' or 'Adios Amigos, from FAB'. Allegedly, in a remarkable deal, five of the FAB's last Catalinas were traded with Americans for a Lockheed C-130 Hercules.

INDONESIA

Below top: A poor quality photo, but a rare view of VH-BDP in late 1948, the former RAAF Cat flown by pilot R. Cobley for fish hauling from Tasmania. The PBY-5 retained its original wartime camouflage and that turned out to be very practical, as under the flag of a quasi airline, Air Indonesia, this Australian Cat got entangled in an illicit arms/ammo/fuel transport to the Indonesian Republican Army, which was supporting an armed assault against the Dutch Army in the Dutch East Indies. On 29 December 1948, this Cat crashed at takeoff in central Java after one such clandestine delivery flight, killing R. Cobley and his crew.

The Indonesian Republican Army must have had more help from foreigners with the setup of their Republican Air Force (AURI). The air force consisted of a fleet of ex-Japanese fighters Mitsubishi Sonia Ki-51, Lilly Bombers, Oscar fighters and the Yokusaka K5Y Willow double-decker trainers that were left by the Japanese forces in August 1945. Some 70 Willows were collected to make 20 of them operational for light bombing raids and scouting flights. Most of their aircraft were soon detected by the Dutch Air Force and destroyed on the ground but it remains remarkable how they could maintain and fly those complex aircraft in such primitive circumstances.

Allegedly, Japanese stragglers were involved with the flight operations as pilots/trainers and mechanics. The ammo, weapons and fuel supply to the rebel forces came in from India and Malaya.

(Info VH-BDP)

Below bottom: This PBY Catalina, reg nr. RI006 (RI stands for Republic of Indonesia), was flying for the Liberation Army of Indonesia (TNI) and had the bad luck of landing on Maguwo airport, near Yogyakarta (Central Java), in December 1948. Just before the Cat landed the airport was re-conquered in a surprise attack by Dutch Korps Speciale Troepen (KST) paratroopers on the TNI – a fact unnoticed by the pilots of the Catalina. The Dutch military must have been as surprised as the Catalina crew that flew the valuable airplane, intact, into the hands of their enemy.

(Photo courtesy of: https://nimh-beeldbank.defensie.nl/foto-collecties)

CIA OPERATED CATALINAS

Below: This photo depicts the ex-TRAPAS Catalina F-BDRN (see photo later in this chapter) that was sold to CAT in August 1951. It is one of the PBY Catalinas operated by CAT or Civil Air Transport Corp (in 1959 converted to Air America). Allegedly, CAT was the covert air support operations agency of the CIA and hence involved in stealthy backups to revolts, uprisings, guerilla arms supply and support, and other activities directed against the advancing communist influence in SE Asia in the 1940s–1950s, and into the early 1960s in Central America and the Bay of Pigs, Cuba.

CAT was created in 1946 by the legendary Claire Chennault, who flew supplies and medicaments into war-ravaged China. CAT soon turned into a support and supply machine for Chiang Kai-Shek, who fought a civil war against the Communists under Mao Zedong, right after WWII. Aircraft crews were selected primarily from the American Volunteer Group (AVG) veterans of Chennault's WWII combat group, aka The Flying Tigers.

In 1958, CAT supplied 20 aircraft (a PBY Catalina, 15 Douglas A-26 Invaders, and P-51 Mustangs) to a totally unknown insurgent movement in Indonesia, named Permesta – a rebel movement against President Sukarno's regime, fighting from Sulawesi (Celebes), in Northern Indonesia. This photo was most probably taken on Clark AF Base in the Philippines, before delivery.

The PBY-5A was flown by CIA-trained mercenaries. With no opposition in the airspace above Sulawesi, Kalimantan (Borneo), and the Maluku Islands, this Catalina had an active role in the revolt as an observation platform. It was a CIA job in which they had to try to topple Sukarno, who was allegedly coming too much under the influence of the Communist Party. The CIA's intentions may have been good, but it was too much of a haphazard insurrection.

For more info and photos about this CIA Catalina operation, read my Dakota Hunter blog: https://www.dc3dakotahunter.com/blog/pby-catalina-26-invaders-p-51-mustangs-cia-rebel-air-force-attacking-indonesia-1958.

Above: This was the first Catalina PBY-5A purchased in New York in 1946 by the Asiatic Petroleum Company Ltd on behalf of Shell's oil exploration activities in the Dutch East Indies. The Shell affiliate Asiatic Petroleum Company had as head of their Aviation Department a legendary war hero – Group Captain Douglas Bader, CBE, DSO, DFC. In November 1948, Bader made an inspection tour on board PK-AKC, from Djakarta to all Shell-affiliated BPM (Bataafse Petroleum Maatschappij) facilities in the Eastern Archipelago. The PK-AKC also flew to Tarakan and Balikpapan in Eastern Borneo, where Shell/BPM had its largest oil-refineries, that were just about to re-establish their production capacity after the destructions inflicted by the Japanese Army and by the Allied bombing raids in 1944–1945.

PK-AKC was built by Boeing of Canada in 1943, and converted to a 16-seat passenger transport. This was the first of four Shell-owned Catalinas bought in the USA for operations between Java and Borneo under the BPM flag. Five others were operated under the Shell/NNGPM flag in the New Guinea–Ambon–Morotai area for the oil-exploration.

Note the very clean and graceful lines of the aircraft, with the waist blisters removed and the smooth clipper bow mounted in front. Small windows were added in two passenger compartments. Each of them had eight seats, one just behind the cockpit (with a single window) and one behind the main gear (with three smaller windows). The area where the blisters were was the cargo stowing area, which could be entered via a hinged hatch, either on both sides of the fuselage or (like in this PBY) only at the port side.

(Photo courtesy of Prudent Staal)

Right: PBY-5A of Dutch MLD (Marine Luchtvaartdienst) P-82 during a patrol mission over the waters around Dutch New Guinea, in the early 1950s. Below is the torpedo boat destroyer HLNMS *Eversten* (F803). From the 1950s, both the Dutch Navy and the MLD were engaged in an increasingly aggressive 'confrontation policy' over the Indonesian claim on Dutch New Guinea. A good reason to keep'em flying!

The affair escalated with the infiltration of Indonesian Commandos in New Guinea, dropped by PT boats and aircraft. The operations were far from successful, as most commandos were hunted by the local Papua tribesmen in what they considered as an infiltration in their backyard. Most of the drops ended quickly, and if lucky and alive, the captured soldiers were handed over to the Dutch Army patrols. They must have felt relieved, realizing that old tribal cannibalism customs had allegedly been revived.

Finally, in 1962, a mini sea battle between this destroyer and three Indonesian PT boats took place. One of the PT boats was immediately sunk by canon fire (it had over 50 soldiers on board); the other two were chased and wrecked. Indonesia's first intended invasion with 150 soldiers failed in its delivery but succeeded on the political front. Under strong international pressure, the Dutch Government handed 'their' New Guinea over in 1962 and it would soon become a province of Indonesia.

(Photo courtesy of Prudent Staal)

Above: KLM's PK-CPA at Amsterdam Airport, starting its long route to Indonesia, November 1949. The San Diego built Catalina was the first of ten KLM Cats, converted in the USA and all flown over the Eastern route to Indonesia. Note the KLM Lockheed Constellation in the left corner, and further in the background, a Douglas DC-3. I was the fortunate son of a worldwide traveling oil-exploration engineer and flew in all three types to, from and in Indonesia in the 1950s.

Above: KLM's PK-CTB 'Bali' built by Canadian Vickers at St Hubert, Quebec for the RCAF.

As a young kid, I came from Trinidad in the West Indies and traveled with my family to the East Indies in 1950. In that year, on 1 January, (after a bloody four-year Independence war), the Dutch flag was replaced by the Indonesian Republican flag.

My Dad arrived with his family in war-ridden Eastern Borneo, which had previously seen the terrible devastation of the Pacific war between 1942 and 1945. I was only five years old, about to enter the best years of youth that a curious and adventurous kid could ever have. The 'Gates of Wonder' opened up for me, right there in Indonesia. I still remember my first view of a Catalina water landing. That plane put a spell on me. I was mesmerized and that feeling is still alive!

For the next seven years, I would frequently fly over the jungle and the archipelago in a DC-3 or in a PBY Catalina. It was the ultimate entertainment for me, way before color TV and the first PlayStation had arrived.

(Photo courtesy of Prudent Staal)

Razor sharp photo of Shell's PK-AKT, which flew for the other subsidiary, NNGPM (Nederlands New Guinea Petroleum Maatschappij). It started its operations in 1947. By the end of 1950 with its C of A expired, the plan was to take her out of service. But, with the unplanned loss of her three sister ships PK-AKS/AKC/AKR this one soldiered on until early 1954. In that year, both engines were taken off and the airframe was scrapped.
(Photo courtesy of Prudent Staal, PK-AKS/-AKC/-AKR)

Above: Catalina CF-GKI during its New Guinea survey visit in Kenting Aviation livery and the KLM DC-3 PH-KOM at the airport of Jefman Island, near Sorong on the West coast of Dutch New Guinea (now West Papua), 1953. That was the time that I lived in Indonesia and I can vividly remember identical sights of a Garuda DC-3 and the Shell-operated PBY-5A standing next to each other on Sepinggan Airport, Balikpapan, Borneo.
(Photo: Paul Howard collection)

Above: After Indonesia got its independence at the end of 1949 eight Catalinas were transferred from KLM IIB (Inter-Insulair-Bedrijf) to the fledgling Garuda Indonesian Airways that hired facilities and pilots from KLM since 1950. Seen here is PBY-5A PK-CPE ex-KLM Catalina 'Emu' with the Garuda bird logo under the cockpit and Indonesian Flag on the horn-balanced rudder. Its last flight was on 8 January 1955. On the left, parked on the Kemajoran Airport ramp in Djakarta, is a Caltex DC-3.

It is quite possible that I have flown in this particular PBY, as she has operated on the Eastern Borneo route and subsequently must have landed often on the Mahakam River near SangaSanga (close to Samarindah), where we lived in the jungle outpost between 1951 and 1953.

Above: Shell's PBY-5A JZ-POD at Biak Airport, Dutch New Guinea from where KLM operated its Lockheed Constellations. In December 1956 we made our final flight back to Holland in a Constellation like this (with wing-tip tanks). That was an eventful flight during which we had a harrowing experience. On the evening after takeoff from Bangkok one of the engines R-3350s exploded and set the engine on fire. With flames licking over the wing, for a moment the capricious reputation of the Constellation as the 'world's best three-engine aircraft' appeared to be shattered and many passengers must have anticipated worse to come. Fortunately, the fire extinguisher worked wonders. There were no more flames, but a much-desired precautionary landing was impossible due to the weight of the full tanks. For two or three more anxious hours, we flew on three engines in the pitch dark over the ocean in order to dump the fuel load.

We eventually landed in Ceylon (Sri Lanka), where we sat it out for three days until a new engine arrived from Holland. Finally, we could continue our flight back to a new winter wonderland in Holland with ice and snow unlike I had ever seen before in my life. Unsurprisingly, there were a number of passengers who refused to take that flight with the repaired Connie. A bad omen, they said, but we had survived it all.

Above: The Jefman Shell Aircraft Operations in Eastern Indonesia and New Guinea 1947–960. Seen here is a pair of Catalinas, and in the center a Grumman Mallard, a smaller mphibian that could handle 10 pax. The Mallard G-73 was built by Grumman from 1946 to 951. Only 59 were made, mainly used by smaller commuter airlines and for corporate use. n the 1990s I flew the Turboprop Mallard quite a few times with Chalk's Ocean Airways rom Miami's Cruiser port to Bimini Island, Bahamas, just 50 miles east of Miami. That was a wonderful flight with a water landing and takeoff in the Miami harbor and in the Bimini lagoon. However, one day in December 2005, Chalk's Mallard crashed in the sea and all 20 occupants were killed. The right wing folded during the climb-out just after takeoff from Miami port, right next to the Cruise ship terminal. The cause of the accident was found to be a poorly maintained aircraft with undetected cracks from corrosion in the wing spar. Overnight, Chalk's operations folded, never to be re-established again.

Above: Shell operated the Catalina all over the Indonesian Islands of Borneo, Sumatra, Celebes and the Eastern side of the Archipelago into New Guinea. This shot was taken on Jefman near Sorong, New Guinea. The Dodge Power Wagon that is shown here as a towing vehicle, was widely used in postwar Indonesia. In Borneo, the American and Australian Forces left most of their trucks behind in August 1945. The transports came available for grabs for the Dutch Army and for Shell, who re-established its oil exploration activities in 1946 and widely used the 'free' Willys Jeeps, the Dodge Command Cars and GMC trucks.

Above: PBY-5A MLD 16-215 at Fakfak, Dutch New Guinea, November 1954. While for most Allied forces, their PBY Catalina fleets became redundant after Japan's capitulation in August 1945, the Dutch Marine Luchtvaart Dienst (MLD) was about to face another 17 years of hostilities in Indonesia and New Guinea. Good reason to keep 'em flying and surely not dispose the war-weary aircraft.

As the good old days of colonialism crumbled all over SE Asia, the Dutch East Indies got their share, and the Army and MLD were confronted with a strong Independence movement, which had germinated during the Japanese occupation (1942–1945). Due to illegal weapons supply and access to ex-Japanese arms, aircraft and ammo stocks, the dispute almost immediately escalated into a military conflict between the Dutch Military and the Indonesian freedom fighters. They were led by Sukarno, who had declared Indonesia a Free Republic in August 1945. MLD's Catalina were much needed to control the archipelago of thousands of islands.

These hostilities came to an end by late 1949 as Indonesia was finally being recognized as an Independent State with Sukarno as the first President. But that was not the end of the problems as Dutch New Guinea was not part of the 'deal' and remained under Dutch Colonial rule. From scratch, Sukarno started to use political pressure to get Dutch New Guinea under his control. It was only a matter of time before Indonesia would try to solve the conflict over their claim through military means. So, it was all hands on deck for the MLD, and their Catalinas were ordered to fly their patrols once again, from Biak Island and the jungle rivers. It would be a further five years after the war ended before peace finally reached the islands.

(Photo courtesy of Prudent Staal)

Above: Dutch MLD PBY-5A Catalina on an idyllic tropical beach in New Guinea near a Papua tribal settlement.

In 1952 the Australian Government announced that it would present six Catalinas to the Dutch Government for use by their Navy (MLD) in Dutch New Guinea. All were PBY-5 amphibians, kept since 1945 in open storage at RAAF Rathmines. Their weathered condition required complete overhauls, which the RAAF no longer had the capacity to carry out, so a contract was awarded to Bristol Aviation Services at Bankstown Airport, Sydney.

The overhauls took place over the next 18 months. A Sydney newspaper report on 27 June 1954 stated that, so far, only one Catalina had been completed and flown to Biak and that the overhaul cost which was estimated to be £192,000 would be closer to £300,000 – a fortune in those days.

Each aircraft was collected by Dutch crews and ferried to Biak, Dutch New Guinea. There they were only operated for a couple of years, until 1956, when they were replaced by the MLD for the Martin Mariner PBM-5A, of which 15 were bought as 'pre-owned' by the US Navy. That turned out to be a real disaster, with so many fatal accidents that in 1960 these flying hearses were taken out of service. They were replaced by 11 Lockheed Neptune P2V-7s, and so ended the flying boat era for the Dutch MLD.

(Photo courtesy of Prudent Staal; info courtesy of: www.goodall.com.au/australian-aviation/civil-catalina-1/Civilcatalinas.html)

Above: The Catalina has appeared on a great number of postage stamps over the years. This stamp from 2015 shows Catalina CC-CNP, owned by the famous Chilean aviator Roberto Parragué.

Above: Greetings from the French Antilles. Air France operated a small number of Catalinas in the West Indies on their 'Reseau des Antilles'. From 1947, three Catalinas were being operated on behalf of the inter-island passenger/cargo transport, as those islands had no land-based airfields yet. They served places such as Fort de France in Martinique, Port of Spain in Trinidad, Pointe-a-Pitre in Guadeloupe and San Juan in Puerto Rico.

Bought from the RCAF stocks, the Canso aircraft were converted by Convair to a capacity of 20–22 seats for passengers. In Air France livery, the Cats were registered F-BBCB, F-BBCC, and F-BBCD.

(Courtesy of http://cansonet.free.fr/Utilisateurs/Compagnies/body_compagnies.html)

Above: Rare photo of the Air France Catalina F-BBCB with running engines and wheels down, climbing up a slipway to lift herself out of the water. Out there in the distance is a very rare Latecoere flying boat model 631. It was F-BANT that first flew in 1945, powered by six Wright Cyclone engines of 1,600 hp (1,200 kW) each. Four of these giant flying boats were purchased by Air France, and entered service on the French Antilles route in July 1947. The aircraft were withdrawn from service in August 1948 following the fourth accident of only eleven built. The final Air France Latecoere 631 was lost on 10 September 1955. This was the last of the flying boat giants – the remaining survivors being scrapped. Ironically, that most reliable and indestructible 'warbird' Canso/Catalina would live on for many more years.

Above: On 14 March 1948, this Catalina F-BCJG was parked at Magenta Airport, Noumea, New Caledonia. It was destroyed beyond repair during a cyclone that came in from the Pacific. Its sister-ship, F-BCJH, was also damaged but would be repaired in Australia.

Right: PBY-5A Catalina F-BCJH of French Noumean Airlines TRAPAS. The nose turret is covered but has not yet been replaced by a more streamlined clipper bow. F-BCJH arrived at the French Pacific Island of Noumea on 14 July 1947 and was named Nouvelle-Caledonie. It visited Auckland, New Zealand on 8 January 1948 and was damaged by a cyclone while parked at Magenta Airport, Noumea on 14 March 1948. After temporary repairs, it was flown to Brisbane for permanent repairs by Barrier Reef Airways situated on the Brisbane River. On 26 January 1949, F-BCJH, along with another TRAPAS Catalina F-BDRN evacuated New Caledonia to Brisbane to avoid a cyclone. It was sold by TRAPAS in 1952 and ended up with Civil Air Transport (CAT) at Taipei as B1403 and got entangled in clandestine CIA operations in SE Asia. For more info see the CIA-operated Cats mentioned earlier in this chapter.

Above: Photo taken in Noumea, New Caledonia after the war in the late 1940s. The leftovers from the war are clearly visible in the background. During the war, New Caledonia was an essential support base and a key location for the American and Allied troops, due to its strategic location. On 12 March 1942, an American Expeditionary Force landed in Noumea in order to make sure that the American, Australian and New Zealand Allies could use New Caledonia during the wartime as a highly effective fixed 'aircraft carrier' against the Japanese Naval forces.

Above: TRAPAS F-BCJG, a PBY-5A built by Consolidated at San Diego for the US Navy. The Cat went to the island of Noumea, starting its operations in July 1947. The Bus looks like a Bedford 1945 OB Coach.

Fortifications and Nissen huts were built all over the Pacific to house the Military. But, New Caledonia never came under attack as the tide turned for the Allies after the Battle of the Coral Sea. The Catalina F-BDRN in the foreground c/n 851 was bought in Honolulu, Hawaii, from the US Navy and converted there into a passenger cabin layout with the removal of the blisters and nose turret before being flown to Noumea in July 1948. It was baptised 'Tahiti'.

Above: 'Le Pelican Noir' Catalina, France, July 1969, operating as a water bomber at the Cote 'd'Azur, Southern France. This one was stationed near Marseille. With very frequent and fierce bush fires occurring in summertime in Southern France's densely populated Cote d'Azur, water bomber operations started with the mass tourism that had been growing rapidly since the early 1960s.

In 1968, Canadair introduced its CL-215, built with the stronger P & W R-2800 radial engines of 2,100 hp. They were the ideal successor for the aging Catalinas and became operational in France in 1970. The last of the Catalinas dubbed 'Pelican' were flying along the French coast in 1976. The Pelicans that served in France were:

- 'Pélican Blanc', F-ZBAQ, entered service in 1963, was lost near Marseille on 8 August 1967
- 'Pélican Rouge', F-ZBAR, entered in 1963, crashed in July 1964, replaced twice by another Cat in 1966–1969
- 'Pélican Gris', was hired in 1966–1967 as F-ZBAX, and in 1968 as F-ZBBE
- 'Pélican Bleu', was hired in 1966–1967 as F-ZBAY, and in 1968–1969 as F-ZBBD
- 'Pélican Noir' (see photo), hired in 1966–1967 as F-ZBAZ, purchased in 1967, operational until 1976
- 'Pélican Vert', F-ZBAV, entered in 1964, crashed in August 1964, repaired and taken out of operation in 1974
- 'Pélican Jaune', F-ZBAW, entered in 1964, put out of service in 1975

Above: This Catalina is a PBY-6A built by Consolidated in New Orleans. The aircraft came from the surplus stocks of the US Navy and was used after the war for passenger transport and later as a water bomber between 1950 and 1960. In 1974, the legendary Jacques Cousteau bought the Catalina for US$ 80,000. With the intention of using her for the 'Cousteau Team' in Oceanographic expeditions, the aircraft was refurbished as a flying laboratory. With living/sleeping space for 10, including kitchen, the aircraft could operate autonomously as a flying platform for aerial photography and was fully equipped for diving operations. This Catalina, named Calypso, was a one of a kind in every aspect.

Right: Very sadly, during a test flight on 28 June 1979, the Calypso aircraft hit a sandbank during takeoff at high speed in the River Tagus, Lisbon, Portugal. The Catalina fatally crashed and broke up in pieces with the loss of Philippe Cousteau, Jacques' son. In the photo the sad remains of the PBY-6A N101CS, aka Calypso.
Photo Earle Johnson via Ron Maki)

GREENLAND

Above right: Grønlandsfly A/S – a Canso and a DHC-3 Otter moored on a lagoon at Kangerlussuaq, at Greenland's west coast, north of Nuuk. The aircraft had been hired from the Canadian operator Eastern Provincial Airways (EPA) since 1958.

The purchase of a PBY Canso amphibian aircraft in 1953 allowed EPA to take larger charter jobs, and with a converted Canso, they flew water-bombing flights on behalf of the government. In addition to regional charter work, international projects were operated as well, including a contract beginning in 1958 to do extensive work for Grønlandsfly A/S with PBY Cansos and de Havilland Canada DHC-3 Otters until July 1965.

The DHC-3 Otter was developed by de Havilland Canada from its predecessor DHC-2 Beaver, another highly successful bush plane family with STOL capacities that had pioneered the opening up of the Northern Canadian outback since its first launch in 1948. Of both types, some 2,300 aircraft were built by 1967. The final family extension is the Twin Otter DHC-6 twin turbo prop, still in production.

Right: This Catalina was operated in Greenland by Grønlandsfly A/S and is seen making a steep entry into the water from the Nuuk slipway in the 1960s. The amphibious undercarriage made such an operation quite easy.

Below: Denmark's Greenland post-war anti-submarine warfare patrol PBY-6A. The Royal Danish Air Force (RDAF) operated Canso As, PBY-5As and PBY-6As on rescue flights and missions to support Denmark's assets in Greenland. In this photo a PBY-6A L-863 taxies into a lake in the wilds of Greenland. Its large radar housing, unique to the RDAF, can be seen above the cockpit roof.

CHILE

Below: Although its serial is not quite legible, this is a Catalina Amphibian of the Fuerza Aéreade Chile (FACh) undergoing maintenance whilst still on the water. The photo shows a rather busy scene with a lot of mechanics working on the engines. The mechanic beside the starboard engine is using the foldable engine work platform. The starboard prop has been removed by a hoist.

VENEZUELA

Below: YV-485C's beautiful livery of a Catalina owned by the Orinoco Mining Company. This aircraft had an important role in the post-war excavation of the lower Orinoco banks for iron and aluminum ore in Venezuela. Photo taken on Los Roques Holiday islands off Venezuelan shore near Aruba. I found this Catalina back in the year 2000 while on a Dakota Hunter expedition in Puerto Ordaz, a town in Venezuela on the lower Orinoco River. She was parked on the local airport, abandoned in a derelict state with all canvas rotten out and not even a shadow of the beauty that you see here off the Venezuelan shore.

But, that is not the end of the story. In 2013, she was rescued by the Rathmines Catalina Memorial Park Association and is being rebuilt to static display condition in the Lake Macquarie area of New South Wales, Australia.

(Photo courtesy of Michael Prophet; info via David Legg)

ICELAND

Below: Icelandic airline Flugfelag Islands operated a number of DC-3s and three Catalinas – one pure flying boat and two amphibians – on passenger flights to remote communities only accessible by water. The flying boat commenced services before the end of WWII and the two amphibs' were acquitted at the end of the war. They were unusual in being ex-Royal Air Force. TF-ISK, illustrated here, was RAF Catalina III FP532, which was eventually taken out of service after an accident in 1958 and scrapped at Reykjavik around 1960. Note the DC-4-style vertical tail bar on the right right and the De Havilland Dragon Rapide on the left. (Courtesy of Olafur Sigurdsson)

SPAIN

Right: Chilean water bomber No 32 operating in Spain empties its belly tanks by opening two hatches, dropping 4,000 litres of water from its internal tanks. This was a very effective way of extinguishing a bush fire: by spraying it out from an airborne engine platform. The Catalina's flight speed of some 90–100 knots ensured the fine dispersion of the water over a large area, in terrain where, often, there were no roads or tracks to easily access the fires with vehicles. Freshwater loads were picked up from lakes, bays or broad rivers, allowing a rapid turnaround time.

Below: Three Chilean Catalinas on hire to the Spanish fire fighting organization ICONA overfly a fleet of Grumman Ag Cats during the late-1980s. The PBY-6A in the back row with its taller vertical tail and rudder is ship nr. 35. This Cat CC-CNP was owned and used for many years by ASPAR as a water bomber in Chile before being chartered to fire fighting organizations in Spain and Portugal. She is now in Australia under long-term restoration with The Catalina Flying Memorial Ltd at Bankstown, New South Wales.
(Info David Legg)

THE LUXURY AIR YACHT CATALINAS

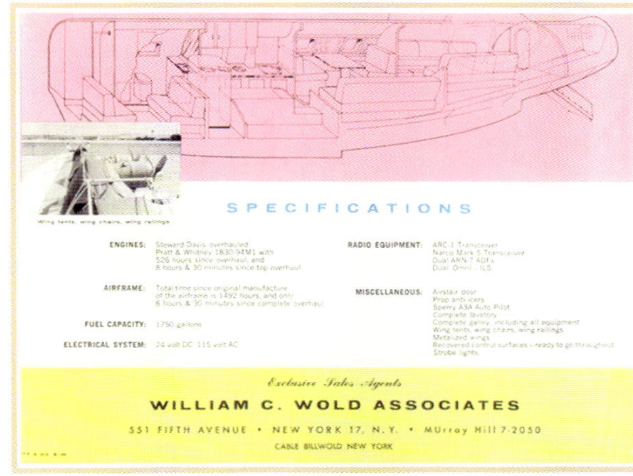

Above left: Not long after the war, with an abundant supply of disposable PBY Catalinas available for grabs, an entrepreneur by the name of Glenn Odekirk saw a new future for the versatile Catalinas as luxury flying yachts. They were to be the ultimate in glamorous travel and were called the 'Landseaire'. As amphibians, they could operate from land, on sea and in the air.

Glenn Odekirk had an established reputation on the Californian Aviation scene: for many years during the war he was the right-hand man of the legendary Howard Hughes, and he was involved with him in the development of the 'Spruce Goose'. By the end of the 1940s, he decided to build 'an aerial luxury yacht in which you can land and live almost anywhere in the world with all the comforts of home.'

The outcome was a lavish Catalina with a luxury interior and a small boat slung under the wing that could be lowered from the cockpit by activating electrically powered winches. After water landings, the 14-ft dinghy could be used as a fishing boat or to get on land in case there was no launch, ramp, or pier available.

Above middle: A sales brochure for a Landseaire PBY Catalina as converted by Glenn Odekirk. A small number were sold, but the idea faded away after its first launch in 1950. In spite of a very sexy report published in *Life* magazine, the extravagance of this flying boat had gone beyond even the wildest dreams of the richest.

Above right: In 1950 William Wold Associates offered this pre-owned Landseaire with mid-life engines (526 hours since overhaul of engines by Steward Davis) and only 1,492 hours of airframe since original manufacture!

Note the airstair door in the rear end, autopilot, toilet and galley and remarkably: the 'metalized wings'. Metalized? Remember that a large part of the rear end of the main wings of the Catalina was originally fabric clad. This made the leisurely walk over the wings (part of the promise in the *Life* magazine and the promotional brochure with folding chairs on the wings!) a bit awkward for the guests. With one bottle of bubbly in the bucket and one for the toast, a single careless step of a guest into the wide, but difficult to recognize, 'NO STEP' area could result in a foot (or two) tearing through the fabric. The weaker canvas cover of the rear end of the main wing was replaced by an aluminum skin plating that was more 'step-proof' and also more resistant to rotting and debris.

For more photos and info see:
www.vintagewings.ca/VintageNews/Stories/tabid/116/articleType/ArticleView/articleId/424/Sweet-Dreams-and-Nightmares.aspx

Left: Adding glamour to the Cat. This photo was part of the promotion that Glenn Odekirk (in front, left) made for his Landseaire PBY conversion. The luxury and the models gave the impression of entering a flying Playboy 'Mansionnette'. No doubt, it would become an epic photographic feature in *Life* magazine.

THE FIRST KENDALL CATALINA STORY

In the mid-1950s, Los Angeles industrialist Thomas W. Kendall and his wife decided to create a similar flying yacht to Odekirk's Landseaire, and so began the Kendall Catalina story. Purchasing surplus Second World War PBY Catalinas, the Kendalls hired famed Los Angeles interior designer George Erb to convert three of the warplanes into a trio of flying and floating luxury suites. Kendall, a retired businessman who made his fortune in air conditioning, planned to create a business converting and leasing the planes, with plans to build 14 similar conversions. In total, he purchased over a dozen surplus PBYs in 1956, one of which still exists today at the San Diego Air & Space Museum.

By sheer coincidence I came in contact with Mrs Ingeborg Kendall Maranto, who was married to Bob Kendall, the son of Thomas W. Kendall. According to Ingeborg, Thomas W. Kendall never worked with Glenn Odekirk.

She wrote to me:

> Thomas Kendall did everything independently here in California as Catalina Limited or Mobil-Marine. Kendall acquired over a dozen surplus Catalinas from the US Navy and gathered them at Orange County Airport in California. No less than thirteen of them were subsequently registered to him and his company. Kendall was a mechanical engineer and obtained all the conversion permits from the FAA.
>
> N5590V is now in the San Diego Air & Space Museum whilst another was left as a wreck in the Gulf of Aqaba (see photos) after doing a lot of trips domestically in the US, moviemaking in Europe (The Guns of Navarone) and Egypt. My late husband Bob helped his father Thomas to ferry them from Arizona.
>
> Some of the damaged planes were never fixed, instead they were shipped to Honolulu and used in the movie 'Tora, Tora, Tora' and blown up! The rest were sold to others for various purposes, sometimes as parts. The gold ship N5590V, (now a static showpiece in SD Museum) had very unusual fabric on the interior walls (see photo)! My sister-in-law and her husband donated the remaining parts, a truckload full which had been in a warehouse all these years, to a PBY museum in Oregon a few years ago.

Above: Inside the Kendall Cat that was offered to the affluent client, the customer had a choice of interior trim. In its original military outfit, the Catalina was very clamorous, not really glamorous! Kendall's conversion changed that radically with more glamour and less clamour. Noise was kept to a remarkably low level by a 4-inch-thick lining of fiberglass, and carpeting as in a hotel cocktail saloon.

Interior designer George Erb gave each of the three Catalinas their own unique color scheme and personality, creating a Gold, a Turquoise, and a Red and Black aircraft. Each of the amphibians had a capacity to sleep eight passengers with covered foam rubber sofas that converted into beds, a full galley, lavatory and even a dining room with a table for eight.

Kendall's Gold Ship is seen here. An upgraded luxury Cat such as this cost a lot of money. $265,000 was the basic price, and in those days, the late 1950s, that was a fortune. This, coupled with heavy operating costs, virtually put the aircraft beyond the reach even of most millionaires. Expected sales volumes were most probably never met, making this Catalina even more desirable as the ultimate dream luxury flight yacht.

Right: Thomas Kendall's Landseaire N5593V seen here in Egypt.

In the footsteps of Jules Verne – a round-the-world adventure

In 1959, the N5593V had flown to London after a filmmaking assignment in Madeira for the 1959 movie *SOS Pacific*. Kendall was in the process of flying this Catalina on an around-the-world voyage with his family. The entire Kendall family joined the Catalina in Croydon, South London – Kendall, his wife and four children (his son Bob was the co-pilot), his secretary and her son. The planned circumnavigation of the globe trip was like realizing Jules Verne's epic adventure novel *Around the World in 80 Days*. It started in London and was bound for Egypt and the Pyramids.

After visiting Cairo, the Suez Canal and Luxor (see photo), they landed at the Strait of Tirana (between Egypt's Sinai and Saudi Arabia) and anchored the aircraft a short distance from the shore to spend the night there. This would be the last landing that the PBY ever made, and the Kendall family had a harrowing near-fatal end to their plans.

Right: Kendall's Catalina Interiors came in a variety of trims. This photo of the interior displays how the waist blister compartment was the real cocktail lounge of the Air Yacht. Sitting on couches and under the cupolas, those guests sitting here enjoying a magnificent view during the flights.

After water landings, the blister windows could be opened up and the platform behind the couches could be used as a step-up to disembark in the dinghy that was slung under the wing. Also a dive from there into the 'Blue Lagoon' waters was an option.

Sleeping accommodation was provided for eight persons in three double beds and two singles. A chemical toilet, a kitchenette and even a small shower cabin were all part of this airborne Super-deLuxe 'Motorhome'. It was like a Magic Carpet ride from the One thousand and One Nights fairy tale, with a speed pack and floats.

Below: Thomas Kendall's N5593V parked at Croydon Airport, UK, in 1959. Thomas Kendall had acquired this Catalina as a stock Consolidated PBY-5A from US Navy surplus at Litchfield Park, Arizona and fitted it out with luxury interior and amenities.
(Photo: Jeremy Hughes Collection)

Above: Soon after their departure from London, the Kendall family arrived in Egypt, where famed photographer David Lees took this photo as the Catalina flew over the Nile and the Giza Pyramids. In a low and slow fantasy flight, the passengers could see the world glide by below them. Who is not dreaming of making such trip one day?

Above: What a day for a daydream! A water landing near a totally abandoned beach. The Kendall family can be seen having a relaxed day at that sunshine beach. The kids found giant shells in the sand and life seemed a breeze. But, suddenly, very dark clouds appeared out of the blue over this idyllic scene.

Above: In this photo, we can see Mr Thomas Kendall sitting on the floor on the right, while recovering from a bullet wound.
(Info via Kenneth Stanford)

On the 22 March 1960 they landed at the Strait of Tirana and anchored the aircraft a short distance from the shore to spend the night there. Thomas Kendall wrote about this memorable day:

> After a late lunch I went up on the wing to check the left engine. Bob was in the water checking some equipment in the nose. Stephen and Paul were wading in the shallows about 60 feet away, playing with our bright blue rubber life raft. Everyone else was in the plane. When I finally buttoned up the engine, I stood up and glanced around. Except for the boys, I saw nothing but rocks, low hills and empty sand. I looked at my watch. It was 4:32 exactly. Then I heard what sounded like distant firecrackers. My first thought was that some local Bedouins were celebrating the Muslim holiday of Ramadan, which was then in progress. In Luxor, Egypt, our last stop, they had celebrated by firing off a cannon. Suddenly, I noticed little splashes in the water beside the rubber raft. Somebody was shooting at the children . . .
>
> As I ran I shouted for everyone to lie down on the floor because we were under fire. Mrs Shearer ran with me to the tail and we watched our small son and his dog paddling very slowly toward the hatch, just their heads above water, towing the raft for cover between themselves and the bullets . . .
>
> By now machine-gun and automatic-weapon fire was hitting the plane, I don't know how long we stood there screaming at the children to hurry – it felt like eons . . . The ambush lasted 30 to 40 minutes, and only the cowardice of our attackers saved our lives. If they had come closer instead of hiding behind a knoll three quarters of a mile away, I am certain we would all have been killed.

(From the original report written by Thomas Kendall)

During the attack, Mr Kendall and his secretary were wounded while trying to start the Catalina. They moved it about 800 metres, but unfortunately it ran aground on a coral reef. The firing lasted 30 to 40 minutes and no fewer than 300 shots hit the aircraft. The fuel tanks were perforated and 4,000 litres of fuel poured from the holes, but miraculously the aircraft did not catch fire. The sea was only about 1.5 metres deep and all aboard managed to leave the aircraft and reach the shore.

On the beach they were captured by a group of Bedouins attached to the Saudi Arabian army, who had taken them to be Israeli commandos. They were eventually taken to Jeddah and interrogated. The US Ambassador protested to the Saudi Arabian government, but they refused to accept any liability for the attack and consequent loss of the aircraft. The group of Americans was brought to Prince Khalid bin Saud, son of King Saud, who interrogated them about the incident. Soon after, they were treated as guests of honor and repatriated with the assistance of the US Ambassador.

Above: The Kendall Catalina N5593V lies there on the beach slowly corroding to the contours of a beached whale. But, in all its beauty of decay, it is still recognizable as a Catalina: that silhouette with the parasol wing, the waist blisters and the shark-shaped fuselage. Sadly, this Catalina has further deteriorated over the years and its wing has collapsed now.

Above: In 1995, 35 years after the incident in which the Kendall Catalina was so badly damaged with 300 bullet holes, the aircraft was still right there on that 'horror-beach'. An American engineer stationed in Saudi Arabia at that time, Mr Kenneth Stanford, visited the derelict Catalina in February 1995 and took some awesome photos of the wreck. He gave me permission to publish those photos. For more pictures, see his website: http://kendo1938.bravesites.com/catalina-pby-n5593v.

Thomas Kendall's daughter, Dr Susan Kendall Maass, wrote to me with this additional information. It is a remarkably detailed story that expresses so well the way the family handled the act of terror that suddenly overwhelmed them. But it seems there was no real panic and everybody on board did the right things to face this threatening situation. Quite probably, this almost calm attitude must have contributed much to their survival:

> Bob and I were both sent together to wade/swim out to the plane to get the passports and a first aid kit. He entered through the blister and I entered from the front, climbing up the side to the hatch. I was able to get Ramona's purse containing both her and Stephen's passports; I don't remember if I got the first aid kit as I noticed that Bob was acting erratically (from the gas fumes) and mother was calling him to come back. I was able to push him toward the blister but unable to get him out. I exited and Bob came behind me, both returning to the beach. We were placed in two pickup trucks and covered with blankets so that we couldn't see where we were going. I was with Bob and Ramona (and probably Stephen) while mother and dad (and probably Kathy and Paul) were in the other truck. Not sure where David Lees (the photographer) was located. The attackers tried groping me but I pulled away much to their amusement. As you say, not a fun experience.

(Dr Susan Kendall Maass)

Above: This Pratt & Whitney R-1830 14-cylinder radial engine ran for the last time in 1960 and on 22 March of that year the attack took place. With over 300 bullet holes and leaking fuel tanks, the story was over for this machine. The family was very lucky to escape alive from this nightmare.

The Beauty of Decay. Over the years Thomas Kendall's Catalina has turned into a sculpture, be it that it has no definite form. The salty environment continues to deteriorate the airframe further down to the sandy beach, where it has sat since 1960.

Dr Ingeborg Kendall Maranto, married to Bob Kendall until he died in 1987, also wrote to me with her account of events:

Hi Hans,
The entire story was written up in *Life* magazine as you know and most of it is accurate. Three 'children' of the Kendall Family are still alive, but my husband, Bob, died in 1987 and told me his version as did his sister, Susan, who lives near me. The other two siblings live in northern California and Idaho. The bullet in the back of Tom Kendall near his spinal cord remained with him to his death. It was a miracle the bullet did not penetrate the bone.

turned and taxied the plane away further from shore and unfortunately go stuck on a sandbar. Father Tom was in the belly, getting the children up the ladder and closing the hatch (which was difficult since the plane was moving) and then trying to get the table up as a shield to protect the family from the bullets. It was a horrible experience! Eventually Bob did get permission to swim out to the plane to get passports and his Rolleimarin, passing out in the belly from the fumes; then his sister came up behind him and pulled him ou to safety. At the time, he was an avid under-water photographer, so was glac to get the camera and housing, but all the film was waterlogged. The Bedouins had no camera and neither did the prince who came the next day

THE SECOND KENDALL CATALINA STORY

The Line Islands Experiment

In 1967–8 the National Center for Atmospheric Research in Boulder, Colorado, collaborated with numerous universities (Colorado State University, Saint Louis University, Texas A&M, University of Hawaii, University of Wisconsin and Woods Hole Oceanographic Institution) on a cooperative field program and gained funding and operational support from various sources (NASA, Department of Defense and National Science Foundation) for a weather experiment over the Line Islands. This north-south island chain approximately 800 miles south of Hawaii was a perfect location to do a meteorological study of the mid-Pacific equatorial trough zone. Here they were able to take advantage of the new ATS-1 geo-synchronous satellite that NASA launched on 6 December 1966 and the accompanying urgency due to the fact that the useful lifetime of the cameras was not known.

Since only one of the islands initially had an operational airport, it was necessary to quickly find an amphibious plane. Tom Kendall's son, Bob Kendall, then a graduate student in oceanography at the University of Houston (UH), found out about the experiment via the UH Chairman, Department of Geosciences, and local coordinator of the activities before the experiment began, Dr Colin Ramage, and faculty member Dr Martin Vitousek. The Kendall PBY-5A was the perfect plane for the tasks of this vital mission, bringing the scientists to the islands for a reconnaissance flight in December 1966 and then handling the subsequent supply missions from February to April 1967. In late 1966, The Catalina was ferried from Cable Airport in southern California to Oakland and then flown about 18 hours to Honolulu via the two Kendalls, father Tom and son Bob.

History

This particular PBY-5 Catalina – N5590V – manufactured by Consolidated Aircraft Corporation, began its service life 23 years earlier at Lindbergh Field, San Diego, as BuNo 48406 on 31 December 1943 for the US Navy. Its first destination was the Western Pacific, specifically the Marshall and Gilbert Islands, and was then transferred to the US Coast Guard. It remained in USCG service until the mid-1950s, when it was placed in storage at the Naval Air Facility Litchfield Park, Arizona.

Soon after the Catalina planes were offered for surplus sale and given civil registration, Thomas W. Kendall purchased N5590V as part of a group sale of multiple aircraft and it received aerial yacht modification. Father Tom and son Bob flew the planes to Orange County Airport where Catalina Ltd's operation was based. Initially, Tom chose to use the 90V for family outings and to help promote the sale and usage of the other Catalinas being converted for specific uses, such as for commercial use (Alaskan Airlines) and missionary work (Brazil).

Catalinas as movie stars

While in England the Catalina had already attracted the attention of filmmakers, and Tom negotiated contracts for the use of N5593V in two movies. The first was the British drama *SOS Pacific* starring Pier Angeli and Richard Attenborough. Next, was the major WWII movie *Guns of Navarone*, filmed in Greece, which allowed father and son to work together, both piloting and providing aerial film footage. This British movie was directed by J. Lee Thompson, starred Gregory Peck, David Niven and Anthony Quinn, and eventually won two Golden Globe awards (Best Drama and Best Original Score) and an Academy Award for Best Effects, Special Effects, in 1961.

In 1961, with the N5593V stranded and useless in the Gulf of Aqaba, Tom selected the California-based N5590V for the next movie assignment. Father and son again cooperated for the film work in Lahaina, Maui, Hawaii. The movie was Columbia Pictures' *The Devil at Four O'Clock* and starred Spencer Tracy and Frank Sinatra. The plane was given a name in the movie – 'Tiare Tahiti' – and that name remained on the hull for the next 25 years until the plane was donated to the San Diego Air & Space Museum in January 1986, revealed fully restored and painted in its original US Navy markings in the Roll-Out Ceremony held on 5 November 1986. The son, Bob, spoke on behalf of the family, presenting the long history of the plane.

The donation

While the initial donation to the San Diego Museum was signed in January 1986, it took 10 months to get the Catalina ready for public view. The initial restoration phase to achieve a ferry permit was carried out at Van Nuys Airport. The ferry flight to North Island, San Diego, in May 1986 was the plane's first flight in 12 years and was piloted by Bob Kendall, appropriately since he had logged in the most Kendall hours since the 1950s! In celebration of the 75th Anniversary of Naval Aviation, extensive restoration to the frame and wings was carried out by NARF volunteers and student trainees, with the Aerospace Museum providing the necessary materials. This major joint restoration project involved the Naval Air Rework Facility, NAS North Island, the General Dynamics Convair Factory at Lindbergh Field, numerous volunteers, and extensive funding from the N. Paul Whittier Confidence Foundation and the Reuben H. Fleet Foundation Fund.

On 21 November 1986, the Catalina made a barge trip across San Diego Bay to the General Dynamics Convair Factory for its final preparation and preservation. To move the plane into the museum the wings were eventually removed from the center section and the Cat's three pieces were carefully transported before dawn on 8 August 1988 by three long flatbed trucks through San Diego's downtown streets up to Balboa Park's parking lot. There it was reassembled, and a heavy-duty crane lifted the plane into the Museum rotunda onto a metal support pedestal. After 43 years of service, N5590V, positioned in permanent flight orientation, was dedicated in the Museum on 11 August 1988 as a testimony to its record as the most successful flying boat ever designed and to being built in San Diego for 10 years between 1936 and 1945.

The Kendall family had several Catalinas. One that survived all adventures is the Catalina N5590V, which is depicted in this photo. It can be seen here, in a battered state, on the hard standing of San Diego AFB, after she had been flown in as a donation to the San Diego Air & Space Museum in November 1986. The registration number N5590V is barely visible on the tail.
(Photo from the Kendall Collection)

An account by Dr Ingeborg Kendall Maranto

Dr Ingeborg Kendall Maranto was the navigator and her husband Bob was the pilot during the Line Islands Experiment in the central Pacific Ocean in 1967. She kindly supplied all photos on pages 125–134 from the Kendall Collection and sent me the following report of their adventures with Catalina N5590V during this expedition:

This luxury Catalina, dubbed the 'Gold Ship', was used in *The Devil at 4 O'Clock* with Frank Sinatra, in Lahaina, Hawaii. Then, in 1967 my husband Bob Kendall and I used that PBY as a support vessel to the National Center for Atmospheric Research's meteorological project in the Central Pacific and took passengers down to Palmyra and Fanning Atoll and Christmas Island for 3 months. I loved N5590V for all the adventures it permitted! It now sits in the San Diego Aerospace Museum if you ever get here to California.

To find Palmyra Island after the 8-hour flight, Bob, as pilot and dead-reckoning navigator, had to use 'squares' twice to the west; the tradewind force was a bit stronger than FAA flight operations in Honolulu had predicted, plus a lot of low-lying clouds made visibility a challenge! The sea landing was easy since the water was calm along the manmade channel.

Since the average rainfall is heavy on this island (up to 200 inches at end of March), it was not surprising that we soon saw full cloud cover and a bit of a 'liquid sunshine' shower after we arrived. After the sun came out, we all hiked on the WWII man-made causeway to the southern side of the island and found a WWII bunker, radio tower and lots of Japanese glass balls from fishing nets.

While visited by various ships (British and American) Palmyra Island was claimed as part of the Hawaiian kingdom in 1862 and privately owned over the years by various owners and in 1966–67 by Leslie and Ellen Fullard-Leo of Honolulu. The US Navy made a preliminary survey in 1938 and finally constructed an excellent seaplane base and clear channel for landing in January 1942. Similar to the Christmas Islands, Palmyra was occupied during the British and American nuclear weapons tests. A simple runway was built using the local hard coral material but was covered with bird nests when we arrived, making it impossible to land on it, and instead required a sea landing and taxing up to the seaplane ramp.

After our reconnaissance flight, a barge was brought down carrying road-building equipment and smoothed out the runway. Our Catalina tried to use the runway fairly soon after it was 'ready' only to end up getting a flat tire. Since we had no equipment to tow the plane to the seaplane ramp, we had to wait until the next AF National Guard C-130 brought us a new tire!

The week of waiting on Palmyra Island was delightful. We scuba-dived, ran an ocean-current study for Bob's dissertation and enjoyed exploring.

Above: Catalina Ltd's PBY-5A is moored in Palmyra Island Lagoon in late 1967, the first of three island landings for the reconnaissance team from the National Center for Atmospheric Research (NCAR) by the Catalina Ltd crew of three: Tom, Bob and Bob's wife Inge
(Photo from the Kendall Collection)

Left: This photo shows the channel that was used for landing and takeoff. It was the deepest area and clear of coral obstructions.
(Photo from the Kendall Collection)

Right: Despite all precautions taken before the landing on Palmyra's runway, the Catalina ended up getting a flat tire.
(Photo from the Kendall Collection)

Above and left: Tiare Tahiti carrying faculty members from the six universities down to the islands.

(Photos from the Kendall Collection)

In early 1967, Tiare Tahiti carried key faculty participants from the six universities down to the islands to review the work and provide additional manpower. The unloading of more scientists, mail and fresh food onto the small vessels, while tricky, went smoothly each time and was thoroughly appreciated by the resident island research teams. Nobody got wet! Cargo included steaks, fresh vegetables and fruit, plus 'liquid refreshment'.

Our second stop in the Line Island chain was Fanning Island: the largest of the three atolls we visited, and its highest rainfall in March, we later discovered, was 100 inches. In November there were a few clouds. We initially flew along the atoll rim to view its structure. We then made our landing into the natural channel that flows into the huge lagoon and taxied up to the dock, where the local British commissioner was there with his island crew to help us unload and re-fuel. The re-fueling took a while since we used a shammie to filter the fuel from the 50-gallon drums. Our pilots wanted to be careful to avoid rust in the wing tanks.

After the initial landing in Fanning, the water was so inviting. The stewardess/ navigator, Inge, indulged in some warm R & R in the lagoon, plus snorkeling to get a preview of the sealife on the atolls. Lots of manta rays was the surprise, but in the deeper water. The British Commissioner John Fleetwood worked tirelessly to have his employees provide sufficient small craft for unloading the cargo and research scientists. .

In terms of a landing, Christmas Island was exceptional since it is a large island with no lagoon and a beautiful 10,000-foot concrete runway in excellent condition, mostly clear skies (annual rainfall averages 10 inches per year and later in March no rain) and a moderate, steady head wind upon arrival. It was so easy to land and unload!

This large island was used by the British for nuclear weapons tests from 1956–1964 with a detachment of RAF personnel remaining until June 1964. The US had nuclear weapons tests in April–July and Sept–November 1962 for five months during Operation Dominic. Besides the numerous large hangers full of equipment, pumps, refrigerators, fuel drums, etc., there were a lot of rusty military vehicles decorating the landscape of this very large island, compared to the atolls we had visited. Lots of land crabs dotted the roadway, a challenge to avoid, or not.

Our 'transportation' to the village at Christmas was a large truck with basic seating, i.e. chairs from the local nearby airport buildings. This island had metal houses, which provided us with sleeping accommodations – much appreciated after the long day of travel visiting the three islands.

Above and below: Christmas Island. (Photos from the Kendall Collection)

All photos: Fanning Island

Right: Fanning Island. Topping off the wing tanks, slow and steady via the shammie! Inge explained: 'We sure appreciated the local "volunteers" who did not even wear sandals on the sun-baked wings.' (Photo from the Kendall Collection)

Above and above right: Fanning Island. The view of the narrow ring around the lagoon showed numerous brackish pools and coral reefs no doubt rich with sealife. One area of the ring was wider; it was where the British had an undersea communication cable station, first established in 1902. Initially it served as a relay station between British Columbia and Suva, Fiji, until the new one was completed in 1963. The Canadian-Fanning link was the longest cable in the world, 3,300 miles long. In 1914 the Germans cut it, but within two weeks it was back in operation. During WWII US military personnel were stationed on all three islands (Palmyra, Fanning and Christmas). In 1963 the cable station was sold, and, currently, the University of Hawaii leases the land from the Gilbert and Ellice Islands Colony for various mid-Pacific investigations.

Below and below right: Kauai Island, Hawaii.

After the Line Island Experiment was completed, Bob and I invited key faculty participants to a celebration flight from Honolulu International Airport to a swim party on Kauai, landing in beautiful Hanalei Bay. Truly an idyllic place to relax and enjoy God's beautiful creation, made possible by the versatile Catalina's ability to land in the bay that day! Takeoff was not easy. The calm water made for strong suction, so it took full power for a long while to get up 'on the step' and get released and airborne at last!

(Photos from the Kendall Collection: text courtesy of Dr Ingeborg Kendall Maranto)

Above: The most important people involved with the civil operations of Catalina '90V are Mr Thomas William Kendall (right) and his son Bob. Thomas bought the plane, designed the reconfiguration, and both father and son piloted it. Bob was part of the initial flight when it was purchased, was rated to fly the plane and of course ran the operation in the Line Islands Experiment and later kept it operationally doing the repairs.

We see them standing here under the tail of the reborn '90V during the handover ceremony at the San Diego Air & Space Museum in November 1986. The aircraft was donated to the Museum and arrived in flying condition. That was made possible by dozens of volunteers who had worked so hard to get the old Catalina airborne for what turned out to be her final flight. With quite a number of Catalinas in the world being resurrected and brought back to flying condition, maybe one day...?
(Photo from the Kendall Collection)

Above: The roll out of the reconditioned Catalina '90V during the official ceremony whereby the Cat was handed over to the San Diego Air & Space Museum. Note that the 'civil' clipper bow has been retained; it was later replaced by a more authentic war-type eyeball gun turret (see the photo in Chapter 5).
(Photo from the Kendall Collection)

SEA RESCUE BY DUMBO CATALINA

Below: In mid-July 1945, the heavy cruiser USS *Indianapolis*, the flagship of the 5th Fleet, sailed out from the US mainland to Tinian, one of the Marianas Islands (a small group of islands southeast of Japan in the Central Pacific Ocean). It was a special mission as the battleship had an ultra-classified and dangerous cargo on board. It was enriched Uranium for the first Atomic Bomb, planned to be dropped on Japan in early August. That bomb, given the name 'Little Boy', was to be delivered by the now legendary Boeing B-29 Superfortress, Enola Gay, which was due to take off from the Tinian Air Force Base for her flight out to the Japanese main islands.

In a strange twist of fate, the ship supplying the atomic explosives that inflicted the Empire's final doom – the USS *Indianapolis* – would itself come to grief by just two Japanese torpedoes. In a matter of only 12 minutes, the mighty ship was ripped apart by the second torpedo that hit amidships and ignited the ammo depots and fuel tanks. The ship was deadly wounded and capsized almost instantly, dragging some 300 sailors trapped inside into the abyss of the ocean. That drama took place under total radio silence, not one single distress call was made or received by the US Navy!

Of the total crew of 1,198 sailors, some 900 survivors were lucky to have surfaced. They found themselves adrift in the open ocean. But there followed a second carnage: three days later, with all survivors left helpless in the water and no rescue operation deployed, only 317 sailors had survived the shipwreck's catastrophe.

Above: Drowned sailors in the waters of the Pacific, fighting against sunburn and dehydration, while encircled by sharks. The predators came to the scene from miles around. A feeding frenzy followed for the ever-hungry sharks, attracted by the countless dead bodies, and later they started attacking the survivors who were still in the water. Estimates of the number who died from shark attacks range from a few dozen to almost 150. Whatever the score of the shark's frenzy, the ordeal of the *Indianapolis*' survivors remains one of the worst maritime disasters in the US naval history.

Above: Lieutenant Adrian Marks (4th from right) and his crew in front of their 'Dumbo' PBY-5A Catalina – the heroes involved in the rescue operation after the shipwrecking of the USS *Indianapolis* on 2 August 1945. Lieutenant Marks paid tribute to the sailors he rescued and to all others who had undergone this horrifying ordeal. Speaking at the 1975 survivors' reunion, he said: 'I met you 30 years ago. I met you on a sparkling, sun-swept afternoon of horror. I have known you through a balmy tropic night of fear. I will never forget you.'

Lieutenant Marks had the Air Medal pinned on him by Admiral Chester W. Nimitz, the commander-in-chief of the Pacific Fleet. He died on March 7, 1998, in his hometown of Frankfort, Ind. at the age 81. For more information about this naval disaster, read my Dakota Hunter blog at: www.dc3dakotahunter.com/blog/pby-catalina-saved-uss-indianapolis-sailors-from-massive-shark-attack.

Left: Dumbo Catalina at work, four days after the USS *Indianapolis* went down. The survivors were spotted almost four days after the shipwreck by the crew of a Lockheed PV-1 Ventura on a routine patrol. They radioed for assistance as they saw the shipwrecked sailors in the water, not even realizing that the pride of the 5th Fleet had gone down a few days earlier. In the total confusion, there was one single PBY Catalina that could fly as a Dumbo rescue plane to the place of horror.

Their Captain, Lieutenant Adrian Marks, flew low and slow over a terrible view of hundreds of men in the water in agony and distress, and many being attacked by masses of sharks. He took a very courageous decision and against all orders landed the PBY on the open ocean. He set his Catalina down and while taxiing the Cat, the crew started picking up the wounded and stragglers from the shark-infested ocean.

The PBY Catalina most probably took serious damage due to the high swell that threw the Cat up, bouncing over the waves. Marks was able to pull a total of 56 drowned sailors out of the water and later shut off the engines to put survivors on the bobbing wings, tying the last of the 56 men down with parachute lines. The sailors would surely have had very little strength remaining after having spent three days in the water, and the effort to get them inside the aircraft via the small side hatch or the higher positioned waist blisters (see photo) must have been immense for both the crew and the exhausted sailors. This rescue operation carried on for the rest of the day, and only after midnight did the destroyer USS *Cecil J. Doyle* arrive on the scene, followed by other ships, all helping to pull the final survivors out of the water.

Right: Surprisingly, after its heroic 'Flight of Mercy' in August 1945, the Catalina Dumbo Rescue boat was sunk on the spot at the end of the USS *Indianapolis* rescue operation. Most probably, the Catalina had suffered serious damage from the harsh landing on the 12ft high swell that could have popped the rivet heads of the lower fuselage skin, allowing water to come in slowly. And, maybe, damage from hard bumps inflicted by the boats that came along later that night to take the 56 sailors from the bobbing aircraft that was no longer under its own power.

The crew must have realized that their aircraft was doomed. They abandoned their Catalina with pain in their heart, but the PBY-5A had sustained too much damage to get airborne again from the open ocean waters. The next morning, the aircraft was gunned or scuttled by the USS *Doyle* before they sailed back.

In a bizarre twist of fate, exactly 70 years later, in early August 2015, yet another PBY Catalina would come to grief in relation to this horrifying event. During the production of the Hollywood movie titled *USS Indianapolis, Men of Courage* (starring Nicolas Cage), the epic Catalina rescue operation was 'reenacted' in the Florida waters. By accident, during the filming, the aircraft's cockpit started to take in water (see photo) and sunk partially, with only the nose down. The precious aircraft was towed into the shallow waters near the beach and laid there for four days with its nose submerged.

Right: The sad end of the Catalina that flew for the film about the USS *Indianapolis* in 2015. In the ensuing rescue operation, they tried to hoist the aircraft out of the water in order to put her on a rescue barge. During this effort, things went catastrophically awry and, unbelievably, the priceless Catalina broke up in pieces. The aircraft was so badly damaged that it was a complete loss. To make things worse, the film also became a flop ending with a mega loss of money.

Amazingly, over the past 25 years or so, a number of Catalinas that were (partially) sunk, but fully intact, came to grief due to incompetent 'salvaging' operations with hoists that tried pulling the precious aircraft out of the water while tons of water were still inside the airframes. Cables become cutters if someone tries to lift that weight. It happened in Southampton, England; in Sitidgi Lake, Northern Canada (see at the end of this chapter); and again, here in Florida!

PLANE SAILING AIR DISPLAYS LTD

Right: Having operated Catalinas since 1985, Plane Sailing Air Displays Ltd can justly claim to be the premier private Catalina operator in the world today. It has built up a huge amount of experience and expertise, operating the type as a display aircraft and for long distance charters.

Its first Catalina was acquired in late-1984 by Royal Air Force fast jet pilots Paul Warren Wilson and John Watts, who were joined by the well-known aviation photographer and Fleet Street character Arthur Gibson. Well-used to displaying 'Warbirds' at European airshows, they wanted to move on to a more unusual type and their sights settled on a redundant aerial survey Catalina that was languishing in South Africa. It was flown to the UK and after being repainted to represent the aircraft flown by Coastal Command's Flt Lt John Cruickshank when he 'won' his Victoria Cross it flew its first air display in Rotterdam, Netherlands, in May 1985. This was followed by its first British show – at Biggin Hill, Kent – later that month. It went on to fly hundreds of shows all over Europe as well as appearing in a couple of movies and carrying out promotional work for Italian wine and beer companies!

Along the way, it was repainted in the scheme of the Coastal Command's other Catalina VC – that of David Hornell of 162 (BR) Sqn, RCAF. This overall white livery made it easy to overlay sponsor logos if required or to paint a commercial color scheme on top. Such an opportunity presented itself when Hans Wiesman used Plane Sailing's Catalina and crew for the second Peter Stuyvesant 'Travel Odyssey' to South America (see photo). Amongst many significant and interesting flights, this first Catalina took part in the 50th Anniversary of VE Day flypast over the Royal Family and Buckingham Palace in May 1995 and took Václav Havel, the Czech Republic's first President, aloft during a visit to his country.

For more photos of this Cat, see chapter 4, The Catalina Odysseys.

(Info David Legg; photo Frans Lemmens)

Below: A remarkable photo. In the summer of 2016 a 're-enactment' of the original March 1945 action in which OA-10A Catalina 44-33915 was lost was staged at Pardubice in the Czech Republic. The Messerschmitt Me 262 is a full-sized flying replica whilst Plane Sailing's second Catalina is painted to represent the original 44-33915 'Miss Pick Up', lost in the North Sea. (Photo and info David Legg)

Above: 'Miss Pick Up' rests on Faxa Sø during 'Operation World First'. Seen here in Greenland is Plane Sailing's second Catalina – a former Royal Canadian Air Force Canso A. She was acquired to replace the first in 2002 and after extensive work was ferried from Vancouver Island, British Columbia, to the UK in March 2004. Since then, it has been operated continuously with winter breaks for maintenance and ongoing structural projects. Not long after being acquired, she was repainted to represent 'Miss Pick Up', a USAAF Catalina that was based in the UK on air sea rescue duties in 1945.

In addition to many air displays all over Europe, it has been used to fly around the coast of Britain on a special project in memory of the Australian aviator Harry Hawker and flown along the line of the Thames as part of the Royal Navy commemoration of the 70th Anniversary of the Battle of the Atlantic in May 2013. A memorable flight from RAF Leuchars had John Cruickshank, the RAF's last living VC holder, on board.

Perhaps the most exciting challenge was in 2015 when the Catalina was used by Worksop College to fly a party of students to Greenland for 'Operation World First'. The Catalina landed on a remote lake in Eastern Greenland (see photo) so that the students could disembark and spend three weeks of climbing, outward-bound exercises and teambuilding before the flying boat brought them back to the UK.

'Miss Pick Up' is owned by twenty shareholders and looked after by a team of employees and volunteers and is now flown more than any other surviving Catalina anywhere in the world. It remains fully capable of water operations. It even has its own fan club The Catalina Society.

In this stunning photo Captain Paul Warren Wilson maintains a wary eye on weather and water conditions. More information about the aircraft, shared ownership and The Catalina Society can be found at www.catalina.org.uk.

(Photo Toby Lee via David Legg; text supplied by David Legg)

Above: Photo of the beautiful nose-art of the original OA-10A Catalina 'Miss Pick Up', which was based at RAF Halesworth in Suffolk England during 1945. The Catalina was lost in the North Sea at the end of March 1945 after being shot-up by a Luftwaffe Me 262 following engine failure after landing on the water. Here, its usual crew are seen posing in front of their 'Miss'.
(Photo and Info: David Legg)

AUSTRALIA'S POST WAR CIVIL CATS

Below: Lord Howe Island, NSW. Some 600 km east off the Australian continent, at a latitude halfway between Sydney and Brisbane, you can find this magical volcanic island. Only 10 km in length, it is a most idyllic place with a reputation for its scenic views over the beaches, lagoons, mountain peaks and the endless Pacific. Arguably one of the most beautiful islands in the world, it started to attract small amounts of tourists from the mainland in the late 1940s. By ship it would take days, but with the huge RAAF disposal inventory at hand, private operator Trans Oceanic Airways (TOA) and Qantas started a tourist shuttle operation from Sydney's Rose Bay with a Catalina and later with the Short Sunderland/Sandringham.

Although the postwar years saw the worldwide demise of flying boats, Sydney remained uniquely placed to take advantage of their waterborne capabilities. With air travel becoming more affordable, the Rose Bay flying boats set their sights on Australia's east coast and surrounding South Pacific destinations. Many Sydney residents enjoyed traveling on the flying boats for holidays to Hayman Island; two-week South Seas 'cruises' to Fiji, Noumea and the Cook Islands; charters to Lake Eucumbene, near the Snowy Mountains; and trips to Lord Howe Island. Thousands of Sydneysiders holidayed on this island, many returning year after year. The journey to Lord Howe Island on the flying boat was an integral part of their holiday experience.

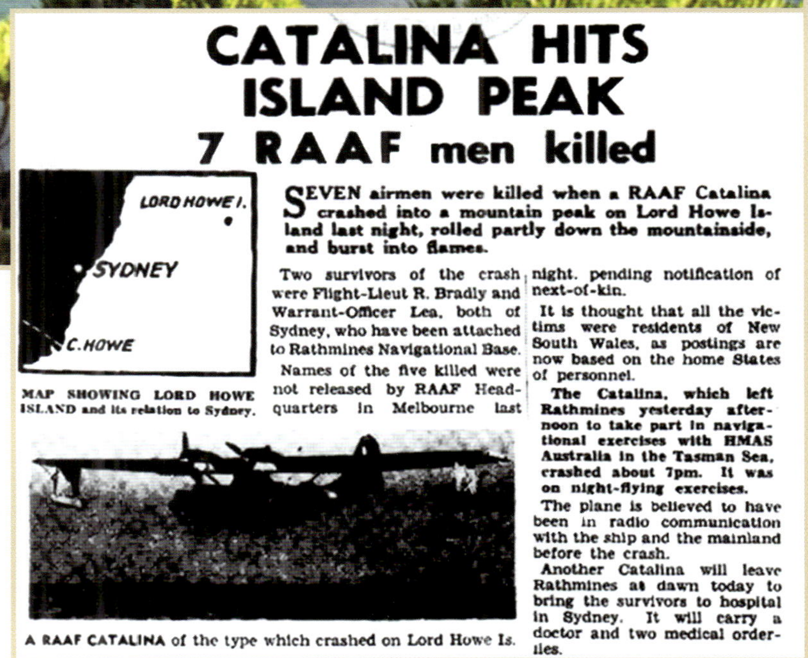

CATALINA HITS ISLAND PEAK
7 RAAF men killed

MAP SHOWING LORD HOWE ISLAND and its relation to Sydney.

SEVEN airmen were killed when a RAAF Catalina crashed into a mountain peak on Lord Howe Island last night, rolled partly down the mountainside, and burst into flames.

Two survivors of the crash were Flight-Lieut R. Bradly and Warrant-Officer Lea, both of Sydney, who have been attached to Rathmines Navigational Base.

Names of the five killed were not released by RAAF Headquarters in Melbourne last night, pending notification of next-of-kin.

It is thought that all the victims were residents of New South Wales, as postings are now based on the home States of personnel.

The Catalina, which left Rathmines yesterday afternoon to take part in navigational exercises with HMAS Australia in the Tasman Sea, crashed about 7pm. It was on night-flying exercises.

The plane is believed to have been in radio communication with the ship and the mainland before the crash.

Another Catalina will leave Rathmines at dawn today to bring the survivors to hospital in Sydney. It will carry a doctor and two medical orderlies.

A RAAF CATALINA of the type which crashed on Lord Howe Is.

Right: On 28 September 1948, an RAAF Catalina crashed on Lord Howe Island. Rathmines-based No 11 Squadron suffered the loss of a Catalina amphibian and seven crewmen in a night crash on Lord Howe Island on this day. The aircraft (A24-381) had completed the outward leg of a navigation exercise to the island and altered course for home when a serious fuel leak began filling the compartment with petrol vapor 20 minutes into the return leg. The captain decided to turn back to Lord Howe and attempt a landing on the island's sheltered lagoon. After crossing the island west to east, the aircraft turned back before clipping the ridgeline below Malabar Hill at about 7.30 pm local time. The Catalina careered down the slope before exploding in flames. Local residents who rushed to the scene extracted two seriously injured crew from the wreck. The death toll was the highest suffered by the RAAF in a peacetime accident up until that time. Today, you can still find the remnants of that crash – pieces of the wings and a radial engine Pratt & Whitney R-1830 – on the hillside.

(Courtesy of RAAF)

Left: On 23 June 1949, Qantas Empire Airways (QEA) Catalina VH-EAX was lost in the lagoon of Lord Howe Island under suspicious circumstances. Its steel mooring cable had been broken during strong winds and the aircraft was blown ashore and badly damaged; it went literally on the rocks (see photo). Investigation on the broken cable showed excessive corrosion between the strands, caused by an alien red substance. Was this sabotage?

Only 2 months later, on 27 August 1949, yet another, even stranger accident happened with a QEA Catalina VH-EAW (see photo below). The Cat was moored in Rose Bay, Sydney at night when a fierce explosion inside the aircraft caused a fire that could not be extinguished by the launches that came in to help. The Cat was damaged to such an extent that she sank within 20 minutes.

In the following investigation, a time-ignitor was found under the flight engineer seat. The Managing Director of the competitor Catalina operator Trans Oceanic Airways (TOA) was tried on the charge of causing malicious damage to the aircraft with a bomb. The director was able to supply a valid alibi and was acquitted. A more plausible motive emerged later pointing to the possible involvement of a number of people who had been expelled and forced to fly back via PNG with that Cat.

Left: A Qantas-operated Boeing of Canada-built PB2B-2 Catalina VH-EAW, Lord Howe Island, Australia, 1949. From 1947 both Qantas and its smaller competitor, Trans Oceanic Airways (TOA), operated in a profitable and emerging tourist flights market, executed with widely available disposal Catalinas from RAAF bases Rathmines and Lake Boga. Flights went from Rose Bay, Sydney, to Lord Howe Island (600 km) in just a few hours. Flights to Noumea (New Caledonia), and to and around New Guinea, were also soon to become the realm of the war-veteran Catalinas.

For the tourists, it was a pleasant experience, but with basic comfort. Once landed in the sheltered lagoon, a small launch was used for the disembarkation. However, with a hard wind and a Pacific Ocean swell just half a mile away, the Catalina and the launch could each bob and roll in their own rhythm. The passenger's boarding over the high threshold of the blister from a rocking boat four feet below must have been a challenge for some. Imagine your planned step up widens in a split second by a foot or more. A majestic entry was sometimes spoiled by an embarrassing 'stumble and fall' act into the cabin. The exits into the small boat could be even more hilarious, with people almost going overboard as they miscalculated their step down. An incoming wave could inadvertently make the gap grow to insurmountable proportions. But that all added to the adventurous character of the Catalina trips to this fantasy island, and it was a great success.

Sadly, the final fate of VH-EAW was far from pleasant. As described in the above caption, she was blown up and sank at her mooring in Rose Bay in August 1949 (see for more info about that accident next photo's caption).

Above: This PB2B-2 with BuNo 44287 (c/n 61193) is Catalina VI JZ834. She came to the RAAF as new, departing San Diego for Australia on 20 May 1945. It was sold and issued to the purchasers on 27 February 1947, having been registered VH-BRA to Barrier Reef Airways, Brisbane, and named 'Beachcomber'. It was converted to a 22-seat passenger configuration.

Short history of Barrier Reef Airways/Barrier Reef Airways Pty Ltd, Brisbane, Qld
Formed by Stewart Middlemiss (formerly in charge of the wartime RAAF Ferry & Acceptance Detachment at NAS Terminal Island, San Pedro, CA, USA) and Chris Poulson in October 1946, this company purchased eight surplus Catalinas from the RAAF, of which five were reduced to spares at Lake Boga without entering civil service. The three others were acquired from Rathmines (NSW) and two went on to be civil registered as VH-BRA and VH-BRB. The third – A24-304 – was probably used for spares. The airline was based on the Brisbane River and started charter flights, mainly with VH-BRA, in April 1947, later operating services to the Lindeman and Daydream Islands. Barrier Reef Airways became Barrier Reef Airways Pty Ltd in April 1950 and merged with Trans Oceanic Airways to form Ansett Flying Boat Services in 1952.

The aircraft was retired and moored engineless at Hamilton Reach on Brisbane River from October 1951. Ownership was taken over by Ansett Flying Boat Services Pty Ltd 1952. The aircraft was WFU by January 1953 and stored on Brisbane River slipway; registration cancelled on 21 May 1953; and later scrapped at Colmslie, Brisbane.

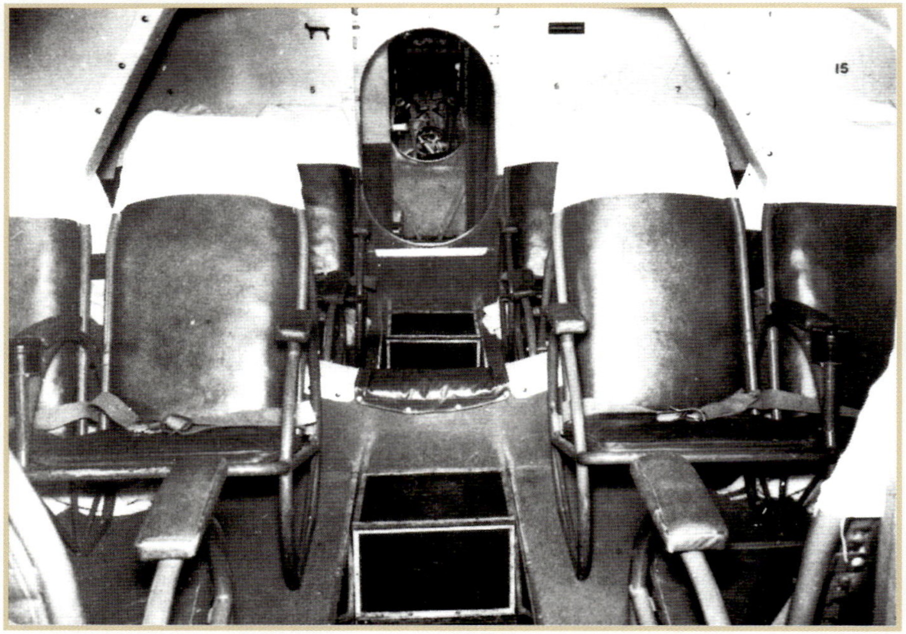

Above: The interior of the Catalina VH-BRA was rather basic with the seats in a thin leather upholstery, but who cared? Any seat would be good enough to make such magical flight in a Catalina to a fantasy island.

(Photo via Martin Collins)

Above: Catalina VH-BRA's interior under the blisters. With four seats and decent cushions, it looks almost like the 'First Class' of the aircraft but it by no means comes close to the luxury of the Kendall Catalina. Considering the relatively short flight to the islands, this seating was of a sufficient standard. Note the ashtrays on the bulkhead wall.

(Photo via Martin Collins)

Above: Photo of Barrier Reef Airways luggage labels, supplied by Martin and Shane Collins. Their father, Flight Sgt Pat Collins of Brisbane, Australia, served as a wireless operator with RAAF ferry detachment, USA, based in Washington, New Orleans, San Diego and San Pedro, CA, USA, from 1943 to 1945. Pat Collins crewed on nearly 50 individual Catalinas of various types during this period. Right after the war, he got involved with the Barrier Reef Airways operations, which included the purchase and conversion of the Catalinas, later operational as VH-BRA and VH-BRB for the company. The logos, brochures and labels were also designed by him.

(Photos courtesy of the Collins family private collection; all brochures and photos of Barrier Reef Airways are copyrighted by Martin Collins)

Above: Barrier Reef Airways luggage label.

(Photos courtesy of the Collins family private collection; all brochures and photos of Barrier Reef Airways are copyrighted by the Collins family)

Above: Catalinas inspire Barrier Reef Airways. On the reverse of this advert is the following text:

> Famous Catalinas inspire Barrier Reef Airways. The idea of a fast, comfortable flying boat service to islands of Queensland's Barrier Reef was inspired by the famous Catalina flying boats themselves. Young Australian pilots, after six years of war service mostly spent in 'Cats' realized that these aircraft, with their amazing war record, their ability to carry big loads and to nose around from island to island, were perfect for the service.
>
> And so Barrier Reef Airways was born. It is a private airline, with all ex-service personnel. The flagship and first aircraft in service for BRA is the 'Beachcomber'. Sister ships are the 'Buccaneer' and the 'Bermuda'. The Catalinas are, of course, completely fitted for civilian transport, being soundproofed and equipped with comfortable adjustable chairs, built-in ashtrays, etc. (See interior photos in this article.)

(Photo courtesy of Martin Collins)

Right: A most attractive newspaper ad for Barrier Reef Airways, with a photo of passengers boarding the Catalina in a small launch in the lagoon of Heron Island. It seems a most romantic holiday and a successful start for the young company. However, in reality, at a very early stage of their operations, one of the founders, Chris Poulson tragically disappeared on 28 November 1947 under strange conditions. A friend had arrived on Heron Island by yacht; Chris went out in a dinghy and enjoyed a welcome party on board. He left in the dinghy later that evening, but never returned to his hotel. The next morning his business partner Stewart Middlemiss arrived with passengers in the Catalina and they discovered that Chris was missing. The Cat was started immediately for a search operation around the island. They found the capsized dinghy but Chris Poulson's body was never found again. That loss turned out to be fatal for the fledgling company. They had all sorts of new plans, but with Chris's death, they had to wind up the company, just as they were getting on their feet.

(Photo and info via Martin Collins)

Above: The promotional tour of VH-BRI in an attractive livery, Essendon Airport, Melbourne, Australia, in 1959. Note the luxurious rear entry with an airstair door and enlarged windows in the cabin for better viewing. Ansett Flying Boat Services was based at Rose Bay flying boat terminal in Sydney. They wanted to take their share of the emerging tourist flight market to the exotic islands.

The Catalina was named 'Golden Islander'. It flew Mackay–Hayman Island services, making a water landing in the bay and taxying up a ramp to the Hayman Island Hotel (Great Barrier Reef). This aircraft was bought in the USA as a luxury Landseaire conversion and ferried by Stewart Middlemiss. He vividly describes the tragic end of this beauty in his memories; an amazing story:

> . . . the Catalina (skin) acted a bit a like a ping pong ball . . . it used to dent (after a rough water landing) and then pop back to its normal position. But when it did, it knocked the heads of the rivets off and you got little leaks in the hull. In the Air Force days, we used to put rubber bungs in the holes. In my civilian flying, I used to carry pencils to plug the holes . . .
>
> We lost the 'Golden Islander' on Hayman Island on 8th July 1962 because the pilot came in with a fairly heavy landing and did not realize that he knocked half a dozen rivets off. He left the aircraft on its mooring and overnight it gradually filled with water. When he went out in the morning, the Catalina was lying with its wing on the surface of the water. In my whole career in flying boats, we lost them only through water landing accidents.

(Photo by Lindsay Wise; info courtesy of: www.goodall.com.au/australian-aviation/civil-catalina-2/civilcatalinas2.html)

Above: Lord Howe Island. A magnificent shot from a Short Sunderland that is about to make a water landing in the sheltered lagoon of the island. That single tourist out there on the beach must have been made up to have created such picture, as would have the photographer of this shot, Matt Holle. Bravo!

Flying boats didn't require expensive land airports and they became the basis for the opening up of tiny islands for tourism, saving passengers the long travel time by boat. Flying-boat operations were always more awkward and required more maintenance due to the frequent contact with corrosive saltwater. Also, the mooring operations needed skilled and experienced crews on the water and in the cockpit. Land-based airstrip constructions, along with the shorter takeoff /landing capacities of post-war aircraft (due to 'reversible' props and speed-reducing wing flaps), made the flying boat redundant.

By the early 1970s increasing maritime traffic on Sydney Harbour had resulted in the restriction of flying boat services, and only two of this Short aircraft remained at the Rose Bay base. After an airstrip was built on Lord Howe Island in 1974, the two remaining flying boats were sold off and finished their working days in the Caribbean. When the flying boat base closed that same year, a unique chapter in Sydney's history came to an end.

However, people who have seen or flown with flying boats speak affectionately of their beauty and romance. Look at this picture: the flying boat is like an elegant swan that flies in to land on the water. For many, it was, is, and always will remain, a most impressive sight that cannot be matched by any land-base aircraft.

(Photo courtesy of Matt Holle)

CANADIAN CIVIL CATS OPERATIONS

Above: Transporting hundreds of thousands of pounds of fresh fish in Northern Saskatchewan. How do you accomplish such a daunting task? The short answer is: buy a Canso! Reindeer Lake and Wollaston Lake are huge freshwater lakes in Northeastern Saskatchewan, Canada. Commercial fishing began on Reindeer Lake in 1937 and the experimental use of small aircraft to transport fresh fish from these northern lakes to market, via Flin Flon, Manitoba, was a rather doubtful affair.

Prior to the end of the World War II, flying goods across the north was not very easy and not very profitable. Many of the northern bush pilots had enlisted with the Canadian Air Force. Also, due to their size, the aircraft that were commonly available for amphibious use during that era were very limited in freighting capacity. After the war ended, the Saskatchewan provincial government embarked on a major effort to promote and enhance the commercial fishing industry in the north. They eventually created the Saskatchewan Fish Marketing Board in 1945, and, in 1946, established the Beaver Lake Fish Filleting Plant at Denare Beach, Saskatchewan, and the La Ronge Fish Filleting Plant (see photo, taken in 1948).

In order to obtain fresh fish from the far north to supply such fish processing plants, they also experimented with using various amphibious aircraft. At this time the Norseman was the aircraft of choice. The Saskatchewan Government Airways (SGA) had a growing fleet of aircraft that included a number of Norseman that were being used for freighting across the north. The challenge was that the payload of the Norseman was still only about 2,000 lbs. When the officials did the calculations, they realized it was going to take a much larger aircraft to transport the million or million-and-a-half pounds of fish that were being planned for. The surplus Canso came into view.

The maximum allowable conservation limits for fish caught in Reindeer Lake and Wollaston Lake in 1948 was 3 million pounds of primarily lake trout and whitefish. To transport a large percentage of that potential poundage, the manager of the Saskatchewan Government Airways, F.R. Glass, wrote a letter of proposal on 12 January 1948 to purchase a Canso aircraft.

(Story and photos by Les Oystryk)

Above: The heading in the regional newspaper was 'Canso Flying Boat Ordered For Run to Reindeer Lake'. The aircraft was ordered from the De Havilland Aircraft Corporation who had originally purchased it from the Canadian War Assets Corporation. It was capable of carrying up to 10,000 pounds of fresh fish. It was also anticipated that the operating costs were only going to be double that of the Norseman, even though the payload was five times as much.

Preparations were begun to accommodate the use of this Canso. Production contracts with fishermen were signed, larger fishing boats were built, radio communications equipment was planned, and loading and unloading facilities were being built. All of these works and facilities were in very isolated locations across the vast northern wilderness of Saskatchewan.

Delivery of the Canso was in April of 1948 and CF-SAT joined the ranks of the Saskatchewan Government Airways (SGA) fleet. The primary purpose of this aircraft was to transport huge volumes of fresh fish, but she was also used for other related freight and transportation purposes. Additionally, the SGA was tasked with providing an adequate air service to the vast expanse of Saskatchewan's northern wilderness.

This photo was taken in July 1950 and shows SGA Canso CF-SAT moored on the water in front of the Beaver Lake Fish Filleting Plant at Denare Beach, Saskatchewan.

(Photographer unknown. Photo courtesy of the Provincial Archives of Saskatchewan Ref. # BE-69; story and photos supplied by Les Oystryk)

Right: Photo of Canso CF-SAT moving Jacobson to Wollaston Lake. The photo was taken by Harold Jacobson at Wollaston Lake in northern Saskatchewan, in the summer of 1948. It is a beautiful photo that shows two men unloading boxes and other freight belonging to Harold Jacobson and his wife Sylvia. They were unloading the freight onto a motorized canoe that belonged to the Jacobson family. CF-SAT was used to transport Mr and Mrs Jacobson and their belongings from their commercial fishing camp on Reindeer Lake to their new commercial fishing camp location on Wollaston Lake.

CF-SAT was manufactured in 1943 in Vancouver, British Columbia, Canada, in the airframe style of a Consolidated PBY/OA-10 Catalina /Canso A. From 21 January 1943 to 18 November 1946 she was taken on strength/charge of the Royal Canadian Air Force with S/N 9757. From April of 1948 until sometime in 1955 CF-SAT was owned and operated by the SGA in northern Saskatchewan and used to transport fish for the Saskatchewan Fish Marketing Board. In 1955 SGA sold her to Transair Limited in Manitoba, Canada. After a number of subsequent ownership changes she crashed and sank off the coast of Maui in the Hawaiian Islands on 14 April 1986.

(Story © by Les Oystryk)

Above, inset: De Havilland Canada DHC-2 Beaver C-GADE on skis in Flin Flon, Manitoba, 1984. A light but very sturdy transport aircraft, built from 1947 until 1967 in over 1,600 pieces.

Above: Wollaston Lake and Reindeer Lake located in the north. These were the main destinations to fly for hauling fresh fish to the La Ronge and Beaver Lake fish filleting plants further to the south. Flin Flon is located on the border between Saskatchewan and Manitoba, close to Beaver Lake.

The area of Northern Saskatchewan is approximately 269,996 square km or 104,246 square miles. This is nearly half of the entire size of the province. It was therefore not unusual to find the Canso being utilized to freight people and goods into this wilderness area with very few outposts or communities. For example, when fishermen were needed on these lakes, the Canso was used to transport these men, along with their families and their associated equipment and supplies.

Often, these flights with people and goods were on the back-haul of loads of fish being transported south to the fish processing plants at Denare Beach, La Ronge or Big River, Saskatchewan. The distances traveled varied (as seen on the attached map), but the common one-way route for CF-SAT from Denare Beach at Beaver Lake (near the town of Flin Flon) to Tate Island on Reindeer Lake was 170 miles, and from Denare Beach to the outpost on Wollaston Lake was 242 miles. These round trips were well within operating range for this Canso.

(Info and map supplied by Les Oystryk)

Above: One of the other commonly transported goods by the Canso CF-SAT was diesel fuel for various pieces of equipment or machinery used for power generation or transportation at the northern outposts. The Canso had huge fuel tanks in each wing. One wing tank was filled with over 700 gallons of diesel fuel for transport north and the other wing tank was filled with regular aviation fuel for the aircraft engines. Upon arrival at the northern outpost, the diesel was off-loaded into barrels and stored for use during the fishing season. The Canso was then loaded with fresh fish and flown to the southern fish plant. One veteran Canso pilot, George Horne, recently commented, 'It was always important to remember not to switch fuel tanks when flying one of those diesel fuel hauling trips.' No doubt there!

The above photo shows an SGA Canso CF-SAT moored in front of the Beaver Lake Fish Filleting Plant at Denare Beach, Saskatchewan (circa 1948). From the Martha Cressey Collection, Flin Flon Community Archives, courtesy of the Flin Flon Heritage Project.
(Photo credit: Martha Cressey photo #1008075 via Les Oystryk)

Left: Photo taken in July 1950 of an SGA Canso CF-SAT moored on the water in front of the Beaver Lake Fish Filleting Plant at Denare Beach, Saskatchewan.

Materials such as cement for the construction of concrete building foundations was commonly transported by Canso. Two men are unloading bags of Portland cement from the barge-type watercraft and into the Canso. The man standing on the left is Canso pilot Don Brownridge. The man inside the Canso appears to be wearing a flight-crew suit and seems to be taking the bags of cement to place within the hold of the aircraft. The bags of cement have a 'Canada – Canada Cement Company' label on them. **(Photographer unknown. Photo courtesy of the Provincial Archives of Saskatchewan Ref. #BE-73, supplied by Les Oysterik)**

Above: SGA Canso CF-SAT. This photo was taken in July 1950 and shows an SGA Canso CF-SAT moored on the water in front of the Beaver Lake Fish Filleting Plant at Denare Beach, Saskatchewan. Three men in a motorized canoe appear to be approaching the Canso with a load of freight to be taken on board. A crew member inside the Canso's hold appears to be ready for them to come alongside.

(Photographer unknown. Photo credit to the Provincial Archives of Saskatchewan Ref. # BE-71 via Les Oystryk)

Left: Junie sitting on top of Canso CF-SAT aircraft. The photo was taken by Maureen Hogan in 1948 while the Canso was moored on the water in front of the Beaver Lake Fish Filleting Plant at Denare Beach, Saskatchewan. Although time has taken away the memory of Junie's last name, Maureen Hogan recalls that she was a co-worker at the fish filleting plant that summer. Junie appears to be quite happy and comfortable as she sits on top of one of CF-SAT's engines and is proudly wearing her 'Flin Flon North of 54' sweatshirt. The Beaver Lake Fish Filleting Plant buildings can be seen in the background. The community of Flin Flon, Manitoba, was located just 20 km away.

Flin Flon was founded in 1927 by Hudson Bay Mining and Smelting Co., Limited (HBMS) to exploit the large copper and zinc ore resources in the region. In the 1920s, HBMS invested in a railway, a mine, a smelter and a hydroelectric power plant at Island Falls, Saskatchewan. By 1928 the rail line reached the mine. The town grew considerably during the 1930s as farmers, who were impoverished by the Great Depression, abandoned their farms and came to work at the mines. The municipality was incorporated on 1 January 1933, and in 1970, the community reached city status.

The town's name is taken from the lead character in a paperback novel, *The Sunless City* by J.E. Preston Muddock. The book is about a prospector called Josiah Flintabbaty Flonatin who explores a bottomless lake in a submarine. When Tom Creighton discovered a high-grade exposure of copper, he thought of the book and called it Flin Flon's mine, and the town that developed around the mine adopted the name. Flin Flon shares with Tarzana, California, the distinction of being named after a character in a science-fiction novel. **(Info and photo via Les Oystryk)**

Above: Canso CF-SAT, Beaver Lake. This photo shows Canso CF-SAT taxiing towards the dock in front of the Beaver Lake Fish Filleting Plant. A barge-type watercraft that was used for loading and unloading freight and fish from the Canso is seen moored to the dock. A small rail cart, which was used for hauling boxes of fish up to the fish plant, can be seen on the dock.

(Photo taken by Doug Pegg in the summer of 1948; supplied by Les Oystryk)

702

Left: The Phoenix that resurrected from Sitidgi Lake, Inuvik, NT, Canada. Following a nine-year restoration, a group of six farmers (FARS) restored to airworthiness a former Royal Canadian Air Force Canso A, originally built by Canadian Vickers.

During WWII, Canadian Vickers (later Canadair) and Boeing Aircraft of Canada produced 194 amphibious Catalinas for the Royal Canadian Air Force. In RCAF service they were known as Canso As, but they were basically equivalent to the US Navy's PBY-5A model. In 1979, as many as 39 Cansos, most of them Canadian-built, were still active in Canada.

A few of these ex-RCAF aircraft still survive and one, Buffalo Airways' Tanker 702 C-FNJE (CV-437), was left sitting submerged in a lake in the Northwest Territories after it had crashed in Sitidgi Lake on 24 July 2001 during a water pick-up on the lake 40 km east of Inuvik.

After serving during World War II as RCAF 11094, this Canso had a long civilian career with Field Aviation, Chiupka Airways, Northland Airlines, Midwest Airlines, Nordair, Ilford Riverton Airways, St Felicien Air Service, Survair and the Government of Newfoundland and Labrador. Buffalo Airways would be the aircraft's last owner after purchase in 1996.

Doug Roy wrote to me: 'Hans, this photo was taken November of 2016 at the first running of both engines at the same time. They sounded wonderful!'

(Story © by Dirk Septer; photo courtesy of Doug Roy)

Above: A submerged Tanker 702 C-FNJE in the process of being lifted from its grave. While landing on the water of Sitidgi Lake, Inuvik, Canada, on 24 July 2001, the water bomber's starboard wing hit the water first. The wingtip collapsed in the process, as can be seen on this photo, and the Canso had started taking on water (but not in the intended way), then sank to a depth of about 100 feet (30m). The aircraft was later raised, floated, and pulled to the shoreline, where it was stripped and left abandoned.

(Story written by Dirk Septer © 2017; photo courtesy Artic Photos, David Musselwhite)

Above: After C-FNJE was lifted from the bottom of the lake it was 'parked' on the lake's shore. For seven years, the Canso would sit there until six aircraft enthusiasts decided to try to salvage the aircraft and restore the Canso to its former glory. Officially organized as the Fairview Aircraft Restoration Society (FARS), but more commonly referred to as 'a group of farmers', they had taken on quite a project.

Once the aircraft C-FNJE was lifted from the lake, it had to be salvaged from the remote location and transported for over 3,000 km by barge and trailer to Westview, Alberta. In 2008, they managed to haul it over the frozen surface of the lake to the Dempster Highway. The original equipment, a donated tractor, proved insufficient and had to be replaced by a snowcat machine with more horsepower.

Camping out in -25 C weather in a canvas tent dubbed 'the wilderness workshop', the men prepared the Canso C-FNJE for the next leg of the journey south. From the Dempster Highway they got the aircraft to the Mackenzie River, where it was loaded on a barge and shipped upriver to Hay River, Northwest Territories. From here the aircraft, its final wing removed, was driven by road to Fairview.

(Photo courtesy of David Musselwhite)

Above: Something definitely went wrong during the lifting from the lake, which resulted in a torn-off main wing. Read here what David Musselwhite wrote about this salvaging operation:

I was flying a Cessna 206 on floats doing a fire patrol with forest people for about 2.5 hours, south and west of Inuvik. On our way back to Inuvik we noticed smoke in the area and called in the water bombers. I left the area because of lack of fuel and shortly after that found out the Canso (nr 702) touched a wing on the water and went down. After much discussion, I guess (XX) was the only one that took the job to raise the plane. Commercial divers from Whitehorse were hired to raise the plane, but they refused and we flew them back to Whitehorse. Then someone hired some amateur divers to do the job along with their staff. It became a circus and because of the way it was pulled out of the water on to the shore more damage was done (see photo). Buffalo Airways was planning to fly it out I think before the damage was done. I only made a few trips with freight and people to the site and most of the time without a camera. You could write a book on how not to manage a job like this.

(Photo and story from David Musselwhite)

Above: The Fairview farmers: Henry Dechant, Joe Gans, Norbert Luken, Doug Roy, Don Wieben and Brian Wilson. For the next nine years they would spend their Wednesday evenings working on the restoration of the Tanker 702. A group of aviation enthusiasts in Newfoundland donated two P & W engines. The farmers drove across Canada in a motor home to pick them up. The test flight in fall 2016 was only delayed due to Transport Canada's strict maintenance schedule, which had to be submitted for a heavy aircraft. FARS made its first flight with the restored water bomber on Sunday 18 June 2017 from the Fairview airport. Special thanks to Captain W.J. (Bill) Brady and his Co-Pilot Gary Wieben for taking the Canso PBY-5A into the air for this official 'first flight'. The achievement of FARS can only be appreciated with greatest respect for their dedication to get this vintage machine back in the air, bravo!

(Story by Dirk Septer, photo and info courtesy of Doug Roy. See also their website www.savethecanso.com)

The Catalina Odysseys

During my lifetime, I have had a passionate relationship with the Catalina. I can say that my youthful experiences from Borneo have forever left a giant footprint in my memory as being one of the truly most exciting experiences that a young boy can have when living in such a totally isolated world in a very small community, surrounded by an endless, steaming hot and sometimes hostile jungle.

Some 40 years after that first memorable experience, I would have a second Catalina experience. One day in 1992, working in my professional career as a Creative Director, I was invited to submit a format/script for an out-of-the-box TV travel documentary. The brief was to come up with a fascinating concept to lure major European TV networks to broadcast a series with 8 episodes in which 12 contest-winning students would discover the world in an adventurous way – in the style of Jules Verne's epic novel *Around the World in 80 Days*.

I entered the competition against other advertising agencies pitching for the same job. Those agencies suggested hiring a Jumbo B-747, or even – in one plan – the supersonic Concorde as the proposed transport for the 'Ultimate Trip-of-a-Lifetime'. Evidently, this Borneo-raised boy had a different idea. I came up with a concept that was based on my Pacific flight experiences of 40 years earlier, and as the transport for this idyllic 'Magical Mystery Tour' I proposed the Catalina, what else? The format won, and, suddenly, I was (again) engaged in a new Catalina adventure, this time under the name 'The Catalina Odyssey'. Boy, was I lucky!

What convinced the TV networks to select this particular aircraft as the dream transport in their documentary series? The vintage Catalina brought back the laid-back feeling of bygone years and the 'romance of flying'. Plus, as a bonus, the unusual ability to land at choice on virtually every single stretch of water – next to a sandy beach, in a blue lagoon, lake or river, or whatever we came across during our scenic flights over the Caribbean and South America. So close to Earth and yet so far away, like 'Fly away with me to another world'. That was, still is and will always be a wonderful concept.

None of the lucky contestants who came along with us had ever imagined they'd experience the thrill of that 'pure' flying sensation, the exciting feeling of soaring low and slow over the mountains, seas, and shores. Like in the fairy tale *One Thousand and One Nights*, flying on a metalized magic carpet, converted with a speed-pack and floats. No more jam-packed airports or cramped modern-day jet aircraft, those flying compression tanks that flash at altitudes of 10,000 meters, at a speed of 1,000 km/h. With the Catalina, we had only 18 people aboard our vintage war bird making the epic 'trip of a lifetime' over the Atlantic and the Americas, and hey, the only compression we felt was when we opened a (blister) window in flight at 1,500 feet altitude. That feels like riding in an open-top sports car at 100 miles per hour, not so bad.

Being the scriptwriter for the TV format and the tour director, the two Catalina Odyssey trips that followed in 1993/1994 took me on a total of twelve weeks of semi-continuous flying in the Catalina. In total, the trips yielded over 300 flight hours, eight TV episodes of 52 minutes each, over a 100 hours of edited footage, and some 1,000 fabulous photos of all sorts of exotic locations. The very best, the most colorful, most fascinating, and most romantic pictures of these trips have been selected for this book.

Catalina Z-CAT has landed on the Rio Negro in the Amazon, for a night stayover in the jungle tree-cabins
(Photo Frans Lemmens)

This magnificent photo of Catalina Z-CAT was taken over the Victoria Falls, located on the Zambia/Zimbabwe border. While it is neither the highest nor the widest waterfall in the world, Victoria Falls is classified as the largest, based on its combined width of 1,708 m (5,604 ft) and height of 108 m (354 ft), resulting in the world's largest sheet of falling water. Victoria Falls is almost twice the height of North America's Niagara Falls and well over twice the width of its Horseshoe Falls. In height and width, Victoria Falls is rivaled only by Argentina and Brazil's Iguazu Falls.
(Photo by Babette Alfieri via Pierre Jaunet; text from Wikipedia)

Aircraft History: Z-CAT Canso A (CV-357)
Currently registered and operated in New Zealand, Catalina ZK-PBY (ex Z-CAT) was built under license as a Canso A (A for amphibian) by Canadian Vickers in Cartierville, Quebec, in March 1944. The aircraft was given the construction number CV-357, and built out of a batch of 339 aircraft built by this plant (30 more were built in the St Hubert plant). CV-357 entered service with the Royal Canadian Air Force and was allocated the service number 11054. It is known to have served with No 5 Squadron from bases in Newfoundland and Nova Scotia. #11054 was declared surplus and struck off charge on 27 June 1947, having accumulated only 1,142 flying hours.

Catalina Z-CAT.
Little is known of its whereabouts and activity between 1947 and 1955 when it appeared in Costa Rica and was converted to a '28-5ACF' (civilian standard) by SALA in San Jose. This involved the removal of controls and gauges from the flight engineer's pylon position and relocation in the cockpit. The front gun turret was removed and a semi-clipper bow was added. Other modifications were added for safety. The aircraft returned to Canada registered as CF-JCV (later C-FJCV) and was operated by at least seven owners/operators including the Eastern Canada Stevedoring Company, Notre Dame Air Transport, Austin Airways, Aero Trades Western Ltd and Air Caledonia.

The Catalina CV-357 then fell into disuse and was placed in storage at Reno, Nevada, until 1988, when it was sold to Pierre Jaunet. He flew the Catalina over to Africa and operated her for the next five years for tourist flights down the Nile River with his Catalina Safari Company from Harare, Zimbabwe. It carried the registration Z-CAT from the summer of 1990. The Safaris continued until 1994 when political unrest in several African nations restricted civil aircraft operations. Z-CAT was hired by me from the Catalina Safari Company to fly the 1993 Peter Stuyvesant Travel Odyssey Atlantic Tour. She was flown to Eindhoven, Holland and received a brand new blue & red color scheme.
(Photo Babette Alfieri)

Catalina Z-CAT bought by the French adventurer Pierre Jaunet. In 1986, just a year or two before that deal was made, I met the same aircraft on Stead Airport in Reno while I was visiting the Reno Air races. From afar, I saw her standing on the apron in the outer corner of the field. I walked across and climbed over a low fence as nothing could stop me from meeting with old 'friends' from my childhood years in Borneo. The Cat looked somewhat dilapidated and I was gently touching her skin, when suddenly a big dude appeared, out of the blue, asking me if I was interested in buying her. I pretended to be a prospect as he showed me the interior with a 16-pax outfit. We stepped out of the cockpit's sliding hatch and walked over the huge wing and sat under the blisters. It was like stepping back into history, entering a time warp of some 40 years. From that moment, something must have germinated in my imagination, the birth of the Catalina Odyssey was imminent, but it would take another seven years before my dream would become a reality.

Pierre Jaunet flew Z-CAT all over Africa, the Americas, and finally Asia. His Catalina must have seen more of the World than most others ever did. In October 1994, Z-CAT left on its last ferry flight, traveling through nine countries, covering almost 10,000 nautical miles, in 90 flying hours, over 13 days, to arrive in its new home, New Zealand.

Today, registered as ZK-PBY, this venerable aircraft is operated by the New Zealand Catalina Preservation Society, a non-profit organization dedicated to keeping it airworthy for all to enjoy. See Chapter 5 for more photos of this Catalina in its current livery.

(Info Michael Prophet, David Legg; photo via Pierre Jaunet, made by Babette Alfieri)

Z-CAT flying over the river Nile. It was operated by Pierre Jaunet's Catalina Safari Company, which flew special luxury travel tours from the Victoria Falls in Zambia all the way up north via the East African route to the Luxor Pyramids in Egypt, with water landings on the Nile and many lakes and rivers. This was not a cheap flight ticket, and was exclusively for more affluent people looking for a very unique and luxurious safari experience.

One of the most famous clients was a man who was CEO of a relatively unknown company at that time, named MS or Microsoft. He made the flight with a group of 12 people, members of the Board of Directors of MS. His name was Bill Gates and he made a remarkable statement about his flights:

> There is nothing in the world that captures the total freedom and pure excitement better than flying in this amphibian airplane; it lands on rivers, lakes, seas and on land. As we flew on average at 1,500 feet altitude, we overlooked Africa as from a balloon, but we were faster and landed on every amazing location that we spotted from our vintage air cruiser, the Catalina.

(Photo Babette Alfieri)

Right: The first Catalina Odyssey's itinerary over the Atlantic and the Americas with Catalina Z-CAT from Zimbabwe. It took place in July 1993 with 40 days to fly 4 legs, with a total of over 170 flight hours, and covering a total distance of 25,000 km (16,000 miles)!

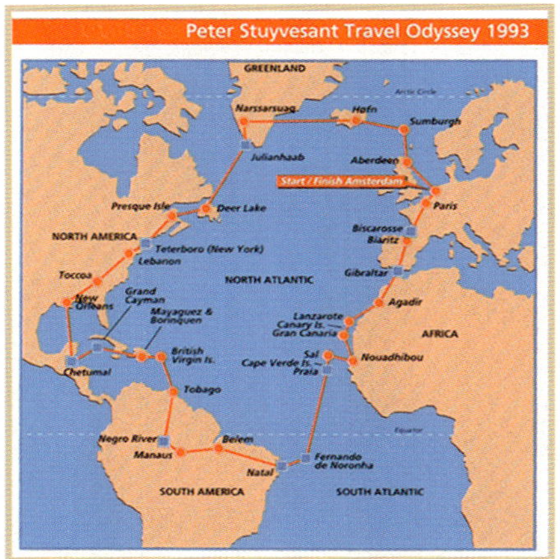

This was a very ambitious flight plan, which started at Schiphol Amsterdam Airport. The next stop was at a lake in SW France, named Biscarrosse, where the French contestants boarded, and where, before the war, the long-distance flights to South America with flying boats began.

We continued on to Gibraltar for a water takeoff then flew into African airspace with a landing in Agadir, Morocco, and in Mauretania. The sea crossing started with a landing on Lanzarote, Canary Islands, and on the Cape Verde Islands. From there, the real Atlantic crossing began with a hop over to Natal, Brazil, and back to the Fernando de Noronha archipelago. The flight over the north shore of Brazil brought us to Belem, and later into the Amazon, Manaus, and the Rio Negro, over the jungle up north across Venezuela to Tobago/Trinidad – the first of a string of Caribbean islands.

The next destinations were the BVI (British Virgin Islands), Grand Cayman, and Chetumal in the Yucatan, Mexico. On to New Orleans and New York City for an epic landing in the harbor, right in front of the Liberty Statue. Then, via Newfoundland, Deer Lake, we made a very chilly hop to Greenland and landed right between the icebergs. From there, we continued to Iceland, with a spectacular landing on a glacier lake near Höfn, and on to the Shetland Islands before we planned to make our final leg back to Amsterdam.

However, on our way over the North Sea, we had a serious engine problem and had to divert to Aberdeen, Scotland, for an emergency landing on one engine with a fully laden aircraft. During that diversion, we lost altitude and barely made it to Aberdeen Airport. From there, the passengers were flown back to their end destinations with regular flights. A week later, with a new engine mounted, Z-CAT flew the leg back to Holland for a final water landing on the Dutch IJsselmeer. It was the end of the first Catalina Odyssey.

From Holland, I flew with Z-CAT to Paris, on her way back home to Harare in Zimbabwe. There are not many vintage aircraft in this current era that have flown such distances all over Europe, the Americas, and Africa in a matter of just over two months. It was also the last time we would do this. In 1994, Plane Sailing's UK-based Catalina was hired for the job, saving us a whole lot of ferrying.

Peter Stuyvesant Travel
DISCOVER THE WORLD
ODYSSEY
THE ATLANTIC TOUR

Above: Our logo for the first Catalina Odyssey in 1993, which was sponsored by Peter Stuyvesant Travel.

Right: Late afternoon, sunset at the Rio Negro.
(Photo F. Lemmens)

Above: The Catalina that I had seen in 1986 in Reno, Nevada, was, in 1993, now subject to inspection at Harare Airport, Zimbabwe. With the aviation expert Edwin Bosman from Holland and the co-pilot Mike Terrell from the USA (sitting on the wing), we went through the aircraft, which had flown several sightseeing trips over Africa to Egypt and back over the previous years.

Schiphol Airport, the Netherlands, Amsterdam. The Catalina Z-CAT started the very first Catalina Odyssey right here in July 1993. The aircraft was flown in from Zimbabwe only a couple of days before departure and had to be re-sprayed in the sponsor livery before it could start its epic voyage – The Catalina Odyssey – over the Atlantic.

Our first stopover was in SW France, with a tight water landing on Biscarrosse Lake. It was the lake from where the pre-war Aéropostale aircraft departed on their long voyages to Rio de Janeiro and Buenos Aires in South America. Before the war, such long flights could only be made by flying boats that were capable of making water landings on the many stopovers, most of which had no airfields yet. Biscarrosse was a well-located lake that also housed the legendary Latécoère aircraft factory and the Air France terminal at Hourtiquets. The leftover buildings and ramp at Hourtiquets could still be found on the edge of the lake. (Photo Frans Lemmens)

Gibraltar was the next stopover before we flew into Africa. From the airfield, the Cat rolled from the concrete slipway at the end of the runway into the Mediterranean and we made a water start for a stunning low flight around the 'Rock'.
(Photo Erik Sampers)

Right: We flew the total 1993 Catalina Odyssey split over 4 legs, equally dividing the total distance and taking us 40 days in total, or 10 days per leg. Each leg, we had six new pre-selected contestants from France, Holland, and Belgium on board. In addition, there was the TV crew and photographers, plus Pierre Jaunet (sitting in front) and myself as the Tour Director (sitting on top of the engine at right).

With a total of 18 people inside the cramped cabin, split into three compartments, and the cockpit, it was like living in a flying submarine. But nobody complained about the basic comfort, the low temperature at 6,000+ feet altitude, the high temperature inside the cabin while waiting on the platform, and the terrible noise-level during the long flights. It was all part of the 'flight-of-a-lifetime' experience.

(Photo Frans Lemmens)

Left: Gibraltar as seen from its east side, with the Spanish seaport of Algeciras behind the 'Rock' and the land entry via La Linea at the right hand side. The water catchments above Sandy Bay are clearly visible, looking like stretched cement-covered slopes. Built in stages between 1903 and 1961, they were designed to cater for Gibraltar's ever-increasing demand for fresh water, as during the war they had been cut off from Spanish supply. By 1993, the total catchment area was no longer in use.

(Photo taken by Erik Sampers from Z-CAT)

Suddenly, there was sign of life below us. Our Catalina made a refuelling stop at Nouadjibou, Mauritania, south of Morocco. In the desert-like scenery, we could see shipwrecks and devastated buildings. It was like a scene from a science-fiction film. (Photo Erik Sampers)

Cape Verde Islands, Praia.
Our Catalina overflying the bay where a water landing was planned. In hindsight, that proved to be not such a good idea, although it was exactly the place where the wartime Aéropostale and Lufthansa aircraft made their water landings. As you can see in the photo, there was a serious ocean swell coming in that would make the water landing tricky, to say the least. The high swell made our aircraft bump a few times over the crests of the waves, and, finally, our captain Bryan McCook decided to make a full stall landing by simply pulling the yoke of the aircraft abruptly backward so that the aircraft pitched sharply up and stalled, as an emergency brake procedure. The result was a kind of controlled 'dropping out of the air' effect with the Cat hitting the water with its tail first. Then, with a ferocious splash, we smacked into in the water, making a hell of a racket inside the aircraft, as if the Cat had broken her back: white knuckles guaranteed for everyone on board, but it all had a happy ending and it was the only water landing during this Odyssey that did not go really smoothly.

Later, Captain Bryan's commented rather laconically: 'In these cases, there is nothing to be done. The sea plane hits the water at nearly full speed, whereupon it is impossible to attempt another takeoff. The only thing to do is believe in her lucky star and hope she does not come apart in the waves. That is why water landings on open sea are rare; it is by far preferable to land on lakes or well-protected bodies of water. But as soon as there are a few waves, you are sure to be in for a rough landing.'
(Photo Frans Lemmens)

After the hop over the Atlantic Ocean from the Cabo Verde Islands, flying to the nearest island on the way to Natal in Brazil, you will meet this awesome view. There, 350km from Natal, in the middle of the vast Atlantic Ocean, we found one of those truly majestic fantasy islands. Named Fernando de Noronha, the archipelago is virtually unknown in Europe and North America, but it has a most interesting history. The island had been an important supply station for vessels that sailed from Europe to Salvador de Bahia in Brazil since the early days of sailing over the oceans that started in the 16th century after the discovery of America. With the arrival of the steamboat, the island lost its function and since the early 1900s, the Brazilian government reshaped it into a huge prisoner camp (their version of Alcatraz) for political prisoners. There was no escape for the exiles, and the only entertainment that they had was the frequent arrival of the Aéropostale and Lufthansa flying boats on their way to Europe or Argentina. The old station building can still be found there. Named Aéropostale, it is a tribute to the pioneer's work of French pilot and adventurer Jean Mermoz.

(Photo Frans Lemmens)

Fernando de Noronha, Brazil.
Jean Mermoz, before he disappeared during his last Ocean crossing in December 1936, frequently landed in this same bay, right under the rocky Spike. This large stretch of water was well protected against the huge ocean swell and was an ideal 'refuge' for the flying boats that landed here for refilling their empty fuel tanks. There was no way for an optional landing if the weather was rough with high swell, so they had to do the landing, no matter what conditions they met. This bay was the ideal spot for such no-option landing in the middle of the Atlantic.
(Photo Frans Lemmens)

Fernando de Noronha, Brazil.
Catalina Z-CAT is about to land in the lagoon. With the two Teton mountains in the distance and the Needle on the left, an epic sea plane water landing is imminent; the first since the war years (the anti-submarine patrolling Catalinas must have landed here before the airstrip on the island was constructed).

Brazil has a rich history in aviation and its Air Force (FAB) keeps a number of shiny warbirds in perfect condition. The Catalina also had a very long career in the FAB until 1984, when their last Cat was phased out. That was only nine years before we arrived! There was a lot of attention surrounding the arrival of our Z-CAT and the aircraft was proudly parked alongside the contemporaries of the Catalina: a B-25 Mitchell bomber and a B-26 Invader were good company for our Catalina for the night.
(Photo Erik Sampers)

Our arrival in Natal was most interesting for a variety of reasons. The river was also the landing site for the inter-war flight routes from Europe to South America. Both Aéropostale and Lufthansa used the river, the station and the ramps at the Potengi River. Where the river ended in the Atlantic, we found an old fortress, 'Forte dos Reis Mages' built by the Portuguese in 1598 and once conquered by the Dutch. By sheer coincidence, our Catalina and the local fishermen used the same colors for their 'boats'.
(Photo Erik Sampers)

Party time at the Aéropostale building in Natal, Brazil. With national television coverage on GLOBO TV, the local VIPs were invited to a welcome party on behalf of the arrival of Z-CAT. You see here the old terminal building at the Potengi River where the flying boats landed on their way to Rio and Buenos Aires. The building was in fairly good shape with many signs from a glorious Interbellum flying boat past. But today's Intercontinental jets fly at 10,000 meters over Natal, never landing again next to the beautiful sand dunes and beaches of Natal, which we enjoyed so much.

(Photo Erik Sampers)

Northern Brazil, overlooking the Atlantic Coast. Hundreds of miles of sand dunes filled with rainwater. Lençóis Maranhenses National Park in Barreirinhas, Maranhão.
(Photo Frans Lemmens)

Belém, Brazil. Catalina Z-CAT together with other aviation legends. In 1993, the Curtiss C-46 Commandos were still found here and there but spent their final days of operations in Brazil. They were put up for sale as their days were numbered: the Brazilian Jet and Turbo Prop Commuter aircraft were taking over the market from the old War Horses. Way too slow and flying too low with non-compressed aircraft, the distances in Brazil are of such proportions that their cruising speed of 250–300 km/h became a serious drawback compared the more modern competition flying at 600+ km/h.
(Photo Frans Lemmens)

In the city of Manaus, I noticed this PBY-6A Catalina of the Brazilian Air Force, placed as a Gate Guard at the entrance of the Naval Base from where they used to fly. PBYs were operational in Brazil until 1984.
(Photo Corine Quarterman-Wiesman)

Z-CAT overflying the immense Amazon River: only jungle and rivers as far as the eye can see. Here and there, we notice settlements or a riverboat. This view would not change for hours. Near Manaus, we came to the junction where the Rio Amazon and the Rio Negro come together. We opted for a landing in the Black River, with definitely fewer mosquitos. (Photo Erik Sampers)

Amazon region, East of Manaus, Brazil. We landed on the Rio Negro to spend the night in the jungle cabanas/huts, hidden in the jungle behind the riverboat. The first thing to do after our arrival was to dive into the black water of Rio Negro from the blister of our Catalina Z-CAT. But our passengers were not used to diving into a pitch-black jungle river, where you can expect the unexpected both in and outside the water. This was the Amazon, remember, but my first dive made them curious. 'Look, he's still alive, so can we follow? Yes, come on in'. And in they went; no one wanted to miss the thrill of swimming in the Rio Negro.

While everybody was out there in the water, we could not resist playing a hilarious trick to get everyone's immediate attention. A simple shout over the water: 'Crocodiles!' was the magic word to get everyone back on board in less than 20 seconds! 'So sorry, there are no crocodiles here; it was only a bunch of alligators. If you want, you can go back in.'

(Photo Frans Lemmens)

Where the Amazon River and Rio Negro meet we landed for a night stopover in comfy tree huts. Curious kids came over in their canoes to watch this spaceship that, out of the blue, had landed in their backyard. It took an hour to overcome their suspicion and meet us in our Catalina Z-CAT.
(Photo Erik Sampers)

Arriving just before sunset over the Rio Negro, it seemed we had landed in Paradise with no sounds other than the millions of birds and animals that were shrieking 'goodnight' to each other. We were sleeping in majestic tree huts, from where this photo was taken, a room with a view. Another lazy Sunday afternoon ended here, but this was one to remember forever!
(Photo Frans Lemmens)

Late afternoon, Amazon sunset over the Rio Negro. The overnight stay on the water carried some risks. The mooring cable, the correct setting of the anchor, and possible leaks created during the last water landing when a couple of rivets popped out under the waterline, were all points of attention which meant that, often, one of the crew members slept on board while parked. A bilge pump, running on a small generator, was always on standby to get the water out. A 50-year-old aircraft has its own little inconveniences with leaks and tweaks that require some special care.

Very early the next morning, we departed from our paradise at the Rio Negro, and made our way north to Venezuela and Tobago/Trinidad. Mike Terryl, our co-pilot, waves at the photographer Erik Sampers and asks him to climb back on board, almost ready for takeoff. No wonder this is named the Rio Negro. The water is really dark.
(Photo Erik Sampers)

Right: Coral Reefs of the Caribbean and the Atlantic Ocean. With our low flight speed and altitude, the Catalina blister makes the best platform to view those wonders of the world.
(Photo Erik Sampers)

Left: After our visit to the Amazon, we flew, via Manaus, up north over the jungles into Venezuela and on to the Caribbean Sea. Trinidad was our stopover for the night. The next day, we flew over Saint Martin/Sint Maarten, on our way to the British Virgin Islands (BVI).
(Photo Erik Sampers)

Above: Z-CAT making a splash while taking off, Virgin Gorda, The British Virgin Islands. Even a moderate chop on the water can cause quite a lot of water being sprayed over the aircraft when hitting a wave with the clipper bow. When sitting in the cockpit or in the blister, for seconds you may see only water coming over, as if you have just boarded a submarine. Also, the old lady had some leaks here and there and water dripped in from many places. It did not have a water-/air-tight compressed airframe with double-glazing and floor heating like a modern aircraft.
(Photo Frans Lemmens)

Right: Tortola, British Virgin Islands. With our flying motorhome, Catalina Z-CAT, we visited another event organized by Peter Stuyvesant Travel. It was the 'Blue Marlin Trophy': a sailing competition for sailing yachts and surfboards, hopping from island to island around the BVI. We followed the tour in the Catalina. From the main island, Tortola, we sailed out to the exotically named Jost van Dyke, Virgin Gorda, and Anegada islands – some of the most idyllic Caribbean islands. There are worse places to fly and to sail in this world.

Life was a Breeze for all participants. Seeing this photo reminds me of the Mary Hopkins song: 'Those were the days my friend, we thought they'd never end.'
(Photo Frans Lemmens)

Peter Stuyvesant Travel

Tortola, The British Virgin Islands, July 1993. With a helicopter hanging overhead, the Catalina Z-CAT cruises over the water after just another landing on the sea.

Grand Cayman, Cayman Islands. Our Catalina Z-CAT was the diving platform from where we went snorkeling to watch the stingrays.

Below: Chetumal, Yucatan, Mexico. We landed on the Mexican Caribbean coast of Yucatan near the city of Chetumal. Armelle and Thomas, our French passengers, were having a pina colada on a little pier with 'les pieds dans l'eau'. With the Catalina moored for the night (in the background), we went for dinner at the Beach Hotel. There was no such thing as boredom during the Catalina Odyssey.
(Photo Frans Lemmens)

Right: New York harbor, USA. In the background is Lower Manhattan with the Twin Towers and Governor's Island right below us. We were about to make the slogan 'Make the Flight of a Lifetime' come true.

From Teterboro Airport, we started with a low fly-pass over the Hudson River. It was a beautiful Sunday morning and nothing could stop us from making an awesome sightseeing tour and a water landing right below us, in the NYC harbor.
(Photo Frans Lemmens)

Above: Big rays came to us, curious and hungry for the small squid that we carried in our hands to lure them. Suddenly, they were all over the place. We could see them approach us as dark patches under water, touching our legs for attention and food. Those leg-shaving techniques scared the girls, not used to dealing with such weird pets.
(Photo Erik Sampers)

New York, USA, July 1993. The unthinkable was about to happen: a water landing with a Catalina in NYC harbor, right in front of the Statue of Liberty! At the last moment, one little snag almost spoiled the party. As we were on our final approach and about to touch the water, there was a sudden torrential summer downpour. If the rain had arrived one minute earlier, the Port Authority (having blocked all shipping in the harbor for our landing) would have canceled the landing permit – which had been so long-debated with them by my sister Corine. The sunny sky had disappeared for 20 minutes or so, but the dark clouds added drama to the water landing. The photo depicts a sort of eerie mist created by the downpour.

(Photo Frans Lemmens)

NYC Harbor, next to Manhattan Island. We were out on the water with Z-CAT, waiting for permission to take off. Suddenly, the sky cleared up, the sun came back in view and we were permitted to make the takeoff run over the harbor, which had been closed to shipping for 20 minutes. We were airborne again, just in time to give way to this beautiful classic cruiser ship that greeted us with a long blow of its horns. All the passengers were waving at us during this coincidental encounter of two icons of the bygone era of majestic air and sea transport. The World Trade Centre's Twin Towers add to the drama of this awesome picture.
(Photo Frans Lemmens)

Z-CAT overflying Manhattan: the New Yorker Hotel is right below us and the sinister dark rain cloud is moving northwards, making way for the first rays of sun to break through. How lucky could we be?
(Photo Erik Sampers)

Manhattan, New York, USA. Our Catalina Z-CAT in a photo that can never be recreated. The World Trade Center in the background is gone forever. Can you imagine making such a low fly pass over Manhattan in a vintage aircraft? All the passengers were totally mesmerized by the view 500 feet below as we slowly passed by. We did it in 1993, and this flight will most probably never ever happen again in this place at this altitude! Too much has changed since then. But we still have the photos as souvenirs.
(Photo Erik Sampers)

Above: This PBY water bomber or aerial firefighter ship, nr 704, flew for the Province of Newfoundland and was still fully operational when we met her in 1993 on our way up north to Greenland. Our Captain, Bryan McCook, met the Captain of the Canadian PBY. The PBY had no blisters but internal water tanks that could carry a total of 1,000 gallons (3,800 litres) for the standard PBY, while the Super Catalina could carry 1,500 gallons (5,700 litres) of water. Under the access ladder, you can see one of the water tank's hatches in open position. Refilling of the tanks could be done on land, or by a 'touch-and-go' water landing on a lake or river. While skimming over the water, an underbelly retractable scoop filled the tanks in a matter of 30–40 seconds max. Once flying over the fire, the lower belly hatches could be opened from the cockpit and the water dumped. With the Cat's 90–100 mph airspeed, the tons of water that were dropped would be pulverized by the impact of the airstream and create a huge rain shower, delivered right on the spot as in a precision bombing run. It is exactly in this role that the PBY Catalina/Canso found its true post-war vocation as the ideal platform for delivering water where no other transport could bring the firefighting load so fast, and recharge so efficiently, with minimum turnaround time needed! It is mainly due to this role that the Catalina/ Canso could survive for another staggering 50 years after the war.
(Photo Erik Sampers)

Left: St John's, Newfoundland, Canada. Catalina Z-CAT meets his 'brother in arms': one of the many firefighting Cansos from Canada that were still operational in 1993. This is ship, 704, is in its typical 1990's orange/green livery of the Canadian Aerial Firefighting fleet.

Above: My sister Corine (right) and Pierre Jaunet (inside the Catalina on the left) completing their paperwork with the Customs Officers before we could leave American air space. The arrival of the Catalina always attracted a good deal of attention from the authorities and from jetliner pilots too. Mostly very friendly and curious to know what our flight plan was. But in a few cases, it was very awkward to convince the officers that we had no evil intention of smuggling drugs. Sometimes, our documents were checked over and over again. It could take a few hours and if you were in a hurry, it was better to keep your temper on ice! And there would be ice galore on the next trip that we were to make – to the Arctic.
(Photo Frans Lemmens)

Qaqortoq, Greenland. The Cat was anchored right in between the icebergs that were scattered all over the inlet. Local Inuits welcomed the plane and passengers – not a sight they saw every day out there in Southwest Greenland.
(Photo Erik Sampers)

Maneuvering the Catalina to its mooring position on one engine in Qaqortoq, Greenland – a Scandinavian-looking fishing town where the Cat was moored for the night.

From Greenland to Iceland: we had a wonderful flight in very sunny weather and arrived in Höfn, a city on the east coast of Iceland. The next day we planned a water landing in the nearby Jökulsárlón Glacier Lake. We went in a little dinghy to the centre of the lake and waited for the Cat to come in, just next to where we were positioned. Captain Bryan McCook found the lake too small for a real water landing and decided to go for a touch-and-go, skimming over the water. With the icebergs in the background, we were able to take some fascinating photos.
(Photo Erik Sampers)

Jökulsárlón Lake, Iceland. Our Captain is about to fully open the throttles again, in order to pull the Catalina out of the glacier lake and clear the hills at the lake's border. Note the 'whipped cream' shaped icebergs behind the Cat.
(Photo Erik Sampers)

Aberdeen, Scotland. In our last leg, from the Faroe Islands to Amsterdam, the nr. 1 engine started to play up. Captain Bryan McCook throttled the engine back over the North Sea, sent an Emergency Call out, and diverted the flight to Aberdeen, Scotland.

For a couple of hours, we were flying at lower speed and steadily losing altitude. Pierre ordered us to make a list of the least valuable goods, which could be dumped overboard in order to save weight and altitude. The tension on board slowly grew; silence had replaced the chatter. The tension grew further when, suddenly, a huge Sikorsky (or Westland WS-61) Sea King helicopter came alongside us. Its orange color and the words 'Sea Rescue' written on the side did not help put us at ease. As we slowly but steadily sank in altitude, the inevitable dumping of fuel was also activated and things became a bit worrying. Maybe we should prepare for a water landing on open sea?

But at an altitude of maybe 400–500 feet we saw land, and we all felt the relief of that sight. Captain McCook had no time to relax: he was focused on the imminent single-engine landing, just over the coastline, at Aberdeen Airport. He realized only too well that he had one single chance to land the stricken Cat; there was no power or altitude left for an overshoot.

Flying over the golf links north of Aberdeen, we followed the river and made a sharp turn to the right. The wheels were dropped out late in order to keep our airspeed. Less than a minute later, they hit the runway. It was a smooth landing on one engine: Bryan McCook and his co-pilot Mike had done an awesome job, bravo!

The Cat was soon surrounded by huge fire trucks. It was an official emergency landing. In hindsight, I guess the flight at the very end was tighter than most of the passengers had realized. They were all so happy and soon chatting away again. Corine was doing her job efficiently and within hours, all our passengers were booked on a scheduled flight back to Holland.

Pierre and his crew stayed behind with the stricken Catalina. They had to wait for their new engine, which was flown in from Paris, and, a week later, they made their belated last flight with the Catalina Odyssey to Amsterdam.

Z-CAT making her very last water landing in Holland on the IJsselmeer near Lelystad, in early August 1993. From here, the Cat flew the following day to Paris, France, and later on to her home base in Harare, Zimbabwe, never to return again to Europe. Shortly after the Catalina Odyssey, this Cat was sold to New Zealand and made another epic flight from Africa over Asia to her new homeland, where she has remained ever since (see also Chapter 5, The Survivors).

The second Catalina Odyssey took place in August 1994. The format of the trip changed in certain aspects. For the contestants we skipped the start and finish in Europe, so the two Transatlantic crossings were this time made with a light-weight Catalina with only crew and fuel on board, which was easier to clear with the insurance company.

The passengers boarded in Natal, NE Brazil, and were flown out to the Brazilian Island of Fernando de Noronha, 350 km north east of Natal. The trip was again divided into four legs of ten days each, making a total travel time of 40 days for the six young passengers per leg from France, Belgium and Holland.

After spectacular water landings in the scenic bays of Fernando, we flew with the Cat to Bahia de Salvador and on to Rio de Janeiro to make another of those epic water landings, this time in front of Sugar Loaf Mountain. Next, we flew – via the famous waterfalls of Iguaçu – to Bolivia's capital, La Paz, and on to Lake Titicaca for another water landing. Next was Cusco, in Peru, where we visited the ruins of the enigmatic Inca city of Machu Picchu. From there, we continued on to Lima and northwards along the Pacific coast to Quito, Ecuador.

Flying over the Panama Canal, we entered the Caribbean and saw the archipelago of San Andrés, Providencia and Santa Catalina – one of the true gems of all the treasure islands that we encountered. The next stopover was in Cayo Coco and Havana, Cuba, before we flew to Bimini Island, in the Bahamas. The Grande Finale took place in Miami, from where the Catalina left (empty again) for Europe, via a direct hop from Newfoundland to Shannon, Ireland, and finally flying back home to Duxford, Cambridge, UK.
(Photo Pascal Baudry)

The Peter Stuyvesant Travel event logo for the second Catalina Odyssey trip in 1994.

Aircraft history: VR-BPS Consolidated PBY-5A 'Catalina' (BuNo 46633 – c/n 1997). This Catalina was one of 59 PBY-5As to be built by the Consolidated Aircraft Corporation at its New Orleans plant at Lake Pontchartrain. It was ordered under contract number NOa(s)-464 for the US Navy and the serials BuNos 46580 to 46638 were allocated. The subject of this profile was given the c/n 1997 and serial BuNo 46633. It was one of the last PBY-5As to be built as, shortly after it rolled off the production line at the very end of 1944, the -5A was replaced by the model -6A.

The US Navy took BuNo 46633 on charge on 5 January 1945, and, between that date and its eventual military retirement, it is known to have served with various squadrons including FAW-14, VPB-100, VP-53, NARTU San Diego, NARTU Los Amitos, and NARTU Memphis. Squadron locations included Pearl Harbor, Alameda, Chincoteague, and Seattle. It was eventually struck off charge in August 1956, and entered a period of storage at Litchfield Park in Arizona.

In September 1964, CF-MIR was sold to Laurentian Air Services and a year later went to Survair. By this time, CF-MIR had been converted for an aerial survey role, and early on in its time with Survair it was fitted with large plates containing electromagnetic survey gear at each wingtip. In subsequent years various other types of geophysical survey equipment were hung arounc the airframe and the wings.

(Photo Frans Lemmens)

In 1956, the Catalina VR-BPS shown here was purchased by Trade-Ayer of Linden, New Jersey, and registered N10023. It was later sold in Canada to Miron & Freres of Cartierville, Quebec, for use as an executive transport. They had it registered as CF-MIR and converted to so-called Super Canso S/C 1000 status. This involved the removal of military equipment including bow and rear turrets as well as the Pratt & Whitney engines. The bow was faired over and the power-plants were replaced with 1,700hp Wright Cyclone R-2600s. The rudder was replaced with a squared-off design of greater area to give more directional control. An airstair was installed in the rear hull to allow easier access whilst on the ground. The modifications were finished off with prop-spinners, wheel hub-caps and a small dinghy under each wing. The conversion work was carried out by Noorduyn-Norseman Aircraft of St Laurent, PQ, who designated it a Super Canso S/C 1000.
(Photo Frans Lemmens)

In mid-1967, the US registration N608FF was briefly allocated but it was restored to the Canadian register shortly thereafter. During this period it was operated by Firefly Inc., Aero Service Corp., and Barringer Research.

Back in Canada, it flew with Questor Surveys and Geoterrex Surveys/Terra Surveys. Geoterrex flew CF-MIR out of South Africa for contract work and in 1984 placed the Catalina up for sale. It was purchased by a consortium of British air show pilots and flown to England in its new marks G-BLSC. Its new owners, Plane Sailing Air Displays Ltd, refurbished it and flew it at hundreds of air displays throughout Europe, initially in RAF Coastal Command colors as JV928/Y of 210 Squadron and later as 9754/P of 162 Squadron, Royal Canadian Air Force. In 1994 it was also flown to South and Central America and back. Just prior to this it was re-registered in Bermuda, first as VR-BPS and later as VP-BPS. In 1995 it represented Coastal Command in the 50th Anniversary of VE Day flypast over Central London and the Royal Family at Buckingham Palace. Whilst taking part in a promotional flight in July 1998 the Catalina suffered an accident on Southampton Water and subsequently sank. The resultant damage led to the airframe being 'written off'.

Can you imagine any other plane that has this feature? Sitting comfortably on a couch placed in the rear compartment, you open up the blister window by sliding its eyelid up and you feel the wind in your face. Flying low (at 500 feet or less) and slow (90–100 mph), it feels like riding in a fast open top sports car. A room with a view, plus that aircraft can land on almost any stretch of water that you spot below you. Once you've landed right there in that blue lagoon, that same couch will become a diving platform for a swim or some snorkeling in the crystal clear water.
(Photo Frans Lemmens)

Fernando de Noronha, the Archipelago 350 km NE of Natal in the Atlantic Ocean. Overlooked by the famous needle, we enjoyed ourselves with some diving from the Catalina wing, swimming, and snorkeling in the warm emerald waters of the island. With less than [illegible],000 inhabitants and no industry, all development and construction activities are restricted. The island has been declared an Environmental Protection Area and has a limited daily influx of tourists. What a relief: there is no mass tourism industry with big multi-story hotels, no port and no cruiser ships with 2,500 tourists on board, so there is no air/water pollution. In that splendid isolation, dolphins and turtles come here to mate and breed by the thousands. You would not believe what you can see underwater with only a simple mask and snorkel. (Photo Pascal Baudry)

Above: The forgotten prisoner island Fernando de Noronha suddenly acquired a new supply role in the early stages of WWII. As General Rommel was invading North Africa in 1941 and threatened the British military presence in Egypt and the Eastern Mediterranean Sea, the US military war machine came to help with massive supply of aircraft that were flown over to the North African theatre of war, via the Southern Atlantic route. Flying over the Caribbean, the route went to Belem, Natal and on to Fernando, before making the hop over the Atlantic to West Africa. Before the big four-engine USAAF bombers arrived in large numbers, the flight range of the two-engine aircraft was much shorter, and they could barely make the hop over the Atlantic without a fuel-stop. Fernando was ideally positioned as a much-needed refuel station but required a landing strip to be constructed over the island's muddy inland. A fixed 'Aircraft Carrier' was built in the Atlantic. Our Catalina stands here on that American-made airstrip, with the island's landmark in the backdrop.

Above: In 1942, the US Military sent over a contingent to Fernando de Noronha for the construction of an airfield and barracks, providing a supply station/emergency base on the air-route from Brazil to Western Africa. Shortly after, the US Navy established on the island a weather station and an anti-submarine patrol base from where the PBY Catalinas and Lockheed Venturas made their long patrol flights over this vital part of the Atlantic Ocean. During our stay on the island in 1993, we slept in one of those barracks, which were still there, now acting as a makeshift tourist hotel. The island has pousadas, or small hostels, and huts/cabanas, but we preferred the barracks. When else would you have the opportunity to sleep in an authentic wartime-built barrack?

Right: Same place, same type of aircraft, but this photo was taken 50 years earlier. Strategically positioned in the Atlantic where so many shipping lines crossed, Fernando was also an ideal station for Allied anti-submarine patrol flights against German U-boats, which were increasingly wandering into the Southern Atlantic.

Opposite: As we left the paradise-like archipelago of Fernando, we flew south along the Brazilian east coast. Our next stopover was Salvador de Bahia. In the bay, we spotted a little island where we thought it would be good to have a lobster lunch on the beach. Brazil still has that laid-back mentality, 'Do what you like as long as you do not bother others'. So, we just landed in the lagoon, dropped the wheels out in the water and pulled the Cat up on the Beach under its own power!
(Photo Frans Lemmens)

Salvador de Bahia, Brazil. The restaurant had no valet parking service so the owner decided to welcome us and waved with wild hand signals where to park the aircraft – as if he had such guests every week and maybe he expected yet another aircraft to park right behind us? He was very determined to reserve some room for the next spaceship to come in. A hilarious little incident, but by the time we were finished with our lunch and Captain Paul Warren Wilson wanted to take the Cat back into the water under its own power, the wheels had sunk deep into the sand by about a foot, and all the sunbathers on the beach had to help to push her out of the sand trap. With the two engines running at full throttle, it was a noisy and windy job but they all loved it and had with us a most memorable 'Lazy Sunday Afternoon' on that Bahia beach.

(Photo Frans Lemmens)

Salvador de Bahia, Brazil. Our Catalina in a low flypast around the palm trees, just after a spectacular takeoff from Bahia Bay.
(Photo Frans Lemmens)

Rio de Janeiro, Brazil. In the bay right under the famous Sugar Loaf, with Copacabana Beach in front of us, and the Mountain of de Corcovado and the Christ the Redeemer Statue in the distance.

Introduction to an Emergency Landing

With a helicopter overhead taking scenic footage of the water landing and takeoff from this legendary spot, the Catalina was about to start its run over the bay waters. As Paul pushed the throttles fully open for maximum thrust, puffs of white smoke suddenly escaped from the exhaust over the wing – an alarming sign that I noticed while sitting in the port blister, but was not yet visible in the cockpit on the gauges. They indicated that all systems were OK.

Our Captain, Paul Warren Wilson, wrote a report in the August 1997 issue of *FlyPast* Magazine about his experiences during the second Catalina Odyssey trip in August 1994. Here he describes what went wrong during the Rio water landing:

Operating from the local commuter airport, Santos Dumont, the program called for a water landing in the bay, just two miles away from the airport. With a full load of excited young people, film crew, and a Bell helicopter hovering overhead to film it all, we touched down as planned – if a little solidly – on the rather choppy water. So far, so good, now reposition for the takeoff run – plenty of water over the cockpit as we do this; with two feet of chop and 12 knots wind we can't help splashing around a bit, especially as we swing the aircraft one way, then the other to turn downwind. Checks after landing, checks before takeoff – co-pilot Ray Coates normally flies Jumbos for British Airways and he's more used to civilized discussions in the cockpit than the highly physical job of getting a Catalina lined up on the sea, opening and shutting the sliding window in the right sequence to let in some fresh air for demisting, but also to stop the next wave from drenching you. You learn fast on this one!

Rio de Janeiro, Brazil. In the bay right under the famous Sugar Loaf.
(Photo Frans Lemmens)

Paul Warren Wilson account continues:

As we are about to apply power to takeoff, the calm voice of Hans Wiesman comes over the intercom. He knows about flying and would not interrupt now unless it was important: 'There are drops of oil coming from the left engine, quite big.'

But there are always drops of oil coming from the engines; we spend our whole life changing seals here, tweaking them to minimize oil-leaks – for the engines were designed in the 1930s and a certain amount of oil leakage is inevitable. Still, Hans would not say this unless he had seen something wrong.

We must either stop the engines, in which case we shall be drifting with only our anchor to hold us, and a threatening shoreline in the distance, or we must try to take off before any possible problem became worse.

Whichever, it must be done at once. Not the kind of decision I like. But the consequences of drifting out of control on this sea are potentially more serious, so the power comes on, the engines are smooth, the temperatures and pressure still good, the Cat responds with a couple of surges of water over the cockpit and then a clear view as she rises up to the step, smacking through the chop, final check, and we have good power indications.

We're safely airborne now above single engine control speed, situation rapidly improving . . . but then, of course, the inevitable falling oil pressure on the left engine . . .

Santos Dumont Airport, Rio de Janeiro, Brazil. Our Catalina's emergency landing, after the left-hand, or nr.1, engine broke down during the water start from the bay.
(Photo Frans Lemmens)

Paul Warren Wilson continued his story:

> . . . Oily blue/white smoke starts to increase from the engine, classic sign of a cylinder problem. But we only have a mile to go on finals to Santos Dumont; a quick 'Pan' call alerts Air Traffic of our problem. We are on the ground almost before there is time to feather the engine. We keep enough speed on the runway to let us taxi off and reach a suitable stopping area – the Catalina cannot taxi far with only one engine running, due to the relative positions of the engines and the brakes.
>
> Once we had made our emergency landing at Santos Dumont Airport in Rio, the next few hours were predictable. 'What's the problem?' – 'How long will it take to fix it?' – 'Why is all that oil on the plane?' and other similar helpful interceptions, all accompanied by an eager film crew and photographers, anxious for that special shot of the crew reacting to a real-life situation. We smile for them and get on with the job, hiding our sinking hearts.
>
> Thirty minutes later, the oil filter produces its telling evidence – a mess of metal particles, very pretty if you like shiny things, but not what we like to see. Whether it is a single cylinder with a broken piston ring (which we believe it was) or something more serious, the fact that we still have 100 hours' tour flying ahead of us means that an engine change is required. The following days were reminiscent of the problem-solving tests I had seen 20 years earlier during my Biggin Hill selection for the RAF, but on a rather grander scale.

Above: Crew checking the engine after the emergency landing, Santos Dumont Airport, Rio de Janeiro. Left-hand Prop is feathered; the fire brigade is on guard.
(Photo Frans Lemmens)

Right: As we all stepped out after the emergency landing on Santos Dumont Airport, we saw this oil spill on the fuselage, not a good sign.
(Photo Hans Wiesman)

Santos Dumont Airport, Rio de Janeiro. After the emergency landing at the airport with a troubled engine, our flight engineer Garry was the first one who tried to diagnose the cause. Reading the expression on his face, we anticipated some devastating news.
(Photo Pascal Baudry)

Paul continued:

> . . . The problem: your aircraft is in South America, your spare engine is in the USA, your crew consists of yourself, your engineer Garry, and your co-pilot. You have only the tools you brought with you, and the availability of any hangarage, work platforms, lifting gear etc. depends upon your ability to negotiate with the Portuguese-speaking staff of the local airline, VASP!
>
> The requirement: get the aircraft back in the air at the earliest possible opportunity or the whole tour will be cancelled. Moreover, provide your estimate to completion now, and it is not good being either optimistic or pessimistic, you have to be right. There were hotel bookings for 20 people to consider, and a rotation by airline of the next set of participants from Europe at Lima, Peru, on the other side of the continent, in 10 days time.
>
> The engine change was successfully completed in seven days, a time which we could not better even at home base. The Catalina was serviceable again and rejoined the tour proper at La Paz and the success of the whole project was recovered. A potentially disastrous situation was saved, and Killer Cat was back in her element again.

So many years later, I offer my compliments and gratitude for what Paul Warren Wilson, Garry Short and all other guys did there in that short time. They saved the total Transamerican Tour, and with that, we made a great success out of it. Bravo!

Once the engine was replaced in Rio de Janeiro, Paul Warren Wilson took the Catalina on a flight to Bolivia in order to continue the Catalina Odyssey as planned. The rendezvous with me was made at El Alto Airport, Bolivia, at an altitude of 13,500ft (4,200m) in the High Andes.
(Photo Pascal Baudry)

Paul Warren Wilson goes on to describe their journey from Rio to La Paz:

> We had flown from Rio to La Paz in the minimum time, two days – with an intermediate stop at a border town between Brazil and Paraguay. The whole operation had been at low level so far. Now, as we confront the Bolivian Altiplano (3,650m–4,250m alt.), there is some serious climbing to be done. A standard Catalina simply would not have the puff to fly this route, but our bigger engines give us a ceiling of 20,000ft (6,100m), more than adequate to cross the Andes and even retain a fair single-engine option.
>
> Approaching 10,000ft (3,050m) the fuel booster pumps come in, as the engine driven pumps need some help at that height. Then, it's time to don our portable oxygen equipment and check our flow settings. At 12,500ft (3,800m) it seems incredible that we still have another 1,000ft to climb to reach landing altitude for La Paz – but then it is the highest (international) airport in the world.
>
> The Cat takes it all in her stride; she has seen it all, done it all many times before in her long career. She is happy to climb and climb, but experience has shown that she is happier making a long, slow climb than being forced up at the last minute, so we let her cruise on up at 100–200ft per minute, always keeping an eye on the engine gauges for any abnormalities. The manifold pressure at full throttle is unusually low – around 25 inches, a consequence of the height – but all is well. Around 15,000ft (4,500m) we are high enough for the approach into La Paz, where the scenery is stark in its beauty – sand-brown land, sand-brown only, duck-egg blue sky pasted with cotton wool tufts, brilliant white snow caps on the mountains, a black tarmac runway 27 ruled out on the ground. It looks so like the simulator, it's hard to believe it's real.
>
> There is a great excitement at La Paz, for the Cat's return has been eagerly awaited. The cameras are running and in quick time we fly out to Lake Titicaca, the highest navigable lake in the world, for a fleeting visit. The following morning sees us filming at the airfield, an incredible piece of the past, with friends from the Cat's own era parked at every corner. DC-3s, DC-6s, C-46s – they are all there, hauling meat to the city from the farms below. A graveyard at first sight, but more like a hospital as you look closer. We look on in awe as buckets of fuel and oil are lifted by hand to replenish for the next flight – say 1,000 gallons, at 2 gallons per bucket, that means 500 bucketfuls!

Above: El Alto Airport, La Paz, Bolivia.
Our participants from Europe arrived to fly the second leg of the 1994 Catalina Odyssey from La Paz all the way up north into the Caribbean. But the promised Catalina was still in Rio, left behind for an engine change that would take a week or so. The show must go on; from La Paz we were heading for Cusco, Peru, in order to visit the sacred Inca hideout Machu Picchu. For that short-distance flight, we wanted to fly in style and hired this immaculate Convair CV 440 Metropolitan from Bolivian-based Lineas Aereas Canedo with Reg.nr. CP-2237.

It was no Catalina, but it was at least an aircraft made by the same manufacturer as the Catalina, Consolidated Aircraft, later named Convair. This aircraft type made its maiden flight in 1955, ten years after the last Catalina was built. It was Convair's last multi-engine piston prop aircraft; three years later the first Intercontinental Jets as Douglas DC-8 and Boeing B-707 were introduced. Their arrival would very soon mark the end of an era for this type of reciprocal engines on big airliners. The Convair survived for a long time on the shorter commuter lines. Even during my last visit to El Alto in August 2017 I again found a Convair, still operational. For more photos of vintage aircraft, follow my blog at www.dc3dakotahunter.com.

Above: Lake Titicaca, Bolivia, at 3,650 m altitude.
With our Catalina, we had planned to make a historical first ever Catalina water landing on the highest navigable lake in the world, Lake Titicaca! Flying in a nearly empty Cat from El Alto Airport, La Paz, we arrived at the sunny landing site on the lake, just in front of the Lakeside Hotel (seen in the backdrop). Suddenly I felt violent gusts jerking hard on the airframe. Captain Paul Warren Wilson seemed to have some doubts about the rapidly changing weather and kept flying in orbits for longer than ever; I could feel he was not at ease. Every time we went down for a final approach, there was that reluctance felt by our Captain as the wingtip floats were never lowered. I knew it was again only a low fly pass to inspect the wind force over the lake with no intention of really landing.

Finally, in the last run, I heard the grinding sound of the electric motors that lowered the floats. I strapped myself into a seat in the back, anticipating a rough landing after all that hesitation. A Bolivian cameraman was sitting next to me and almost fainted from fear, not capable of doing what he should be doing: filming the landing from inside the aircraft.

We must have been some 15 feet above the water level, and, in spite of the hefty turbulence, it felt good to be landing on the sacred Inca lake. But just before we were about to touch the water, with both engines throttled back, a micro burst with an extreme downdraft wind came rolling in from over the mountain ridge behind the hotel. The Catalina was slammed violently onto the chilly waters, and as I looked outside, I saw the radio aerial snap like a kite rope. The very harsh touch on the water made an immense crushing sound, as I remember so well. The five of us were lifted up in our safety belts and pushed back into our seats. The cameraman peed his pants instantly and passed out while his expensive TV camera fell out of his hands; not a single piece of film was ever made during that epic flight!

Luckily, our expert pilot, Captain Paul, saved the day and the Cat. He instantly aborted the water landing, and with full throttles and roaring engines each at peak power of 1,700 hp, he was able to climb out from under the huge but invisible pushing hand of the downdraft, or maybe, was it rather the perturbed Mountain God?

Strangely, this mishap had been predicted the evening before by an old local Inca Shaman who we had met in the hotel. He told us that the gods would not like us to land on their sacred lake; it had never been done before and for good reasons, he said. The cameraman was also there, filming the old Shaman. He heard the story and did not sleep that night, totally convinced that this was a bad omen and that we would crash in the lake. Well, why did you step on board? The Boss had told him to, poor bastard; there was a lot of cleaning to be done after the flight in that seat of his. Seconds before that harrowing experience, nearly being slammed into the lake, this picture was taken by the hotel director from his speedboat.

As we flew back to La Paz, the lake showed a very different face: it was nasty, cold and dark. I shivered at the thought that we just had escaped from the wrath of the Mountain Gods. Paul later commented: 'We were lucky to have had no cargo or passengers on board. If this would have happened during a wheels-down landing on the ground, we quite likely would have crashed the plane.' Years later, I came back for a visit to the hotel and found this photo on the wall at the entry. Amazing picture, it could have been the very last flight of the Cat.

(Photo and account taken from my book The Dakota Hunter)

Below: All of our contestants were invited to sit in the co-pilot seat for a while and get some flight instructions on how to fly the Catalina. Our British captain, Paul Warren Wilson, was the perfect pilot for this trip. He is an ex-RAF Harrier jet pilot and later flew the B-747 Jumbo as his daily routine.

According to Paul in his *FlyPast* interview, the Catalina was in her element on this tour:

> (The Cat) was built for long-range flying and has a ruggedness not found in aircraft design these days. We also have the benefit of 16 modern passenger seats, a proper toilet and, of course, all the wonders of modern avionics – no less than four transceivers, and we have two transponders, as well as three GPS Receivers, Loran, fuel/air data computer, VOR, ILS, DME, ADF . . . In fact, getting lost in this Killer Cat is inexcusable, though I would never say impossible!
>
> Most important are our upgraded engines – Wright Cyclone R-2600s of 1,700 hp replacing the original Pratt & Whitney R-1830s with max 1,200 hp engines. These give a margin of safety that I personally consider important, for the aircraft can fly and climb happily on one engine, even at maximum weight and considerable altitude, whereas the standard Catalina will only climb on one engine under favourable circumstances.
>
> We carry life jackets and dinghies for all, as well as several sets of portable oxygen equipment for use on high altitude flights.

(Photo Frans Lemmens; text from the August 1997 issue of FlyPast magazine)

Above: Huaraz, Peru, with Mount Huascarán in the background. This place was the scene of one of the worst natural disasters in post-war history. In 1970, the village of Yungay was completely wiped out by a huge landslide triggered by an earthquake. The quake destabilized the glacier on the face of the 6,800-m high Mount Huascarán causing millions of pounds of solid rock, snow, ice, and mud to break away and rush over the glacier into the valley below. In the modern day Pompei-like disaster that followed the landslide buried the highland town of Yungay, killing most of its 25,000 inhabitants. At that time, it took days for the world to hear about it. Argentina sent a DC-6 with tents and blankets to help the 3,000 survivors but under their horrified eyes, that plane came in flying too high into the valley, right where our Catalina stands here. Sadly, in the overshoot, they were not able to make a turn in that narrow valley and the aircraft crashed, taking the lives of the crew as it burnt for hours and no one was able to help.
(Photo Frans Lemmens)

Otavalo, Ecuador. Our Catalina is flying in what seems almost an eclipse.
(Photo Frans Lemmens)

On our way out from Peru to Ecuador, we made a landing in Tumbes in the north of Peru. Just a couple of days prior to our arrival, a DC-6 from Bolivia came to a sad end. The plane had engine problems and landed here for repairs and when all was thought to be clear, the pilots started their engines again. As one engine played up, a small engine fire started from the exhaust pipe flame. With no fire extinguisher on hand at this airport, they called for the fire brigade from the town. It took some 15 minutes for them to arrive and meanwhile the flames had reached the second engine. The pilots jumped out of the cockpit and could only watch the Avgas fueling the fire that was slowly taking the 4-engine giant down on its knees.

As I stepped into the intact cockpit lying on its side, I found the original maintenance manual. It turned out to be an ex-Pan Am aircraft that once flew as a proud airliner all over the world, way back in the 1950s. I saw this same mishap later again in El Alto, Bolivia, also with a DC-6.

It is a sad experience to see such vintage aircraft being eaten by flames, while everyone around shouts and cries, and no one is able to stop this horrific scene. No fire extinguisher, not even a bucket of water around – that is Third World aviation. But it is that same world that makes me experience the nostalgia of those aircraft in their difficult survival against all odds. It is a time warp that brings back sweet memories from my childhood years in Borneo

Above: Overflying the High Andes mountain ridges from Peru to Ecuador, on our way to Otavalo, Ecuador. Passengers were dressed in fleece jackets to keep warm in the chilly temperatures at 12,000 feet above sea level. Note the respirator's inhaling tubes required at that high altitude. The oxygen bottle stands in between the contestants' legs, and the walls and ceiling of the aircraft are soundproofed and thermally insulated with special blankets. The comfortable seats came from modern airliners.

Above: On our way up northwards, we flew over Panama. Catalina Passengers looking at Panama Canal below them.

Above: Landing on Laguna San Pablo, Ecuador. Our captain, Paul Warren Wilson, wrote the following account of his experiences of this moment during the 1994 Catalina Odyssey trip:

> Here in Ecuador, we landed at the glassy waters of the Laguna San Pablo – some 8,500 feet above sea level and offering just 9,000 feet of landing run. Volcanoes up to 15,000 feet on both sides, a marginal single-engine escape route and a land where some day the Gods will not welcome the first ever visit by a flying boat to their lake, so nothing less than perfection will do for this approach. Approach speed at 72 knots, steady shallow approach. Power set, concentrate. Surprisingly, the Cat is very slippery on finals, there will be no forgivingness now for a dirty dart on the water. We still have 90 knots ground speed due to the thin air up here. Must be ready for a big suck-down as we touch the mirror-surface water at that sort of contact speed. But we're in the groove, same as the last few practice approaches, everything is looking good, our after-touchdown plan is ready. Ken Emmott taught me that and he learned the hard way in the good old days of BOAC, when his captain brought in a Short Solent too fast, landed nose low, bounced three times and then nose dived under water, breaking the fuselage in half. They lived!

(Text: Report from the August 1997 issue of FlyPast magazine)

Right: In the Caribbean: Isla de Santa Catalina, next to Isla de Providencia, Colombia. After a dive from our Catalina, we headed for the beach of Santa Catalina Island, and discovered a hidden gem with not a single tourist around us. It was like a Treasure Island with sandy beaches, huge palm trees and on top of its mountain, the remnants of an age-old pirate nest with rusty gun barrels and fortifications.

Treasure Island? Yes, the local people told us that the famous buccaneer Captain Sir Henry Morgan had lived on this island for many years. He was a Welsh privateer, the real 'Pirate of the Caribbean'. After attacking and looting the Spanish silver ships that sailed from Cartagena to Spain, Captain Morgan allegedly acquired a fortune and it is rumored that much of it was hidden on this island. He took his slogan 'To Life, Love and Loot' with him to his grave. To this day no one has ever found his – no doubt – immense treasure trove, although once in a while locals still dig big holes, like moles, hoping to find what was left behind from Morgan's raiding trips.

(All photos on this page by Frans Lemmens)

Above: The PBY Catalina in its element, flying low and slow over the waters around Santa Catalina and Providencia in the Caribbean. The islands are barely known in Europe and USA. We met hardly any tourism. Yet, the beaches, waters and reefs of those islands are in my opinion ranking in the top 10 of the most scenic I have ever seen in my life; unspoiled and serene. And believe me, I have been to many places in the world.
(Photo Frans Lemmens)

Above: Providencia, Colombia: a bar near the beach, standing on a pier in the lukewarm waters of the Caribbean Sea. The Catalina flew us in for a pina colada, we did some swimming and sunbathing – what more would you like to have, Sir?
(Photo Frans Lemmens)

Right: Santiago de Cuba. At our landfall in Cuba, we made a majestic water landing in the bay of Santiago at the eastern side of the island and were struck by the quiet environment. There were no boats and only a small village of timber houses on the waterside, right on the other side of the bay of Santiago. We stopped the engines right next to the small pier to take some photos of the scene. Suddenly, a school of some 60–80 children arrived on the pier, all in their school uniforms. They lined up right in front of us and as the teacher arrived they started singing a Cuban song named 'Santa Catalina'.

I remember that little intermezzo so well, the sound of all their voices swelling over the water as more and more voices joined the a cappella, 'Adios, Santa Catalina, adios'. Slowly, we drifted away from the pier, all of us sitting on top of the wing, totally mesmerized. All the kids started waving 'goodbye' to us enthusiastically – an emotional impression from that awesome island in the sun, entangled in its outdated social political system. That was Cuba in 1994; ever since I have loved that island and have returned there quite a few more times.
(Photo Pascal Baudry)

Santiago de Cuba, Eastern Cuba. After a six-hour flight from San Andrés Island (the Caribbean Colombian Island), we arrived with our Catalina in the bay of Santiago de Cuba and made a water landing in a weird place. There were only a few yachts in the marina and hardly any shipping. Cuba has a long way to go but the government-owned Cubanacan Travel Agency gave us a warm welcome as we were towed to our mooring place in the harbor.

Cayo Coco, the island of a thousand flamingos, Cuba. It was a resort under construction with marinas and hotels. We landed in the sea and were wading through the water, taking our luggage out to the nearby hotel. Paul wanted to have the Cat on the beach, more or less out of the water, but did not want to ride up to it as we did before in Bahia. There, we were lucky that we could escape the sand trap, so this time we were better prepared and had the Cat parked on a sandy 'slipway' close to the water, facing the open sea. We needed the locals to pull the aircraft partly out of the water. It worked wonderfully: the next day, Paul started the engines and rode the Cat right back into the sea before we all waded through the water and boarded.
(Photo Frans Lemmens)

Cuba, Havana. Our final stopover in Cuba was Havana, where we stayed for a couple of days. The Catalina is seen here flying over the fortress standing on the entry of the bay of Havana. We were accompanied by an old Russian Mil helicopter that acted as the camera ship.
(Photo Frans Lemmens)

Alice Town, Bimini Island, Bahamas – with two streets, three hotels, four pubs and one small airstrip on the smaller island, just across the inlet of the lagoon that you see here in the photo.

Bimini, only 50 miles east of Miami, is the smallest of all the islands in the Bahamas. In the 1970s and 1980s it was also one of the hottest places, due to the large-scale drugs smuggling from here to Florida. Old propliners such as the DC-3/C-47 and the Curtiss C-46 Commando flew in by night from Colombia and landed on the strip, lit by torches. The contraband that they brought in was unloaded while the aircraft was parked just next to the beach along the airstrip. Fast Cigarette/offshore Powerboats took over the illicit cargo, and, in the heat of the night, departed full-speed in a wild ride to the hidden lagoons and beaches of Florida where the trucks and vans waited for the cargo to be brought over.

The locals rented their 'Big Game' marlin fishing boats to the tourists from Miami but soon got engaged in a more lucrative and even bigger game. Their small fishing boats were replaced by huge black powerboats with 4x150hp outboards and such appropriate names as 'The Midnight Express'. But, such extravagance attracted the attention of the US Coast Guard and the DEA, and they soon started a mini-war-on-drugs against the nightly operations from Bimini.

(Photo Frans Lemmens)

The victims of that mini-war-on-drugs around the Bahamas were still to be found, like relics of an Indiana Jones film. While out there with the Cat we could fly over the often-submerged wrecks; it was most interesting for us to take a look at them.

Two vintage aircraft from Colombia crashed in the direct vicinity of the Bimini airstrip. There is a story that one of the aircraft (a C-46) was on its final approach at night, very close to the landing strip but suddenly the pilots picked up an alarming message that a US Coast Guard ship was nearby. The pilots, in their panic, aborted the landing and tried to pull away from the scene, but with an overloaded aircraft and too-low speed, they stalled over the bay south of Bimini. The plane flipped over its wing and landed on its back in the shallow waters. The wheels are still protruding from the water as a tombstone for the two pilots who were killed in that action.

Later, the US Coast Guard started survey flights over the Caribbean with fast turbo prop aircraft stuffed with electronics and infrared cameras. They could detect low-flying drugs-runner aircraft that skimmed at night over the waters south east of Miami. In this way, they were able to track suspect aircraft before they approached the Bahamas. As they came flying over Cuba, their presence was picked up and with the superior speed of the tracking surveillance aircraft they were easy to follow. Some pilots of the detected aircraft panicked and tried to avoid a forced landing and their apprehension. This Colombian Tagua DC-3 perhaps opted to land on the nearest beach they could find in the pitch-dark night and ran away. Allegedly, the plane was found the next day but was empty: maybe a pre-planned landing out there, with the loss of the aircraft calculated as transport costs?

Bimini, Bahamas. Our Catalina landed next to an old stranded ship that for years was used as a target in shooting practicing by US Military aircraft that came flying over from Florida. With the ship well perforated now, it is an ideal artificial reef and breeding place for all sorts of ocean life, and a wonderful spot for scuba diving and snorkeling.

Catalina PBY-5A before landing in Bimini Bay, Bahamas.
(Photo Frans Lemmens)

Catalina PBY-5A flying over coral reef, Bimini, Bahamas.
(Photo Frans Lemmens)

Catalina PBY-5A landing in Bimini Bay, Bahamas. It was here that we suddenly got stuck and felt the sandy bottom scratch the keel below us. With some extra power on the engines, we came loose again from yet another sand trap.
(Photo Frans Lemmens)

Our final flight over the Bimini Lagoon before we flew out to Miami on our last official tour leg. With the blister slid open, everyone on board wanted to sit for a while in that windy seat and experience the open ride/flight at 100 mph. No wonder: everybody understood that such experience would never ever happen again.

Our arrival at the cruise ship port in Miami, where we disembarked at the (now defunct) Chalk's Airways ramp, right across from where all huge cruise ships depart and arrive.

Two days later, we said goodbye to Captain Paul Warren Wilson and his crew. For the first time during the Catalina Odyssey, it started raining, as we stood on the ramp for a sort of a farewell ceremony and party. But everybody suddenly felt very 'triste'. While there were at first touches of laughter and cheers, they all faded away as the Cat started its engines for the last run over the waters of Miami Sea Port.

The Cat comes on its step just before she gets loose from the water and Paul gives a short wave with his hands. Garry Short sits in the blister and we see him also raise his hand. The girls stand there and start weeping; holding each other for consolation. It is all over now and we all realize such trip will never happen again. We were the fortunate ones to have lived this trip-of-a-lifetime.

Vaya con Dios, Catalina.

The Survivors

According to a recent list compiled by David Legg, the number of Catalinas/Cansos surviving by the end of 2017 totals 94 airframes. That number includes significant remains in collections; wrecks on land (but not the many wrecks that still lay at rest at the bottom of the seas); the derelicts standing forlornly in a corrosion corner of a remote airfield with no future; and the projects with airframes, parts and pieces that wait in hangars and backyards for better times, and which hopefully will one day become a complete PBY again. Plus, there are the refurbished, renovated or reconditioned aircraft owned by foundations, groups, and private owners/collectors, to be found mainly in the inventories of museums as static displays – most with and some without public access.

Finally, in addition to this list, there is the *fine fleur* of the Cat survivors: those that are still operational, i.e. they can fly or will fly in the near future. Some of those Cats operate on a (semi-) commercial basis as touring aircraft for paying passengers but they no longer fly cargo and/or passengers as 'tramp boats' with (non)-scheduled flights to remote settlements in the tundra/jungle or fishing camps alongside lakes and shores.

The longest lasting post-war commercial activity of the PBY was in its water-bombing role. The Catalina had a prominent forerunner role as a forest firefight that started back in 1960. It was successful in that role in Canada, the USA, Chile, and many countries in the Mediterranean such as Spain, Portugal, and France. The Catalina survived as a water bomber until the early 2000s but that is also over now. Most of the retired water bombers have come into the caring hands of museums and private collectors, saved for posterity.

The largest number of Cat/Canso survivors can be found in the USA (40), Canada (14), Australia (12), and New Zealand (3), but this list is subject to change with Catalinas occasionally being brought over to other countries. There is a host of countries that have one or two airframes or complete Catalinas/Cansos. In South America, there are examples in Brazil, Chile, Colombia, and Ecuador, whilst in Europe, we find Catalinas in the UK (2), France (2), Norway (2), Spain (2), The Netherlands (2), Sweden (1), Denmark (1), and Greece (1). Finally, in Indonesia (2, one of which is a full-sized replica!) and Israel (1). For more information see David Legg's regularly updated list on this site: www.catalina.org.uk.

With regard to airworthy Catalinas – those that are in, or close to, flying condition – we see the list of Cats shrink dramatically to around 16 aircraft (all are PBY-5A, PBY-6A or Canso A models). They can be found in USA (6), Canada (4), the UK (1), France (1), Australia (1), New Zealand (1), The Netherlands (1), and in Greece (1).

The list of survivors has come down over the past years, but a remarkable number of restoration projects have started or been completed recently, some of them bringing derelict or abandoned Catalinas back to static display status for museums. There are even a number of long-term projects, in progress or being planned, to bring a small number of Cats back in the air again. Conversely, however, some surviving hulls are, at the time of writing, under threat from firms using Catalina aircraft parts for other purposes than restoring airframes.

It is clear that the serious preservation efforts to save Catalinas/Cansos come right in time, now that the number of airframes has slowly declined to under the 'one-hundred' tally worldwide. It is a revival driven by private enterprises such as the FARS group from Canada, by museums like HARS from Australia, and by enthusiastic vintage aircraft groups/operators such as the Commemorative Air Force (CAF) in the USA.

One of these 'back-to-airworthy-condition' projects in Canada has resulted in an astonishing 'first flight' after a magnificent job done by FARS members. They brought the ex-Buffalo Airways Water Tanker nr 702 back into the air after it had crashed in a lake in 2001 and sunk. The ensuing salvage operation and renovation of that Canso is described in Chapter 3.

More of such projects are underway in Australia, USA, and New Zealand. The Consolidated-Vultee factories started mass-producing the PBY Catalina over 80 years ago in 1936. They cranked out a total production, of the various types, of 3,281 aircraft, including those built under Canadian license. The production of the final versions the PBY-6A ran until late-summer, 1945.

Unlike its contemporary, the Douglas DC-3/ C-47/ Dakota, the Catalina often operated in very unfavorable conditions with (salt) water landings; under heavy 'wear & tear' conditions in warm sea waters (the Pacific, the Caribbean, Brazil); or cold lakes and rivers (Alaska, Northern Canada etc.), often encountering ice, hidden debris and sandbanks that have inflicted many accidents. The higher corrosion factor due to that frequent (salt) water contact, the higher accident rate inherent to water landings (being more accident prone than 'hard' airstrip landings), the operational use of the Cats in remote coastal/forest areas, have all resulted in a statistically lower life expectancy for the aircraft when compared with its 'cousin', the more viable C-47, which had lower maintenance costs and higher pax revenues due to having more seats.

Therefore, during the first years after the war, with the Military Surplus Aircraft depots filled to the brim, the C-47 was the Blockbuster selling out quickly, while the surplus PBY met a more sluggish market in sales to civil operators. With the ex-Military Catalinas requiring some investment in airframe modifications to get her fit for cargo/pax transport, this was a major setback against its 'competitor' the C-47, who had a much simpler conversion to civil status (for the C-47, it was often merely a matter of popping rails in the floor to install 28 seats, making her ready-to-go with some interior insulation and dress-up). Hence, many Cats were bought cheaply just to retrieve their aeroengines, while the airframes were chopped up in a massive extinction effort, their value being reduced to the price of 5 tons of recycled aluminum ingots and two Pratt & Whitney R-1830 radials.

According to the book *Survivors* by Roy Blewett, in 2012 there were approximately 1,000 C-47s/DC-3s/Dakotas left in the world. He wrote: 'I believe the actual number of DC-3/ C-47s etc. remaining is 1,008. Of these, 629 are still in use (245 are flyers, 344 on static display, 21 under active restoration and 19 are grounded airframes). The remaining 379 are out of use, although 198 are in a condition that suggests they could still be put to use again.'

Presuming that in the past five years the numbers mentioned by Roy Blewett will have come down due to accidents, tornados and decay, it remains a fact that the DC-3 has had a much higher 'survival rate', even taking into consideration that the production figures are more than three times higher (in total 10,660+) than that of all PBY variants altogether. Seeing David Legg's figures of the remaining Cats, the flying boat has indeed a substantially (but explainable) lower survival rate, roughly three times lower than that of the C-47/DC-3.

Having said that, we must be grateful for every Catalina/Canso that is still around. The aircraft has become a precious gem, while only twenty years ago she was still operational in a commercial role in numbers. That role is forever over, but just before total extinction of the Catalina from the air seemed to become a reality, the reverse happened. Many groups, sponsors, owners, museums, shareholders, and, not to forget, countless volunteers, have given their passion, their determination and their time, or simply their devotion, to making the Catalina/Canso preservation projects happen. They all deserve our profound appreciation and respect for their efforts in keeping the legacy alive.

The Final Act

The Catalina started as a patrol bomber, a far-flying naval airborne spy-eye with a couple of depth charges or a torpedo on board, The reliable and rugged Cat' developed itself during the war years into a versatile weapons-platform that carried .50 machine guns, bombs, rockets, depth charges, Magnetic Anomaly Devices, Radar, sonic buoys, and a Leigh lamp for nightly surprise attacks. Plus it had dinghies and flares for its role as a Dumbo relief aircraft for rescuing downed aircrews.

The development in five years from a basic two-engine patrol flying boat into an electronically stuffed early warning, tracking and assault aircraft was dazzling, while the aircraft always kept its distinctive archaic looks. Mind you, she was considered obsolete before the war had even started! But its combat/rescue performance proved the critics wrong. Due to its staggering flight range and its excellent durability, the Catalina became a true flying paradox – a multi-tasking living legend during its wartime career, and that was not even the end of the Catalina tale.

After 1945, the aircraft soldiered on into the Cold War with naval patrols in the anti-submarine warfare and in the Coast Guard duties. At the end of its military career by the mid-1950s, the Jet Age had taken off, swept wings and jet propulsion became the norm, and there was no longer a place for piston props and old-school design features such as strutted wings with mixed aluminum and fabric coverings.

But there was a second career looming, not only as a transport for passengers and cargo to remote settlements and islands where no airstrip was available but also in the specialty role as a firefighting aircraft. It was in this role that the Cat found its true post-war vocation that would take her into a second career up into the new century. The PBY went on for another 50 years, serving the communities that relied on its missions, not only as a Naval Patrol and Rescue aircraft but also as a passenger/cargo transport and, last but not least, as a flying Fire Brigade.

This aircraft deserves a top ranking in the Hall of Aviation Fame. I can only hope that this book will contribute a little to keeping the Catalina and her rich history alive for many more years to come. But that is not all, the Cat could not fly on its own, it needed people to perform. It is time to reward the thousands of crews and mechanics for all the missions accomplished during and after the war, and time to show the greatest respect for those who did not come back from their missions.

When I made my first flight in a PBY, back in the early 1950s in an outback post in the Borneo Jungle, the aircraft put a spell on me that remains with me to this day. The experience was so deeply carved in my soul that 40 years on, it was my inspiration for writing a winning TV travel series format. In the realization and the filming of those eight episodes of the Catalina Odyssey, I flew another 250+ hours with the Catalina over SW Europe, NW Africa, the Americas, the Caribbean Sea and the Atlantic Ocean.

I could never have experienced the trips so intensely in any other, more modern aircraft. It was the ultimate trip-of-a-lifetime with the laid-back feeling of flying low and slow over the most fabulous seas and exotic islands, shores, lakes, mountains, glaciers, and rivers – as if I lived in a dream about a new version of Jules Verne's *Around the World in 80 Days*. The flights brought me some of the most awesome experiences an aviation buff can have, including some fabulous water landings in blue lagoons, in the NYC port, and between the icebergs of Greenland.

As a final word, I can say univocally that this book is my personal tribute to the most fantastic transport that I ever met in my life – the flying boat that opened the Gates of Wonder for me, way back in the 1950s and in the 1990s. Maybe one day I'll fly again with her, to another world.

I hope you enjoyed my book with all photos and tales about the Catalina.

Hans Wiesman
For more info and remarks contact me at
www.dc3dakotahunter.com or www.catalinaphotoalbum.com

Signature Pages by Duncan Fenn

VH-PBZ is the sole airworthy Catalina in Australia and as such it commemorates the crews who flew them with the RAAF during WWII. A New Orleans-built PBY-6A, it is painted to represent a 43 Sqn PB2B-2 Catalina coded OX-V, serial A24-362. In its time it has flown as a patrol aircraft with the US Navy, and as an airliner and fire bomber in Chile, Spain, and Portugal. Now based at Albion Park, NSW, it is operated by HARS (Historical Aircraft Restoration Society) and in recent times has undergone progressive restoration including the re-installation of bow turret and rear hull blisters.

Kendall's Catalina 90 V has found a good home in San Diego under the glass cupola of the Air & Space Museum. It has been there on display since 1988 and has undergone a number of modifications as you can see in this photo. The late model nose gun turret with double machine guns in an eyeball setup was added later. The Kendall Catalina 90 V (see Chapter 3) on its last tour of duty (inset), photographed on Christmas Island in the Mid Pacific 1966–67. After its return to USA via Hawaii, this Cat went in storage for years and was finally donated to the San Diego Air & Space Museum in 1984, where it remains today as a static display.

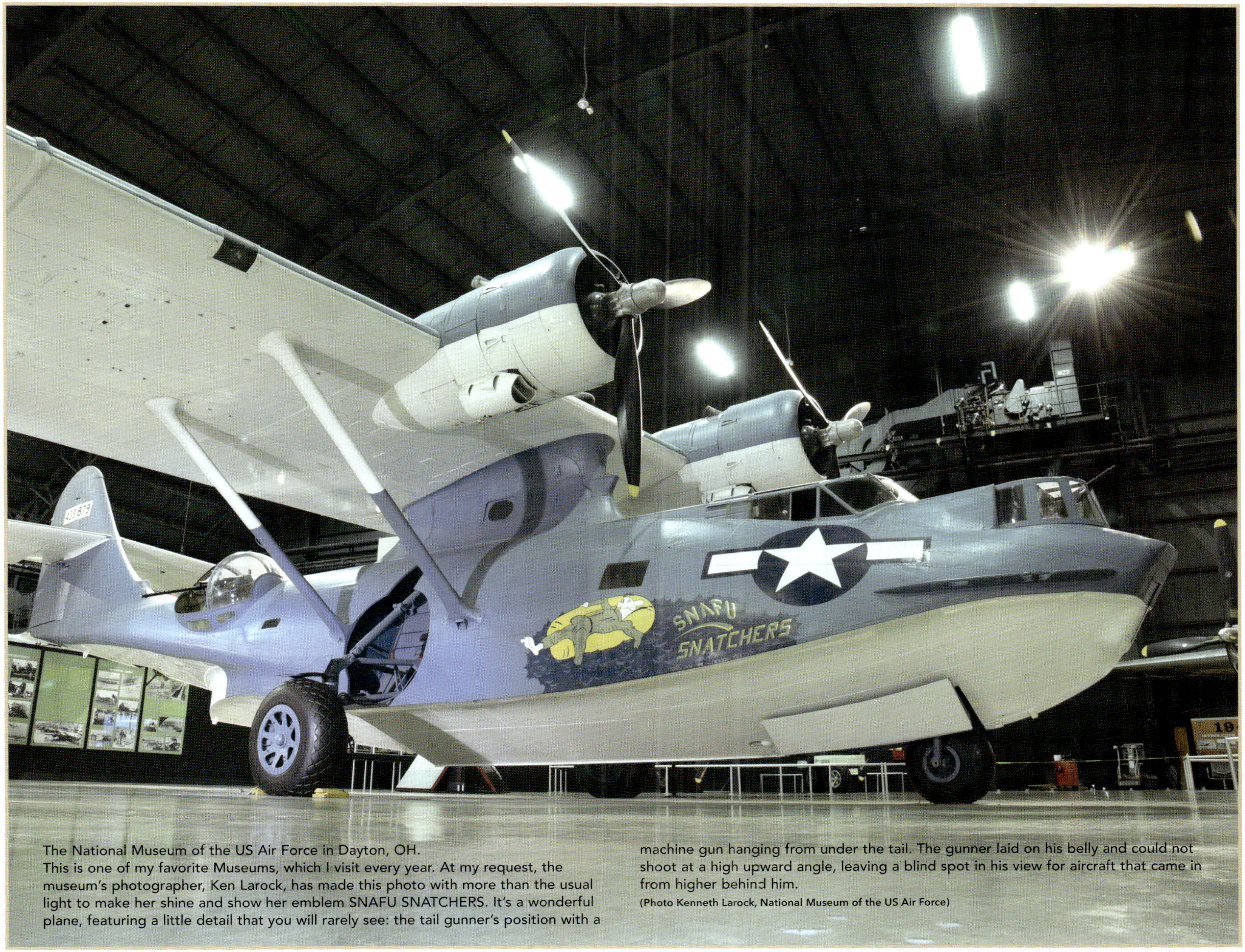

The National Museum of the US Air Force in Dayton, OH.
This is one of my favorite Museums, which I visit every year. At my request, the museum's photographer, Ken Larock, has made this photo with more than the usual light to make her shine and show her emblem SNAFU SNATCHERS. It's a wonderful plane, featuring a little detail that you will rarely see: the tail gunner's position with a machine gun hanging from under the tail. The gunner laid on his belly and could not shoot at a high upward angle, leaving a blind spot in his view for aircraft that came in from higher behind him.

(Photo Kenneth Larock, National Museum of the US Air Force)

WWW.CATALINA-PBY.NL
16 218

The Dutch MLD or Netherlands Naval Aviation Service operated various types of Catalina, both during and after World War Two. The 'Stichting Exploitatie Catalina', or Catalina Foundation, operates a PBY-5A in post-war Dutch military markings from Lelystad, specializing in 'splash and go' passenger experience flights on the IJsselmeer in the central Netherlands.

Seen in a nautical diorama at the Pima Air & Space Museum in Arizona, this aircraft served during World War II with the Royal Canadian Air Force as a Canso A, serial 9742. At the war's end it was sold onto the civil market and had a long career with numerous American owners and operators, even 'starring' in the film *Mysterious Island of Beautiful Women*! Prior to that it had traveled widely in Australasia and the Far East. In 1991 it was acquired by the Lone Star Flight Museum, Galveston, TX, but was damaged there by Hurricane Ike in September 2008. Neglected thereafter, it was rescued by the Pima Museum and transported there in December 2015.

Right: PBY-5A N607CC at the National Museum of Naval Aviation, Pensacola, FL.

Below left: PBY-5B FP216, The Cutaway Catalina, at the National Museum of Naval Aviation, Pensacola, FL.

Below right: PBY-5A N2172N of Erickson Group Ltd, Madras, OR Consolidated PBY-5A Catalina, Bu. No.46522, Constr. No. 1886. This particular aircraft was built by Consolidated Aircraft Corporation in San Diego, California, and delivered to the US Navy in February 1944. It flew with VPB-45 (flying PBYs between March 1943 and June 1945), and VJ-16 out of Guantanamo Bay, Cuba, and San Juan, Puerto Rico. From the 1960s, it was in the hands of several private collectors, flew as a tanker, and was acquired by Jack Erickson to become part of the Erickson Aircraft Collection in 1990 when the collection was at Tillamook Air Museum, Oregon. The collection is now in Madras, Oregon. The aircraft is painted in Insignia White such as was approved for anti-submarine aircraft in 1942 and with Naval Aircraft Insignia of the same period (1942–43).

(Photo: Randy Malmstrom)

Signature Pages by Caliaro Luigina

There are very few PBY-5A Catalinas still flying that boast both bow and blister turrets. Apart from its horn-balance rudder, N9521C looks virtually 'stock'. It is owned by Gerald Yagen of Virginia Beach, VA.

AEROPHOTO.IT
LUIGINO CALIARO

Canso A N315KM of Sea Link Aviation Inc., Stamford CN, USA, but based at the Hellenic Air Force Museum, Dekelia Air Base in Tatoi, Athens, Greece.
(Photo: Bernard Krieff)

Right: Smithsonian Air & Space Museum, Washington, DC. This Catalina PBY-5 is currently not on display at the Museum.

PBY-5A N31235 of Palm Springs Air Museum, Palm Springs, CA.
(Photo: Collection Michael Prophet)

Now preserved as a static exhibit at the Evergreen Aviation & Space Museum in Oregon, N249SB came close to an ignominious end at Nanaimo, BC, after plans to use it for tourist flights in Zimbabwe came to nothing. A veteran of wartime and post-war service with the Royal Canadian Air Force as a Canso A and subsequent use for many years as a water bomber in Canada and France, it was rescued from dereliction and flown on a one-way delivery flight to McMinnville where it now masquerades as a US Navy PBY-5A of patrol squadron VP-44. The location is the Evergreen Museum in McMinnville, Oregon, USA, where the Hughes' Hercules/Spruce Goose is also on display inside the main hall.
(Photo by Eric Kilby)

Photo of the Dutch Catalina PBY-5A, PH-PBY – the oldest Cat still flying – during its formation flight on behalf of the 100 Years Commemoration of the Dutch Marine Luchtvaart Dienst (MLD). On 5 July 2017, the Catalina flew to the Aviation Museum Aviodrome at Lelystad Airport, Lelystad, with MLD veterans on board. The MLD commander-in-chief, who opened an exposition in the museum, came by helicopter, an NH-90. It made a beautiful picture of vintage and modern naval aviation aircraft.
(Photo Remco de Wit, editor/photographer at 'Up in the Sky')

Signature Pages by David Stoddart

Based at Duxford, Cambridgeshire in the UK and operated by Plane Sailing Air Displays Ltd, G-PBYA *Miss Pick Up* is the 'busiest' Catalina in the world, flying mainly air shows throughout Europe between April and October every year.

Miss Pick Up makes a fine sight as she banks for the crowd at a UK air display. Expertly flown, she can show off her various configurations – upper and lower wing surfaces, floats up and down and gear up and down – whilst giving air show audiences a graceful performance.

Above: Colombia. During one of my visits to Villavicencio, Colombia, around 2010, I was invited to a local airshow. That old DC-6 Fenix, standing more or less abandoned at the end of the ramp, was buffed and towed to the center part of the ramp where the grandstand for the public was erected. Even the derelict Catalina (right) was cleaned up a bit: its tires were inflated and the weeds growing all around were trimmed down. All rubbish removed, the show could take place and it felt like the city was finally freed from the years of internal struggles in which the FARC had taken control over the many DC-3s that still fly here every day in and out of the Amazon jungle. The FARC's drugs and weapons transports via Villavicencio had made the city a no-go area for foreigners. Only in October 2006 was I finally allowed to go in there, but ran straight into a full-fledged war-on-drugs, experiencing weird encounters with DEA agents, military roadblocks, and armed choppers flying patrols along the airport perimeters. However, the Catalina and the DC-6 survived it all. The bad news is that the DC-6 has recently been scrapped; the good news is that the Catalina has been picked up, and, allegedly, will come up for sale soon.

For more info about the 'Wild West' scene in Southern Colombia in the years 2000–2008 and the role of the DC-3 in that war-on-drugs, you should read my book *The Dakota Hunter*, which includes awesome photos and background information about that war.

(Photos Hans Wiesman)

Right: HK-2115 PBY-6A is one of the very few Cat survivors that flew as a Jungle Tramp 'boat over Colombia and the Amazon region South of Villavicencio. I dubbed her 'The Queen of the Amazon'. Her former role came so close to what I had seen in the early 1950s in Borneo on the Mahakam River. It was like a sentimental journey back to my childhood years and I hoped that she would never come to her end by the cutting torch. She has stood there on the apron for some 15 years or more, and, like with the DC-6, the fatal day can come without prior notice. Amazingly, in mid-December 2017, the Cat was dismantled at Villavicencio and put on transport by ship to Germany, allegedly for display in a museum. More information will be available soon via my blogs.

Above: A nice photo of the Brazilian Air Force Catalina (FAB) Canso A s/n 6527 now in Museu Aeroespacial, Rio de Janeiro, Brazil.
(Photo: Hebmuller)

Above: PBY-5A N287 – at the time with Charlie Clements, Miami, FL, but since sold and currently dismantled awaiting rebuild in FL.
(Photo: Graham Robson via Michael Prophet)

Below: OA-10A CC-CDT of Ibero Chilena de Aviación, Santiago, Chile.
(Photo from Chile owner Gonzalo Parragué, via Jose Ramon Salgado)

Below: These are OA-10As N2763A (foreground) and C-GFFC (rear) while they were with SLAFCO at Moses Lake, WA, but both have moved on. N2763A is now stored with Yanks Air Museum, Chino, CA, (nothing happening with it) and C-GFFC is now N483CV with Flying Cat LLC, Sanford, Maine.

Signature Pages by Graham Robson

The USA still boasts a number of surviving Catalinas, including former RCAF Canso A N222FT Flyin' Turtle (opposite top right), Wright Cyclone-powered Super Cat N287 (opposite top and bottom left) and Buckeye, Arizona-based N413PB (opposite bottom right)

Left: The author on a visit to Lelystad Airport, Netherlands, in January 2017, where both the Dutch Catalina PH-PBY and the DC-3 PH-PBA were in winter storage, getting their yearly maintenance in a hangar that the 'Stichting Exploitatie Catalina' shares with the Dutch Dakota Association (DDA). The Cat's nose wheel that you can see on the left got stuck after the Cat had made a touch-and-go on the water in summer 2017. Presumably a piece of driftwood was hit and, subsequently, the doors were jammed – which they discovered in the approach flight to Lelystad Airport. It was decided to make the landing on the airstrip rather than on the water. The emergency landing went very smoothly but repairs on the doors prevented the aircraft from flying again during the 2017 season.
(Photo: Peter Schutte)

Above: Canso A C-FPQL in its early 1990's livery as a tanker flying for Conifair. Some Catalina tankers were also used for aerial crop/woods spraying with nozzles along the full wingspan at the trailing edges. It is now in a new white color scheme of RCAF flying for the Canadian Warplane Heritage.
(Photo: Collection Michael Prophet)

Above: Canso A C-FOFI, then registered as C-FOFI of Buffalo Airways but now with Hans Lauridsen, Glendale, Arizona, located at Buckeye Municipal Airport, Buckeye, AZ, as N413PB. This same aircraft can be seen in its current state on page 264 in the lower right-hand corner.
(Photo Henry Tenby)

Above: PBY-6A VH-PBZ of HARS, Illawarra Regional Airport, Sydney, NSW. This photo is from the RAAF Memorial Flight on 28 November 2016 and shows four generations of Naval Patrol aircraft of No 11 Squadron in one flight. It was an historic occasion: a Lockheed Neptune, a Consolidated PBY Catalina, a Lockheed AP-3C Orion, and a Boeing P-8A Poseidon flying in formation over Adelaide to mark a new era for the RAAF. Between 1941 and 1952 the RAAF operated a total of 168 Catalinas, flown by four frontline squadrons, two communications units, and three air-sea rescue flights. (Photo: RAAF)

Signature Pages by Lawrence Acket

New Zealand Catalina Preservation Society Inc

New Zealand is home to ZK-PBY (above), a former RCAF Canso A, famous for the Catalina Safari Company trans-African flight and the Catalina Odyssey in 1993 (see previous chapter). Now used for air show appearances and passenger flights on both North and South Islands, it usually flies in replica RNZAF colors but for a while masqueraded as a French Navy Catalina. N222FT Flyin' Turtle (opposite top left) is based in Texas with Wilson 'Connie' Edwards – one of two Catalinas in his 'fleet'.

Above: The Catalina PBY-5A N7238Z that, for years, stood derelict in San Juan, PR, finally had found its new destination and went out for transport to Australia in 2013. Now at the Rathmines Catalina Memorial Park in NSW, Australia.

Below: PBY-5A N7238Z at Kilaben for Rathmines Catalina Memorial Park Trust, Rathmines, NSW. Rathmines became the largest RAAF flying boat base in the southern hemisphere with almost 3,000 RAAF personnel based there during 1944–45. Over the last few years, a Catalina Festival has been held at the base site each November. The airframe they acquired from San Juan has a bit of corrosion, which needs to be repaired in this tight makeshift tarp hangar.
(Photos above and bellows courtesy of Rathmines Catalina Memorial Park/War Bird News)

Above: PBY-5A N9502C at the RAAFA Aviation Heritage Museum, Bull Creek, Perth, Australia. Note the nice late-war eyeball front turret.

Below: PB2B-2 VH-ASA Frigate Bird II in the Powerhouse Museum, Sydney, Australia. The Museum's Catalina saw service in several air-sea rescue squadrons and in the New Guinea administration just after the war, before being selected by Captain Taylor to fly the first uncharted air route between Sydney and Valparaiso, Chile. The Catalina had the appropriate civil registration VH-ASA (Australia-South America) applied and was presented to the museum in 1985.
(Photo: from collection.maas.museum/object/207900 via David Legg)

C-47 Skytrain and Canso A ZK-PBY of The New Zealand Catalina Preservation Society Inc., Auckland, NZ. Same engines, same era, this photo brings together two aviation classics that originated in the mid-1930s and endure today, albeit in limited numbers. Would their designers have thought this possible?
(Photo: Gavin Conroy)

Miss Pick Up is a regular visitor to the pre-war trans-Atlantic flying boat base on the lake at Biscarrosse, south of Bordeaux. G-PBYA travels from its home airfield in the UK to perform at occasional air shows there and to carry out regular pilot training on the large stretch of water. She makes a magnificent sight.

Left: Canso A s/n Fv47001 at Flygvapenmuseum, Malmslätt, Sweden. The Royal Swedish Air Force, or Flygvapnet, operated three ex-RCAF Canso As. In their service, the type was known as the Tp.47. One of the three, Fv.47002, was shot down into the Baltic by a Soviet MiG-15 jet on 16 June 1953 whilst engaged in a search for a Swedish C-47 that had disappeared during an intelligence-gathering flight. Canso A s/n Fv47001 is now preserved at the Flygvapenmuseum, Malmslätt, and reminds visitors of the Cold War incident that saw its sister aircraft shot down.
(Photo: Stefan Kalm)

Left: PBY-6A N4NC of Wilson 'Connie' Edwards, Big Springs, TX. In 1986, this restored PBY Catalina, flown by Connie, reenacted the first successful transatlantic flight by the Navy's NC-4 flying boat in 1919. That was 75 years earlier, hence that impressive 'nose art' decoration. Note also the extra fuel tanks under the wings and the spray of water that comes from the fuselage just after the takeoff from a lake – a mist that adds drama and speed to this fine picture.

PBY-5A N9521C of Training Services Inc., TA, Virginia Beach, Virginia. Owned by Jerry Yagen, this Catalina also features on the back cover of this book.
(Photo Calliaro Luigino)

One of the reassuring aspects of surviving Catalinas and Cansos is that the airworthy population in Canada has increased in recent years. From a low point of just one, there were four flying by mid-2017. The superb example shown here is C-FUAW, veteran of RCAF and fire fighting service, and now flying with Bob Dyck's Pacific Flying Boats Ltd out of Victoria, BC, just a stone's throw from the wartime Canso base at Patricia Bay.

K
11024

Above: The Royal Danish Air Force donated this ex-US Navy PBY-6A to the RAF Museum back in the early-1970s having acquired it in the USA in late-1956. It had been built at the Consolidated Vultee Aircraft Corporation (Convair) factory in New Orleans and flew with the US Navy as BuNo 63993. It was used by the Danes to support its military interests in Greenland. In 1975 it was moved to the RAF Museum collection at RAF Cosford, where it has resided since. At present, it is on outdoor display, although it is hoped it will go 'back indoors' in due course. The sister ship of this PBY-6A can be seen on page 114.
(Photo: Alastair T Gardiner)

Right: The Royal Canadian Air Force Canso A serial 9767 is a real 'warbird', having attacked and sunk the U-boat *U-342* on 17 April 1944. Later it became an airliner and a firefighter before being acquired by Canadian Air Legend and flown to France where, at the end of 2017, it was still to be found. In late-1998 it started a lengthy trip to South America to commemorate the 1930's mail flights carried out by Air France. The Canso wore that airline's livery for the duration of the exercise.

Now part of the extensive collection of aircraft owned by Kermit Weeks in Florida, N96UC's moment of fame was not during its wartime service with the US Navy but in the 1950s when operated by the Paraguayan military. On 2 October 1955, it was used to fly General Juan Peron, the deposed Argentine president, into exile in Paraguay. The Catalina was flown to Argentina where it landed on the River Plate close to the Paraguayan gunship *Paraguay*. Peron was transferred from the warship, taken aboard the Catalina and flown to Paraguay's capital, Asunción. Another facet in the amazing history of the Catalina flying boat.
(Photo by Mike Ellis)

Proving that a Catalina is just as happy operating from grass as water and hard surfaces, Jerry Yagen's PBY-5A N9521C is seen doing just that in the photo above, whilst to the left she makes a great sight parked amongst other 'warbirds' as the sun goes down. Jerry's Cat has a so-called 'eyeball' style bow turret and horn balanced rudder, as well as a pair of original hull blisters.
(Photo: John Lackey, www.flyby.photography)

The Restoration of PBY-5A N427CV, by Brendan Odell, the reputed vintage aircraft restorer from South Africa

I first laid eyes on the aircraft that would become a defining project for me, in the early 2000s. It was big, it wasn't particularly beautiful, and it wasn't in great condition…

By 2006, the aircraft was looking decidedly sorry for itself. Its flanks had been blackened by years of dripping oil, its dubious white and blue paint had dulled, Perspex had crazed, its fabric controls had been beaten to long wispy shreds, the tires were going flat, and worst of all, corrosion was starting to creep through the seams, from salt water operation. Yes, it was a sad thing to see.

None of us really knew what would happen to it. As all the aircraft around it here in South Africa at Rand Airport – a motley collection of flea-bitten, ragged DC-4s and DC-6Bs – were slowly scrapped, towed or flown away, the poor old Cat stayed put. One day in late 2006, the telephone rang. 'Would you like to help us get the Cat going? We have a customer that wants to rebuild it, and he's negotiating the sale now – he wants us to see if it's worth the effort'. That was Captain Vermeulen calling. 'I know you'll like it,' he said.

Captain Vermeulen had, not too long before, purchased a historic hangar in Art Deco style at Rand airport, built for South African Airways in 1939. It was a lovely hangar – large and light inside – but very cold and oddly low-roofed. It had been built to accommodate an aircraft that had never arrived – the Junkers Ju 90. The aircraft had been due to be delivered in mid–late September 1939, but evidently never turned up. This explained the wide but low hangar. For years afterwards, DC-4s would be brought inside by a complicated means involving raising the nose of the aircraft up onto a dolly to lower the tail and allow it to come inside, and then, after the nose had been lowered again, the tail of said DC-4 could settle amongst the roof rafters of the hangar.

That morning, when I arrived, the Cat was to be moved down nearer to the hangar. After a time getting the wheels inflated, some of the team members, led by the workshop manager 'Spook', helped drag the old Cat from its longtime resting place with a small red Massey Ferguson tractor. The Cat was a heavy thing for the little tractor, and eventually, we had it down at the hangar, ready to start.

Now it was time to take stock of what we had. The interior was musty and dusty after six years in the open. Some seats had been installed in a haphazard sort of fashion – it wasn't as easy as it looked. Corrosion was definitely present, although without getting into the fuel tanks the extent of the seriousness was unknown.

We started with the most expensive bits – the engines. They were, as expected, hydrauliced. After scratching around a bit, we finally found the stands for the engines (these clip onto the wing leading edge and cowlings) and got to work. The first job was to drain the massive 78-gallon oil tanks of all the old, cold and sludgy-acidic oil. Now – anyone who has ever worked on a PBY will tell you that this is a peculiar job at best. The tank is airframe mounted of course, and cannot be removed – being an integral part of the nacelle – thus cleaning it requires an assortment of drums, stands, pipes, fittings and a determination not to make a mess. Eventually, we had the tanks cleaned and filled with fresh oil – after removing bird nests from the exhausts, removing all the spark plugs to clear the hydraulic lock, and pressurizing the carburetors to rest for 24 hours to soften the diaphragms, we went home.

Next day, bright and early we turned on the pre-oiler to start warming up. It worked; the pre-oiling process went well. The oil would take up to three hours to heat through. After several coughs, splutters, and hiccups both engines eventually ran – the left hand one's carburetor jamming up solid (we later found it ruined with corrosion) and the right one ran beautifully. The small crowd that had assembled from nowhere cheered in excitement.

After some more investigation and days of collating and inspecting the aircraft's French-language records we made our recommendation – the project was viable. At long last the project would begin – the aircraft was taken into the hangar for structural work to get started. From here on in, Spook led the project, assisted by Captain Vermeulen's son, Ben, and I, having found other employment, carried on with my life until I was to be called again when the structural work was near to finished.

Over the next three years, progress stepped up. The aircraft was paint stripped, scaffolding was built, the outer wings were removed, the Janitrol heater was removed, all the flight controls were removed, and the massive fabric-covered trailing edges were removed. Spook and an able team of sheet metal workers (Spook, Thinus van Staden, Ben Vermeulen) conducted a massive amount of structural work to get the old Cat airworthy again: the wing rear spar was spliced and massive corrosion needing multiple repairs was fixed in the wing center section. Door modifications were done, all the instrumentation was removed for overhaul, and a new instrument panel was made.

In 2009, I returned to the project – sadly 'Spook' had become very ill and passed away some time afterward. In between restoring DC-3 ZS-NTE, the Catalina project was finished up. To this end, I recruited a team of Zimbabwean mechanics to assist: Albert, Bundo, and Washington. Together with Thinus and Ben, the Zimbabweans and I started to apply as much effort as possible to get the aircraft finished. We removed the engines and fitted

overhauled engines into the engine mounts, we fitted propellers and components, and refitted the overhauled fabric surfaces and outer wings. We (after much effort) repaired the cantankerous hydraulic system and returned the electrical system to operation – including getting the AC-powered instruments working again; we finished rebuilding the 'blisters' (refitting the glazing and getting them completely water-tight was a hard job); and set about building the luxurious interior our customer demanded.

By February 2010 – we had the aircraft pretty much buttoned up and everything working well. Captain Flippie Vermeulen and I took her out for a run and she performed impeccably, especially considering that most of the aircraft had been taken to pieces and re-assembled. The Catalina was finally restored and airworthy – completing this mammoth task to a high standard and in compliance with the US Certificate of Airworthiness requirements. It was heartening to see the aircraft on its maiden flight, nearly six years after we first began work on it!

Right: PBY-5A N427CV during its first roll-out on Rand Airport, SA, and its maiden flight after six years of restoration. The aircraft departed to the USA in 2012, where she is now a flying aircraft participating in air shows and part of the National Museum of World War II Aviation in Colorado Springs, CO, USA.
(Photo Brendan Odell)

Below right: Long before its restoration at Rand Airport, PBY-5A N427CV was hired for a commercial for the FA deodorant brand. The aircraft was flown to Mozambique where they found this little treasure island for the shooting. For years, the ad campaign was publicized all over Europe, using this same photo but with a man walking on top of the wing.
(Photo Chris Simpson)

Left: PBY-5A N427CV in the hangar at Rand Airport, South Africa. Interesting details in this photo are the upward folding hatches in the engine cowlings and the red trapeze-like benches, which allow the mechanics to wrench on the engines while on the water without the use of scaffolds. Also, note the nose of this particular PBY, converted with a circular manhole on top and a rubber bumper nose, while retaining a rudimentary bomber-aimer window in the lower front of the nose. Most post-war converted Catalinas received a more streamlined nose design, deleting the stubby nose of the military version with its original front gun turret and bomber-aimer window.
(Photo Brendan Odell)

New Zealand's ZK-PBY is one of few Catalinas/Cansos in the world that can fly fare-paying passengers – and on water too! The scenery of the country makes a fantastic backdrop as she approaches a lake and then, having alighted, takes off again.

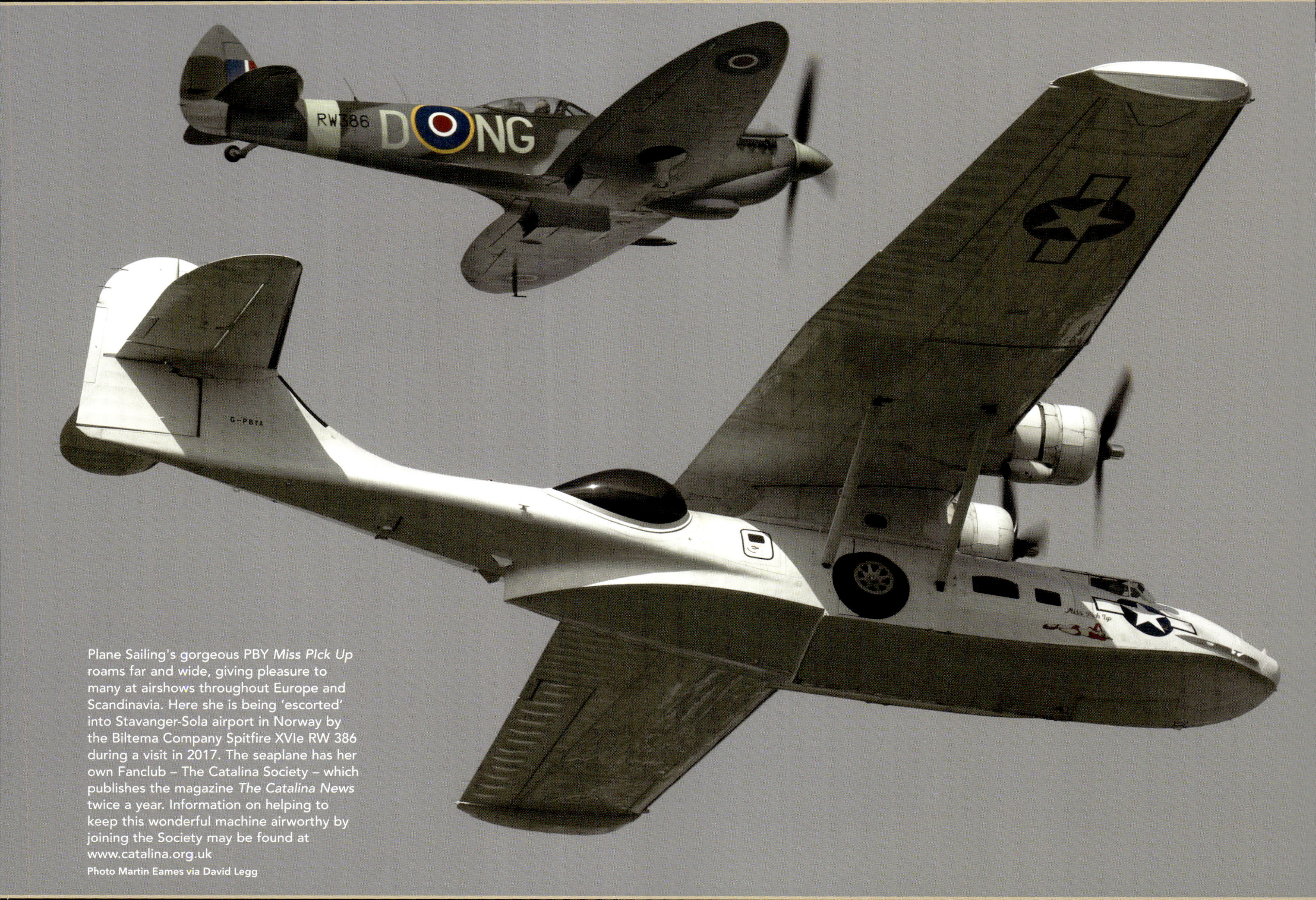

Plane Sailing's gorgeous PBY *Miss Pick Up* roams far and wide, giving pleasure to many at airshows throughout Europe and Scandinavia. Here she is being 'escorted' into Stavanger-Sola airport in Norway by the Biltema Company Spitfire XVIe RW 386 during a visit in 2017. The seaplane has her own Fanclub – The Catalina Society – which publishes the magazine *The Catalina News* twice a year. Information on helping to keep this wonderful machine airworthy by joining the Society may be found at www.catalina.org.uk

Photo Martin Eames via David Legg

Acknowledgements

A large number of people have contributed to the completion of this photo album; to all of them, I would like to express my sincere appreciation and gratitude. I have tried to list all the book's contributors, but there were so many that I may have overlooked some names – I would like to apologize for any omissions if they have occurred.

It was impossible to depict every single Catalina still in existence, or to publish all (often heroic) tales that came to me via my extensive social media network. In addition, some of the photos that were sent had to be rejected due to the low resolution or the small size of the old photographs. I feel sorry if that has happened, but I received such a staggering number of photos that I was urged to extend the book's format from the initial 180–200 photos and 150 pages to double that amount with almost 300 pages and over 400 photos. (My thanks to Erica for encouraging me to carry on!)

Alongside the list of contributors mentioned in the introduction of this book, there are a number of people who have delivered (sometimes substantial) information and photographs from their own collections, their family photo albums, or their digital library. They all deserve my greatest appreciation for making this book what it has become. In no particular order, I would like to thank the following:

Dr Ingeborg Kendall Maranto from the USA, who I met. She was so kind to supply me her account and many nice photos from the Kendall family album for the two Special Stories (see Chapter 3). Prudent Staal, my Dutch friend, who supplied me with so many fabulous photos of the Catalina operations in Indonesia; he is also deeply involved with PH-PBY operations in Holland. Dirk Septer, Flying Dutchman, who lives in Canada and supplied me lots of goodies, books, and data about C-47s and PBY Catalina crash sites and operations. Harry Follas, my pen pal from New Zealand for many years, has contributed some spectacular photos. From South Africa, Captain Fiippie Vermeulen and Brendan Odell have contributed an outstanding report of their PBY restoration project.

The following have supplied me with fantastic stories and photos of Catalina operations in USA, Canada and Australia (see my Chapter Special Stories):

Brendan Odell/Capt. Flippie Vermeulen
Martin Collins
Les Oystryk
Lance Reed
Con Campbell
Dave O'Malley
Ken Berner
Phil Hougland
Dan Shirey
Bill Bailey

To follow is a list of photographers who supplied their photo(s) and the names of collections where photographs have come from:

Kendall Family Collection
Frans Lemmens
Erik Sampers
Michael Prophet
Babette Alfieri
Ken Stanford
David Legg collection
Prudent Staal collection
Kenneth Larock
Martin Eames
John Lackey
Mike Ellis
Heath Moffat
Stefan Kalm
Pierre-Etienne Langenfeld
Gavin Conroy
Lawrence Acket
RAAF
Henry Tenby
Peter Schutte
Graham Robson
Jose Ramon Salgado
Randy Malmstrom
Caliaro Luigina
Duncan Fenn
Pascal Baudry
Doug Roy
David Musselwhite
Doug Pegg
Martha Crossey
Matt Holle
Lindsay Wise
Jeremy Hughes Collection
Olafur Sirgudsson
Earle Johnson
Ron Mak
Paul Howard Collection
Graydon West
Geoff Goodall Collection
Ben Danneker Collection
Eric Allen
Greg Banfield Collection
Larry Milberry
Onno Wieringa
Chris Simpson
Kermit Weeks

I would also like to thank the following museums, foundations and operators that have supplied information and photos of their Catalinas:

The Smithsonian Institution, National Air and Space Museum, Washington, DC, USA
The San Diego Air & Space Museum, San Diego, CA, USA
The National Museum of the US Air Force, Dayton, Ohio, USA
The Pima Air and Space Museum, Tucson, AZ, USA
The National Naval Aviation Museum, Pensacola, FL, USA
Fantasy of Flight Collection, Polk City, FL, USA
Palm Springs Air Museum, Palm Springs, CA, USA
Evergreen Museum, McMinnville, OR, USA
Erickson Aircraft Collection, Madras, Oregon, USA
Rathmines Catalina Memorial Park, NSW, Australia
Historical Aircraft Restoration Society, Albion Park, Sydney, NSW
The New Zealand Catalina Preservation Society, Auckland, NZ
Swedish Museum/ Flygvapenmuseum, Malmslatt, Sweden
Stichting Vrienden van de Catalina, Lelystad, Holland
Museu Aerospacial da Forca Aerea Brasileira, Rio de Janiero, Brazil
Hellenic Air Force Museum, Dekelia Air Base, Tatoi, Athens, Greece
Imperial War Museum, Duxford, Cambridgeshire, UK
The Catalina Society, Duxford, Cambridgeshire, UK

Also by Hans Wiesman

The Dakota Hunter

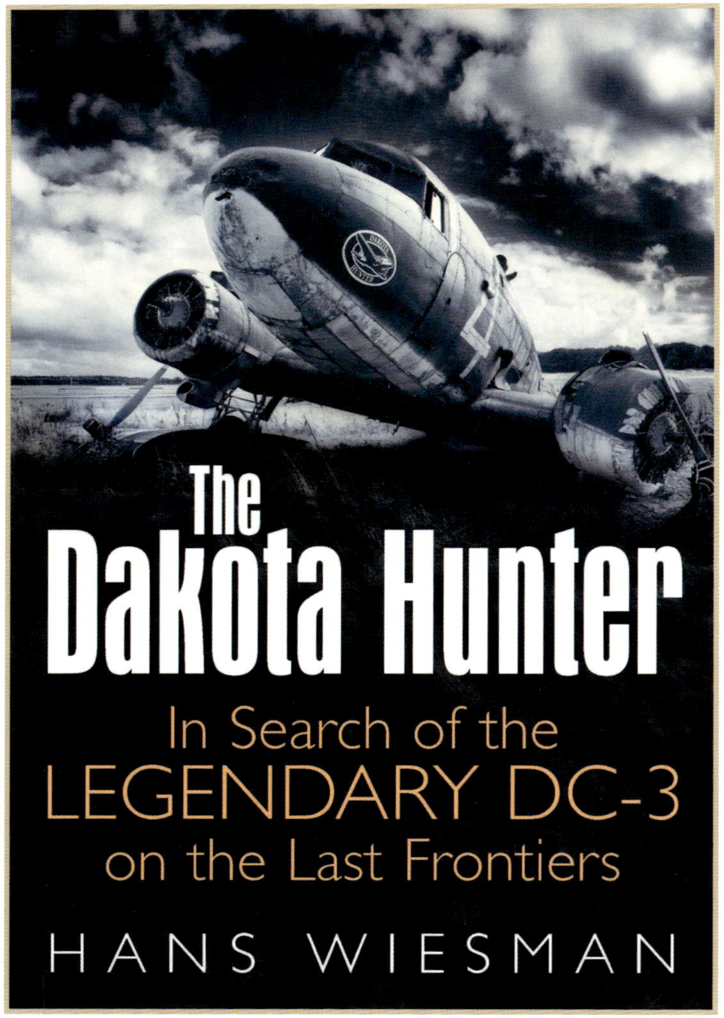

Hardcover: 320 pages/240 photos
Publisher: Casemate Publishers USA/Casemate Publishing UK
ISBN: 978-1-61200-258-3
To order online, go to:
www.casematepublishers.com
www.amazon.com

This book tells the story of a Dutch boy who grew up during the 1950s in post-war Borneo, where he had frequent encounters with an airplane, the Douglas DC-3, aka the C-47 Skytrain, or Dakota, of World War II fame. For a young boy living in a remote jungle community, the aircraft reached the proportions of a romantic icon. As the essential lifeline to a bigger world, it was the beginning of a special bond.

In 1957 his family left the island, and all its residual wreckage of World War II, and he attended college in The Hague, NL. After graduation he started a career as a corporate executive, and met the aircraft again during business trips to the Americas. His childhood passion for the Dakota flared up anew, and the fascination pulled like a magnet. As if predestined, or maybe just looking for an alibi to come closer, he began a business to salvage and convert Dakota parts, which meant first of all finding them.

As the demand for these war relic parts and cockpits soared, Hans began to travel the world to track down surplus, crashed or derelict Dakotas. He ventured deeper and deeper into remote mountains, jungles, savannas and the seas where the planes are found, usually as ghostly wrecks but sometimes still in full commercial operation. In hunting the mythical Dakota he often encountered intimidating or dicey situations in countries plagued by wars or revolts, others by arms and narcotics trafficking, warlords and con men.

This book describes his multiple expeditions in search of the remains of the Dakota legend. It takes the reader to some of the remotest spots in the world, but once there one is often greeted by the comfort of what was once the West's apex in transportation, however now haunted by a passionate adventurer who tries to travel back in time.

Reviews of *The Dakota Hunter* selected from Amazon's readership

"Highly entertaining and not just for DC3 fans. Mr Wiesman has many interesting stories to tell about the countries he has visited searching for DC3 parts. Some may see irony in the fact he only wants the parts to build office desks but there is much more to his story and his affection for the plane shines through."

"Best book I ever read. Fascinating, exciting, heart-pounding, tear jerking, this story of the quest for C47 Dakota survivors, wrecks and relics is great for any aviation enthusiast or lover of a good story. Like tales told around a campfire this book gives a great story. Experiences only few can live but many dream of, I give it high praises."

"A great addition to your aviation literature collection! Wiesman not only manages to convey his love for this venerable aircraft but also provides the wannabe world traveler with valuable insights. A must-read for the aviation enthusiast and those whose work or passions may lead them down paths less traveled around the globe."

"Great adventure story. A ripping yarn that travels all over the world from jungles to tundra, filled with interesting characters. Well worth your time."

"A brilliant story of a man on a mission to track down the whereabouts of these old aircraft whether decommissioned, wrecked or still flying. He takes you to parts of the world where most tourists would not dream of visiting. A very well-written read."

"Great book! Completely enjoyed reading of the author's worldwide quest for these old warbirds! Thanks for writing it Hans!"

"Excellent book and am so glad it was offered to comment."

"An excellent read."

"I thoroughly enjoyed this book, and especially appreciated the numerous photographs that accompany the stories of adventure and discovery as the Dakota Hunter traveled the world in search of DC-3 aircraft and parts."